HEAVENLY PARTICIPATION

Heavenly Participation

THE WEAVING OF A
SACRAMENTAL TAPESTRY

Hans Boersma

WILLIAM B. EERDMANS PUBLISHING COMPANY
GRAND RAPIDS, MICHIGAN / CAMBRIDGE, U.K.

Published 2011 by

Wm. B. Eerdmans Publishing Co.

2140 Oak Industrial Drive N.E., Grand Rapids, Michigan 49505 /

P.O. Box 163, Cambridge CB3 9PU U.K.

Printed in the United States of America

19 18 17 16   8 7 6

2020-06

Library of Congress Cataloging-in-Publication Data

Boersma, Hans, 1961-

Heavenly participation: the weaving of a sacramental tapestry / Hans Boersma.

p.   cm.

Includes bibliographical references (p.   ) and indexes.

ISBN 978-0-8028-6542-7 (pbk.: alk. paper)

1. Sacraments — History of doctrines. 2. Nouvelle théologie (Catholic theology)
3. Evangelicalism — Relations — Catholic Church. 4. Catholic Church —
Relations — Evangelicalism. I. Title.

BV800.B64 2011

234'.16 — dc22

2010040499

www.eerdmans.com

To the Faculty and Students
of Regent College

In æternum, Domine,
verbum tuum permanet in cælo.
In generationem et generationem veritas tua;
fundasti terram, et permanet.

Ps. 118 (119):89-90

Factum audivimus, mysterium requiramus.

St. Augustine,
In epistolam Ioannis, 50.6

Contents

Contents

Contents

Preface

The Italian painter Fra Angelico (c. 1395-1455) had a preoccupation with heaven. The Dominican friar recognized that life lived on earth carried eternal implications. No doubt the Renaissance painter's fervent hope was for the seraphic angels to take him to heaven on the final day. Therefore, in one of his most famous paintings, *The Last Judgment*, angels and saints join hands in a heavenly procession, ready to enter the bliss of paradise. From then on, the saints would be joining the divine liturgy in the singing of the heavenly *Sanctus* (Isa. 6:3; Rev. 4:8). Heavenly participation was the vision that animated Fra Angelico's work, and it is that same vision that also inspires this book (hence its cover).

Heavenly participation does not mean that we should ignore earthly concerns. Far from it! As this book will make clear, it is only otherworldliness that guarantees an appropriate kind of this-worldliness. However, heavenly participation does mean that Christ, the eternal Word of God, provides the created order with stability and makes it trustworthy. As the psalmist puts it, in the words quoted in the epigraph, "Your word, O LORD, is eternal; it stands firm in the heavens. Your faithfulness continues through all generations; you established the earth, and it endures." Prior to the advent of modernity, few people would have been able to read these words of the psalm without thinking of Christ as the eternal Word, who himself was the faithfulness of God and who himself had established the earth. They were convinced that created objects found their reality and identity in the eternal Word of God. It is this link between heaven and earth that allowed premodern Christians to see God's own truth, goodness, and beauty in the world around them.

The broad consensus of the church fathers and medieval theologians — which in this book I am calling the Great Tradition — was not satisfied with merely observing "facts." People were convinced that they could perceive the eternal mystery of the Word of God in these facts. This sacramental vision lies behind Augustine's words quoted in the epigraph: "We have heard the fact; let us seek the mystery." Over the past number of years, this Augustinian vision has captured my imagination, to the point that I have become persuaded that the church's well-being depends on the recovery of this sacramental tapestry.

The twentieth-century French Catholic renewal movement that has been called *nouvelle théologie* has shaped my thinking tremendously over the past few years. Its recovery of a sacramental mindset has become an inspiration to me, and a year-long reprieve from my teaching duties has allowed me to immerse myself in the thought of the *nouvelle* theologians. I am most grateful to both the Association of Theological Schools and the Henry Luce Foundation for appointing me Henry Luce III Fellow in Theology for the 2007-2008 academic year, and also to Regent College for granting me a year off to study the *nouvelle* theologians. Part 2 of this book, in particular, will make clear that *nouvelle théologie*'s recovery of the Great Tradition has had a deep impact on my thinking. Upon reading my book *Nouvelle Théologie and Sacramental Ontology: A Return to Mystery,* two dear colleagues, Richard Mouw and John Stackhouse, urged me to write a somewhat more popular account, which — with a particular eye toward an evangelical audience — would spell out the theological implications that I believe *nouvelle théologie* continues to have. This book, especially the second part, is my attempt to do so.

In a very significant way, my friends at Regent College, both faculty and students, have enabled me to write this book. Among the many wonderful experiences at Regent has been an interdisciplinary team-taught course that touched on many of the topics I address in this book. I am deeply grateful for the lively engagement on these issues, with both fellow faculty members and students. Whenever we found ourselves disagreeing — at times perhaps even vehemently — the result was growth in insight, in wisdom, and in affection. I suspect that there are few places where it is possible to engage in the kind of principled discussion that we thoroughly enjoy at Regent College. With deep appreciation, therefore, I dedicate this book to my colleagues and students.

Several friends, colleagues, and students graciously agreed to read the entire manuscript and have provided me with invaluable suggestions. I am grateful to Gerald Boersma, Fritz Dewit, Bruce Hindmarsh, Matthew Levering, Matt Mattoon, Dick Moes, and Jens Zimmermann for taking the time to work through the manuscript. Their numerous comments have greatly improved the readability of the book and have corrected a number of awkward shortcomings and mistakes. I thoroughly enjoyed the self-styled "nerdish" conversations with several of my students — Alex Abecina, KC Flynn, Matthew Martin, Ben Paulus, and Nomi Pritz — who helped me tremendously by picking apart the manuscript over burgers and beer. May the tradition always hold out to them eternal vistas of truth, goodness, and beauty.

I am also indebted to Dennis Danielson, Mark McConnell, and Bert Moes for their kind input at various stages of my work. Alex Abecina, my research assistant, has kindly crafted the diagrams and the bibliography, while my son, Gerald, has skillfully put together the indexes. I appreciate the permission of several journals — *Books and Culture, CRUX,* and *Evangelical Quarterly* — to reprint material from my previously published essays, each of which is mentioned in the bibliography.

Finally, I am surrounded by the love of my wife and family. They are a great source of joy, and they keep inspiring me to devote myself to the knowledge of God.

Introduction

The past few decades have witnessed two remarkable developments in evangelical theology. First, the nature of the theological discipline appears to have undergone a change. Propositional truth, once a hallmark of evangelicalism, is making way for more elusive means of expression, such as narrative, image, and symbol. Postmodern worry about essentialism, along with a suspicion of absolute truth claims, is affecting younger evangelicals' willingness to stand by the rational apologetics and theological edifices erected by a previous generation.[1] Second, increasing doubts about our ability to capture the essence of absolute truth have placed in question the legitimacy of the scientific method and are thus turning more and more evangelicals away from the various methods of higher biblical criticism.

This mounting opposition to critical exegesis is all the more remarkable considering the fact that its acceptance among evangelicals is only about half a century old (while, all this time, heirs to the fundamentalist detractors of liberal theology have never let go of their opposition to higher criticism). Of course, the younger evangelicals are by no means identical to the fundamentalists of the 1920s and 1930s. Still, they do share with them an aversion to rarefied academic biblical interests and to some of the excesses of higher criticism. The younger evangelicals seem intent on restoring theological or spiritual interpretation: a search for deeper, spiritual levels beyond the historical or literal mean-

---

1. For a discussion of the "younger evangelicals," see Robert E. Webber, *The Younger Evangelicals: Facing the Challenges of the New World* (Grand Rapids: Baker, 2002).

I

ing of the text, hidden in the inner recesses of the biblical text itself.[2] Both the nature of theology and the interpretation of Scripture are experiencing the effects of our postmodern cultural mindset.

Let me make clear from the outset that I do not consider myself a postmodern younger evangelical. At the same time, I do think that some of the criticisms that younger evangelicals are directing against "modern" approaches to theology and interpretation are largely on target. Theology has suffered — among evangelicals as well as elsewhere — from an undue desire for clarity and control, something to which the often abstract and rarefied distinctions of Scholastic theology have contributed. And the same mindset has caused not only a proliferation of biblical theological methods intent on recovering the historical meaning of the text; it has also entrenched the separation between biblical studies and dogmatic theology, between exposition and application, and between theology and spirituality.

While consenting to the ever-louder evangelical criticism of a modern theological and interpretive paradigm, the underpinnings of this book nonetheless do not stem from the same postmodern attitudes toward reality. Rather, I agree with the common perception that postmodernity is little more than modernity coming home to roost. Both, I believe, are predicated on the abandonment of a premodern sacramental mindset in which the realities of this-worldly existence pointed to greater, eternal realities in which they sacramentally shared. Once modernity abandoned a participatory or sacramental view of reality, the created order became unmoored from its origin in God, and the material cosmos began its precarious drift on the flux of nihilistic waves.[3]

2. See my more detailed discussion in chap. 8 below.

3. Craig M. Gay makes a similar point. Speaking of the attitude of suspicion engendered by postmodernism, he comments: "And yet as correct as the hermeneutic of suspicion may be about many of the oppressive qualities of modern existence, it does next to nothing to allay our fear that life may in the end be meaningless and absurd. Indeed, it only exacerbates this fear, for radical postmodernist theory simply extends the typically modern assumption that meaning is something that we must willfully construct for ourselves to its logical — if depressing — conclusion" (*Dialogue, Catalogue and Monologue: Personal, Impersonal and Depersonalizing Ways to Use Words* [Vancouver: Regent College Publishing, 2008], 122).

Introduction

Ressourcement of Heaven

Saint Paul's theology is an otherworldly theology. He is much more concerned about heavenly participation than about earthly enjoyment. For the apostle, heaven is the place we come from, the place we currently inhabit, and the place we aim for. In short, according to Paul, our past, present, and future lie anchored in heaven (Heb. 6:19). In contemporary Western theology, however, discourse on "heaven" has lost its central place. Evangelicals and Catholics alike have become more focused on the here-and-now than on the then-and-there. To speak of creaturely participation in heavenly realities ("heavenly participation") cannot but come across as outlandish to an age whose horizons have narrowed to such an extent that bodily goods, cultural endeavors, and political achievements have become matters of ultimate concern. Nonetheless, in line with the apostle Paul's otherworldly theology, this book will present a plea for a retrieval *(ressourcement)* of a theology of heavenly participation.

In a recent book, *Surprised by Hope,* N. T. Wright speaks for an increasingly common trend among evangelicals when he derides what he believes to be a widespread understanding of the afterlife: "So far from sitting on clouds playing harps, as people often imagine, the redeemed people of God in the new world will be the agents of his love going out in new ways, to accomplish new creative tasks, to celebrate and extend the glory of his love."[4] Admittedly, the combination of harps and clouds makes for a rather otherworldly outlook on the life hereafter. But I am intrigued by the concrete, *this*-worldly character of the expectations of the life hereafter with which evangelicals seem to be increasingly comfortable. There is often little anticipation of surprise: we seem to know a great deal about the future life, both in terms of what it will *not* be like, and what it *will* be like.

We seem to have forgotten C. S. Lewis's wise word of caution that "heaven is not really full of jewelry any more than it is really the beauty of Nature, or a fine piece of music."[5] I am not sure who, in the

4. N. T. Wright, *Surprised by Hope: Rethinking Heaven, the Resurrection, and the Mission of the Church* (New York: HarperOne, 2008), 105-6.

5. C. S. Lewis, "The Weight of Glory," in *The Weight of Glory, and Other Addresses* (1949; reprint, San Francisco: HarperSanFrancisco, 2001), 33. In the preface to his commentary on the Song of Songs, the great third-century Alexandrian theologian Origen made a similar point when he excoriated people who "believe that even after the resurrection cor-

Christian tradition, may have argued that in the hereafter we will be playing harps on the clouds (though it would not be an entirely unpleasant business). However, I am fairly confident that the extent of our eschatological transfiguration will be much more thoroughgoing than many of us suspect and that even our biblical language will literally prove infinitely inadequate to the task of describing the earthly reality that will have been transformed or divinized into our heavenly home.[6]

For Saint Paul, heaven is our home. After all, he insists that our citizenship papers carry the stamp of heaven. "[O]ur citizenship is in heaven," he plainly remarks (Phil. 3:20; cf. Eph. 2:12). This citizenship of Christians is incompatible with attempts to turn earthly ends into ultimate concerns. Speaking of enemies of the cross, the apostle observes: "Their destiny is destruction, their god is their stomach, and their glory is in their shame. Their mind is on earthly things" (Phil. 3:19). The heavenly identity of believers is, according to Paul, already a present reality. The rather realized eschatology of the letters to the Ephesians and the Colossians is emphatic about this present reality. For Paul, it is not as though believers here on earth somehow identify with a faraway place called "heaven." Rather, they have a real or participatory connection with heaven. The central paschal event — Christ's death, resurrection, and ascension — is something Christians participate in: God "made us alive with Christ," Paul insists (Eph. 2:5). He "raised us up with Christ" (Eph. 2:6; Col. 3:1). The result of this sharing in Christ is

---

poreal foods will be necessary, and that drink will have to be derived not merely from that 'true vine' (John 15:1) which lives forever, but also from vines and from fruit that grows on trees" (quoted in Richard A. Norris, ed., *The Song of Songs: Interpreted by Early Christian and Medieval Commentators,* The Church's Bible (Grand Rapids: Eerdmans, 2003), 5.

6. There is a great deal in Wright's eschatology that has my warm endorsement. I appreciate, for instance, his understanding of the resurrection as "life *after* life after death" (*Surprised by Hope*, pp. 148-52), his insistence that heaven and earth are not antithetical realities (pp. 104-6), and his belief that the resurrection entails the transformation of earthly realities (pp. 100, 162). Wright also makes clear that he does not know how exactly our positive contributions will make their reappearance in the final kingdom (though he is sure that Bach's music will be there — p. 209). Still, the consistent focus is on this-worldly realities. As an aside, on the issue of justification, Wright defends the "participationist" element of soteriology, which a strictly "juristic" view ignores (*Justification: God's Plan and Paul's Vision* [Downers Grove, IL: InterVarsity Academic, 2009], 32, 72). It seems to me that Wright's helpful participationist emphasis on union with Christ requires a much greater emphasis on participation in *heavenly* realities.

that believers participate in heavenly realities. We are seated with Christ "in the heavenly realms in Christ Jesus" (Eph. 2:6; Eph. 1:3).

To be sure, St. Paul's otherworldliness does not stand in absolute opposition to every this-worldly orientation. Rather, heavenly participation means that life on earth takes on a heavenly dimension. The church, through her participation in heaven, is called upon to make known the wisdom of God "to the rulers and authorities in the heavenly realms" (Eph. 3:10). Heavenly participation implies a battle "against the spiritual forces of evil in the heavenly realms" (Eph. 6:12). Precisely because heaven is already present on earth, the moral lives of Christians on earth are to reflect their heavenly participation. "Since, then, you have been raised with Christ, set your hearts on things above, where Christ is seated at the right hand of God. Set your minds on things above, not on earthly things" (Col. 3:1-2). The apostle then comments on the vices that are connected to the "earthly nature" (Col. 3:5) and encourages believers to follow the virtues of Christ (Col. 3:5-17). Participation in heaven changes life on earth: paradoxically, only otherworldliness guarantees proper engagement in this world.

Not only is heaven the "place" in which Christians are already at home today, but it also marks their origin and aim. Believers are blessed "in the heavenly realms" because heaven is the place of their eternal predestination "in Christ" (Eph. 1:4, 11). The origin of the Christian hope lies in Christ — and thus in heaven. Likewise, the prize for which Paul aims and toward which he "strains" is the "heavenward" call in Christ Jesus (Phil. 3:13-14; cf. 2 Tim. 4:18).[7] One of the reasons Neo-Platonism has been so attractive to theologians throughout the centuries is that the Neo-Platonic view of the cosmos "going out" from God and "returning" to him — the so-called *exitus-reditus* schema — was broadly compatible with Pauline Christianity.[8] According to the well-known Pauline hymn of Philippians 2, the pattern of Christ — who

7. Again, C. S. Lewis seems to echo this Pauline theme: "I have come home at last! This is my real country!" cries the Unicorn toward the end of *The Last Battle,* while stamping his right fore-hoof on the ground. "I belong here. This is the land I have been looking for all my life, though I never knew it till now. The reason why we loved the old Narnia is that it sometimes looked a little like this" (*The Chronicles of Narnia* [New York: HarperCollins, 2001], 760).

8. To be sure, the Neo-Platonist *exitus-reditus* schema involved the doctrine of necessary emanation, which Christian theology universally rejected. See chap. 1 below, under subheading "Christianity and the Platonic Heritage."

humbled himself by coming to earth and was exalted by returning to heaven (Phil. 2:6-11) — must be the pattern of the church. Contemporary theology needs, it seems to me, a recovery — a *ressourcement* — of this Pauline focus on our "heavenward" call.

In line with this Pauline focus, Saint Augustine borrowed from the Platonic tradition when he centered his account of the history of the city of God on the reality of heaven. Heaven, Augustine explains, was the source and destination of the city of God. The bishop begins his treatment of "the rise, the development and the destined ends of the two cities" by referring to "two classes of angels," namely, the angels of light and the angels of darkness.[9] The Fall in paradise ensured that both cities had their counterparts in human history. While Cain belonged to the city of man, Abel belonged to the city of God. Unlike Cain, Abel never built a city, because "the City of the saints is up above, though it produces citizens here below . . ." (XV.1). Christians are pilgrims on earth, since their citizenship is in the heavenly city of God. This city, Augustine maintains, "is said to come down from heaven because the grace by which God created it is heavenly. . . . This City has been coming down from heaven since its beginning, from the time when its citizens began to increase in number . . ." (XX.17). For Augustine, already today, heavenly participation is a reality for the citizens of the city of God.

Augustine concludes his account of the pilgrimage of the citizens of the heavenly city with a discussion of the eschatological reality in which believers will see God face to face (1 Cor. 13:12; 1 John 3:2). This beatific vision will produce a peace far transcending human understanding (Phil. 4:7):

> It surpasses our understanding: there can be no doubt of that. If it surpasses the understanding even of the angels, so that St. Paul in saying "all understanding" does not make an exception of them, we must then take him as meaning that the peace of God, the peace that God himself enjoys, cannot be known by the angels, still less by us men, in the way that God experiences it. (XXII.29)

Here Augustine has an eye for mystery: he recognizes that the full reality of heavenly participation far transcends the categories of the earthly

---

9. Augustine, *Concerning the City of God against the Pagans,* trans. Henry Bettenson (London: Penguin, 1984), XI.1. Hereafter, references to this work appear in parentheses in the text.

city. Heaven — the place of Christ's eternal dwelling place — is the place
where the church finds both her origin and her destination. Heaven is
the Christian home. Augustine sketches his account of the heavenly city
without worrying about whether the Platonic and the Christian traditions are compatible on this point. Along with nearly all Christian theologians prior to modernity, he was convinced that the Christian faith is
about heavenly participation and that this biblical insight allows for
some kind of Platonist-Christian synthesis.[10]

Let me clarify that the language of heavenly participation in no way
downplays or undermines the significance of the earthly city. Our identification with the heavenly city should not tempt us to disparage
earthly concerns. "[I]t is altogether right," the Bishop of Hippo claims
in *The City of God,* "that the soul should learn to look for those temporal blessings from God, and from him alone . . ." (X.14). Indeed, Augustine argues, "it would be incorrect to say that the goods which this
[earthly] city desires are not goods" (XV.4; cf. XXI.24). For Augustine,
we should not despise temporal blessings; Christians should not view
the ends of the earthly city as inherently evil or tainted. Nonetheless,
Augustine — and most Christian theologians following him — does
carefully distinguish between the ends of the earthly city and the aim
of the heavenly city. The former ends are on a much lower scale of significance than are the latter: "Now physical beauty, to be sure, is a good
created by God, but it is a temporal, carnal good, very low in the scale
of goods . . ." (XV.22). It is thus altogether appropriate to have a certain
kind of "contempt of the world" *(contemptus mundi).* Augustine claims
that the "inferior goods of this world . . . although essential for this
transitory life, are to be despised [*contemnenda*] in comparison with the
eternal blessings of that other life" (X.14).

The contempt with which the great African bishop speaks is not an
absolute contempt; it is a comparative or relative contempt. Earthly enjoyment pales in comparison to heavenly participation. Augustine's relative contempt for earthly goods was also that of the latter-day
Platonist-Christian C. S. Lewis: "But what, you ask, of earth? Earth, I
think, will not be found by anyone to be in the end a very distinct place.

10. Throughout this book I use the phrase "Platonist-Christian synthesis." I do not
mean to suggest with it that Platonism and Christianity merged to form an entity that
was greater than either of the two. As will become clear, it is my conviction that the
Christian faith judiciously appropriated certain elements of Platonic thought in the
process of Christianizing the Hellenic world.

I think earth, if chosen instead of Heaven, will turn out to have been, all along, only a region in Hell: and earth, if put second to Heaven, to have been from the beginning a part of Heaven itself."[11] Paradoxically, earthly realities carry significance only when we refuse to rank them first.[12] Far from downplaying or undermining the significance of the earthly city, heavenly participation is its only warrant. Throughout this book I will make the argument that when we abandon Augustine by turning created realities from objects of penultimate interest into objects that have ultimate importance, we ironically end up losing their significance.

The subtitle of this book speaks of the weaving of a sacramental tapestry. The Russian Orthodox theologian Alexander Schmemann presents a lucid picture of what I mean by the "sacramental tapestry" that characterized the Christian consensus of the fathers and the Middle Ages (the Great Tradition).[13] In his book *For the Life of the World*, Schmemann rejects the opposition between nature and the supernatural, and he attempts to reintegrate the two sacramentally. The "sacramental tapestry" of the subtitle speaks of a carefully woven unity of nature and the supernatural, according to which created objects are sacraments that participate in the mystery of the heavenly reality of Jesus Christ. Schmemann makes the point that everything in the so-called world of nature is meant to lead us back to God. In that sense, created matter is meant to serve eucharistically. By treating the world as a eucharistic offering in Christ, received *from* God and offered *to* him, we are drawn into God's presence. Schmemann puts it this way: "The world was created as the 'matter,' the material of one all-embracing eucharist, and man was created as the priest of this cosmic sacrament." Thus, when he discusses baptism and the Eucharist — the two material elements for which we usually reserve the term "sacrament" — Schmemann makes a point of connecting the water, as well as

11. C. S. Lewis, *The Great Divorce* (1946; reprint, New York: Simon and Schuster, 1996), 11.

12. John Calvin, in his discussion of meditation on the future life, also insists on such relative contempt of the present life: "Whatever kind of tribulation presses upon us, we must ever look to this end: to accustom ourselves to contempt for the present life and to be aroused thereby to meditate upon the future life" (*Institutes of the Christian Religion,* ed. John T. McNeill, trans. Ford Lewis Battles, Library of Christian Classics, vol. 20 [Philadelphia: Westminster, 1960], III.ix.1).

13. I will discuss the notion of "sacramental ontology" in greater detail in chap. 1, under "Sacramental Ontology as Real Presence."

the bread and the wine, with the rest of the cosmos: "Baptism," he insists, "refers us inescapably to 'matter,' to the world, to the cosmos."[14] In baptism and Eucharist we witness the restoration of matter to its original function. Elsewhere, Schmemann puts it beautifully:

> Christ came not to *replace* "natural" matter with some "supernatural" and sacred matter, but to *restore* it and to fulfill it as the means of communion with God. The holy water in Baptism, the bread and wine in the Eucharist, stand for, i.e. *represent* the whole of creation, but creation as it will be at the *end*, when it will be consummated in God, when He will fill all things with Himself.[15]

Schmemann, in this quotation, laments the way in which we often oppose nature and the supernatural to each other. In the church's sacraments — baptism and Eucharist — we witness the supernatural restoration of nature to its original purpose. The purpose of all of matter, as I have already mentioned, is to lead us into God's heavenly presence, to bring about communion with God, participation in the divine life. Thus are the church's sacraments simply the beginning of the cosmic restoration. The entire cosmos is meant to serve as a sacrament: a material gift from God in and through which we enter into the joy of his heavenly presence.

Ressourcement for Evangelicals and Catholics Together

This book is a project of retrieval *(ressourcement)*. By that I mean that it looks to the history of the church for resources to give theological direction to people in the twenty-first century. I do not look to any particular period as a "golden age" that we should recover. However, I do believe that the increasing trend among evangelicals to look for inspiration to the church fathers is a healthy one.[16] The sacramental ontol-

14. Alexander Schmemann, *For the Life of the World: Sacraments and Orthodoxy* (1982; reprint, Crestwood, NY: St. Vladimir's Seminary Press, 2004), 22, 15, 68.

15. Alexander Schmemann, *Of Water and the Spirit: A Liturgical Study of Baptism* (Crestwood, NY: St. Vladimir's Seminary Press, 1974), 49.

16. I am thinking, for example, of Baker Academic's Evangelical Ressourcement series; of the increasing interest in PhD-level patristic studies by younger evangelicals; and of the burgeoning theological interpretation among evangelicals, which I discuss in chap. 8 below.

ogy (or outlook on reality) that characterized theology for a full millennium is worthy of renewed exploration, and this book will make clear why I think this is the case. If we take seriously the *ressourcement* of the sacramental tapestry (along with the Platonist-Christian synthesis that it implies), I believe that we will discover great ecumenical opportunities, particularly ecumenical dialogue between Catholics and evangelicals. I have become convinced that a common rediscovery of the depths of the Great Tradition will, as a matter of course, lead to genuine rapprochement between evangelicals and Catholics.

Some time ago Richard Mouw, president of Fuller Seminary, recommended to me a book by the University of Arizona sociologist Andrew Greeley, entitled *The Catholic Imagination*, a fascinating exposition of what the author thinks is typically Catholic. "Catholics," Fr. Greeley says,

> live in an enchanted world, a world of statues and holy water, stained glass and votive candles, saints and religious medals, rosary beads and holy pictures. But these Catholic paraphernalia are mere hints of a deeper and more pervasive religious sensibility which inclines Catholics to see the Holy lurking in creation. As Catholics, we find our houses and our world haunted by a sense that the objects, events, and persons of daily life are revelations of grace.

This Catholic imagination, Greeley goes on to say, "can be appropriately called sacramental. It sees created reality as a 'sacrament,' that is, a revelation of the presence of God." I believe that Greeley is on to something. The Catholic mindset is different from that of evangelicals.

> Catholic theologians and artists tend to emphasize the presence of God in the world, while the classic works of Protestant theologians tend to emphasize the absence of God from the world. The Catholic writers stress the nearness of God to His creation, the Protestant writers the distance between God and His creation; the Protestants emphasize the risk of superstition and idolatry, the Catholics the dangers of a creation in which God is only marginally present. Or, to put the matter in different terms, Catholics tend to accentuate the immanence of God, Protestants the transcendence of God.[17]

17. Andrew M. Greeley, *The Catholic Imagination* (Berkeley: University of California Press, 2000), 1, 5.

If Greeley's description is correct, we have to conclude that the Protestant Reformation was part of a shift that had been in the making for centuries, and of which the desacramentalizing of the cosmos was the most significant feature.[18]

To be sure, Greeley's observation is in need of several qualifications. I am not convinced, for example, that Catholics lack an appreciation of divine transcendence. Nor is it clear to me that Protestants — especially those of the Pentecostal and charismatic persuasion — do not know what to do with God's presence in the world. Furthermore, Greeley's polarized description of Catholicism versus Protestantism conveniently overlooks the fact that a sacramental ontology has suffered not just in Protestantism, but also in Catholicism.[19] As a Dutch immigrant to Canada, I was struck by the fact that in the 1960s secularism was just as successful in Quebec in supplanting Catholicism as it was in the Netherlands in displacing Protestantism. In many ways, both Protestants *and* Catholics have succumbed to the onslaught of a desacralized modernity. Furthermore, as I wish to make clear in chapters 3 and 4 of this book, the desacramentalizing of the cosmos had its origin long before the Reformation. If this interpretation is correct, we may expect to find the deleterious effects of the loss of a sacramental ontology not just in the Reformation but also in Catholicism. Unfortunately, I will argue, neither side of the Reformation debate came out unscathed.

Ressourcement of *Nouvelle Théologie*

I have mentioned C. S. Lewis several times. The great novelist and lay theologian recognized the problems inherent in the desacramentalizing of modernity. He was also aware that we are often so attuned to our own cultural surroundings that we simply take them for granted. Lewis cautions against the danger of such "cultural snobbery" and, as a result, urges people to read not just contemporary books but also — especially — books from the past.[20] They can help us see the limitations

18. See chap. 5 below for a detailed discussion of this point.

19. Greeley, *Catholic Imagination*, 173-80.

20. C. S. Lewis, "On the Reading of Old Books," in *God in the Dock: Essays on Theology and Ethics*, ed. Walter Hooper (Grand Rapids: Eerdmans, 1970), 200-207. See also D. Bruce Hindmarsh, "Retrieval and Renewal: A Model for Evangelical Spiritual Vitality," in *J. I. Packer and the Evangelical Future: The Impact of His Life and Thought*, ed. Timothy George (Grand Rapids: Baker Academic, 2009), 101-2.

of our own context while opening us up to the wider vistas of the Great Tradition. One of the results of Lewis's reading of the classics of the Great Tradition was his great appreciation for the Platonist-Christian synthesis. For Lewis, *ressourcement* of the tradition means that he took seriously the sacramental ontology that was the result of Christianity's encounter with Platonism.

In the 1940s and 1950s, the French Catholic renewal movement of *nouvelle théologie* ("new theology") engaged in a project of *ressourcement* much like Lewis's and much like the one on which I am embarking in this book. Or, to put it more modestly and accurately, I simply am taking my cue from *nouvelle théologie*'s much more in-depth and wide-ranging project of *ressourcement*.[21] And for *nouvelle théologie,* too, *ressourcement* of the tradition meant taking seriously Christianity's encounter with Platonism. In the French city of Lyons, Henri de Lubac (1896-1991) and his student Jean Daniélou (1905-1974) engaged in a tremendous effort to recover the church fathers, particularly the Eastern theologians, well known for their Platonist-Christian proclivities. The two scholars began republishing the fathers in a series entitled *Sources Chrétiennes,* which over the years has published well over five hundred volumes and has gained great renown for its scholarly character. The faculty of the Jesuit scholasticate in Fourvière-Lyons also published a monograph series under the title *Théologie,* which, though it did not focus strictly on patristic texts, did much to advance the theological interests of the *nouvelle* theologians.

Meanwhile, especially since the 1930s, de Lubac had been reading his way through an enormous amount of material from the church fathers and medieval theologians. The result was that he began to chart a new path in various areas of theology, and he did so consistently on the basis of his reading of the Great Tradition. This was the case with his wide-ranging book *Catholicisme* (1938), with his study of the history of the Eucharist entitled *Corpus mysticum* (1944), with his controversial work on the nature-supernatural relationship entitled *Surnaturel* (1946), and with his four-volume discussion of the spiritual interpretation of Scripture, *Exégèse médiévale* (1959-1964).[22]

---

21. For a more detailed discussion of *nouvelle théologie,* see Hans Boersma, *Nouvelle Théologie and Sacramental Ontology: A Return to Mystery* (Oxford: Oxford University Press, 2009).

22. Henri de Lubac, *Catholicism: Christ and the Common Destiny of Man,* trans. Lancelot C. Sheppard and Elizabeth Englund (San Francisco: Ignatius, 1988); de Lubac, *Corpus*

Daniélou stepped into his mentor's footsteps with a 1943 monograph on the Platonism and the mystical theology of Gregory of Nyssa. Daniélou, widely recognized as the father of contemporary Nyssa scholarship, also published broadly on typological exegesis in the church fathers, on Origen, and on the relationship between cosmic and Christian revelation.[23] The well-known Swiss theologian Hans Urs von Balthasar (1905-88) also spent four years studying theology at the Jesuit scholasticate of Lyons-Fourvière, and as a result he deeply respected de Lubac as his primary mentor. This was reflected in his monographs on church fathers such as Origen, Gregory of Nyssa, and Irenaeus, as well as in numerous other publications on the patristics and the medieval tradition.[24] Finally, the historical theologian Henri Bouillard (1908-1981), who in 1941 was appointed to teach at the Jesuit scholasticate, in 1943 published his (rather controversial) dissertation on conversion in Thomas Aquinas. Fourteen years later, he earned a second doctorate, this time writing on the theology of Karl Barth.[25]

Mysticum: The Eucharist and the Church in the Middle Ages: Historical Survey, trans. Gemma Simmonds with Richard Price and Christopher Stephens, ed. Laurence Paul Hemming and Susan Frank Parsons (London: SCM, 2006); de Lubac, *Medieval Exegesis: The Four Senses of Scripture,* 3 vols., trans. Mark Sebanc and E. M. Macierowski (Grand Rapids: Eerdmans, 1998, 2000, 2009). De Lubac's *Surnaturel* has not been translated, but the essential argument of the book can be found in translations of two later works: de Lubac, *Augustinianism and Modern Theology,* trans. Lancelot Sheppard, introd. Louis Dupré (New York: Crossroad/Herder and Herder, 2000); de Lubac, *The Mystery of the Supernatural,* trans. Rosemary Sheed (New York: Crossroad/Herder and Herder, 1998).

23. Jean Daniélou, *From Shadows to Reality: Studies in the Biblical Typology of the Fathers,* trans. Wulstan Hibberd (London: Burns and Oates, 1960); Daniélou, *The Bible and the Liturgy,* Liturgical Studies, no. 3 (Notre Dame, IN: University of Notre Dame Press, 1956); Daniélou, *Origen,* trans. Walter Mitchell (New York: Sheed and Ward, 1955); Daniélou, *Holy Pagans of the Old Testament,* trans. Felix Faber (London: Longmans, Green and Co., 1957); Daniélou, *The Advent of Salvation: A Comparative Study of Non-Christian Religions and Christianity,* trans. Rosemary Sheed (New York: Paulist, 1962); Daniélou, *The Lord of History: Reflections on the Inner Meaning of History,* trans. Nigel Abercrombie (1958; reprint, Cleveland: Meridian/World, 1968).

24. Hans Urs von Balthasar, *Origen: Spirit and Fire: A Thematic Anthology of His Writings,* trans. Robert J. Daly (Washington, DC: Catholic University of America Press, 1984); von Balthasar, *Presence and Thought: An Essay on the Religious Philosophy of Gregory of Nyssa,* trans. Mark Sebanc (San Francisco: Communio/Ignatius, 1995); von Balthasar, *The Scandal of the Incarnation: Irenaeus against the Heresies,* trans. John Saward (San Francisco: Ignatius, 1990).

25. Neither of these works has been translated in its entirety. Parts of Bouillard's

Introduction

The Dominican studium of Le Saulchoir, located near Paris, was a second center of *ressourcement* scholarship. There Marie-Dominique Chenu (1895-1990), an outspoken figure much engaged in social activism, did meticulous work on medieval theology, especially on the twelfth and thirteenth centuries.[26] From the outset of his career, Chenu was interested in the relationship between contemplation and action, which was clear from his dissertation on Thomas Aquinas, published as *De contemplatione* (1920). As rector of the Saulchoir studium, Chenu wrote on the nature of theology, and he was particularly keen on reintegrating theology with experience.[27] Chenu was always interested in drawing out the contemporary implications of Thomas's historical work. Especially does his popular book on the "angelic doctor," *St. Thomas d'Aquin et la théologie* (1959), read as though Thomas were walking the streets of Paris as one of the socially active worker-priests in the 1940s or 1950s.[28] Meanwhile, Yves Congar (1904-95), Chenu's one-time student and later colleague, was mostly interested in ecumenical studies and ecclesiology.[29] But Congar, too, was engaged in the work of *ressourcement:* he was noted for his careful historical theological work, especially his monumental two-volume study *La Tradition et les traditions* (1960, 1963).[30]

Although the *ressourcement* project of *nouvelle théologie* ultimately gave rise to the renewal of the Second Vatican Council (1962-65), it was

---

work on Barth can be accessed in Henri Bouillard, *The Knowledge of God*, trans. Samuel D. Femiano (New York: Herder and Herder, 1968).

26. See, for example, Marie-Dominique Chenu, *Nature, Man, and Society in the Twelfth Century: Essays on New Theological Perspectives in the Latin West,* preface Étienne Gilson, trans. and ed. Jerome Taylor and Lester Little, Medieval Academy Reprints for Teaching, no. 37 (1968; reprint, Toronto: University of Toronto Press, 1997).

27. See Marie-Dominique Chenu, *Is Theology a Science?* trans. A. H. N. Green-Armytage (New York: Hawthorn, 1959), which I discuss in detail in chap. 10 below.

28. Marie-Dominique Chenu, *Aquinas and His Role in Theology*, trans. Paul Philibert (Collegeville, MN: Liturgical, 2002). See also his extensive work on Aquinas, *Toward Understanding Saint Thomas,* trans. Albert M. Landry and Dominic Hughes (Chicago: Regnery, 1964); see also Chenu, *Faith and Theology*, trans. Denis Hickey (New York: Macmillan, 1968).

29. On Congar, see Gabriel Flynn, *Yves Congar's Vision of the Church in a World of Unbelief* (Burlington, VT: Ashgate, 2004).

30. Yves M.-J. Congar, *Tradition and Traditions: The Biblical, Historical, and Theological Evidence for Catholic Teaching on Tradition,* trans. Michael Naseby and Thomas Rainborough (San Diego: Basilica, 1966); see also his much more accessible *The Meaning of Tradition,* trans. A. N. Woodrow (San Francisco: Ignatius, 2004).

initially met with a barrage of criticism, leading to the temporary si-
lencing of nearly all of the theologians mentioned above. While in
some cases (especially Chenu) social activism was the cause of concern,
the broader angst of the Catholic establishment regarding *nouvelle
théologie* stemmed from its *ressourcement,* its return to the broad consensus of the fathers and the Middle Ages — that is, the Great Tradition.[31]
This may seem surprising, at least from an evangelical perspective;
however, within the Catholic context of the time, the disquiet was per-
fectly understandable.

A strongly intellectualist system of thought known as Neo-Thomism
dominated Catholic theology at the time. This school had come into
prominence especially because of the 1879 publication of Pope
Leo XIII's encyclical *Aeterni Patris.* Leo XIII loved Thomas Aquinas and
had put forward the thirteenth-century philosopher-theologian as the
great model for the church to follow. For Leo, Saint Thomas was not
just an interesting figure of the High Middle Ages; he was *the* abiding
source of philosophical and dogmatic truth. Pope Leo insisted that
Aquinas had gathered together the teachings of the medieval Scholastic theologians in a brilliant way, and had added his own additional insights to this medieval body of thought, thereby creating such an
amazing synthesis that the angelic doctor was "rightly and deservedly
esteemed the special bulwark and glory of the Catholic faith."[32] What
Leo's encyclical did was entrench Thomist philosophy and theology as
the one normative system of Catholic thought.

Nouvelle théologie was a protest against this unified Neo-Thomist approach. Thus, when the Jesuits from Fourvière and the Dominicans
from Le Saulchoir engaged in their *ressourcement* project, they were
reaching back past the ossified Scholasticism of the previous centuries.
Nouvelle théologie's turn to the fathers and the medieval theologians was
an effort to reintegrate faith and theology; it was an effort to go back
to Scripture itself; and it was an endeavor to allow theology to speak to
people's everyday lives. In particular, as we shall soon note, the
ressourcement movement tried to reweave the sacramental tapestry of
the Great Tradition by reintegrating nature and the supernatural, the

---

31. The term *nouvelle théologie* is one that the theologians in question never appropriated for themselves. Rather, it was the Roman Catholic establishment that branded
these French theologians as "new."

32. *Aeterni Patris,* no. 17.

two realms that the Neo-Thomist Scholastics — with their much-debated appeal to Thomas Aquinas — had kept hermetically sealed and separate from one another. By contrast, when the *nouvelle* theologians read Aquinas, they often highlighted his patristic roots, his Platonic proclivities, and the christological starting point of his theology. This meant that, in part, the controversy between *nouvelle théologie* and Neo-Thomism was about the interpretation of Saint Thomas. The program of *ressourcement* and reinterpretation of the tradition was required, the *nouvelle* theologians were convinced, in order to counter the secularizing trends that were making inroads in twentieth-century France.

The Neo-Thomists interpreted the *ressourcement* of the Great Tradition as a betrayal of Saint Thomas and as a novel way of doing theology — hence the designation *nouvelle théologie*. In reality, however, there was little that was novel in *nouvelle théologie*'s approach. A deep love for the church fathers and medieval theology drove the scholarly interests of the *nouvelle* theologians. They recognized in the Platonist-Christian synthesis a sacramental ontology that they believed had been lost through the modern separation between nature and the supernatural. As a result, *nouvelle théologie* set out to reintegrate the two by pointing to the sacramental participation of nature in the heavenly reality of Christ. The *ressourcement* theologians were convinced that the vision of sacramental participation was the only viable answer to the secularism of the modern age.

Therefore, after I have sketched the decline of the sacramental tapestry of the Platonist-Christian synthesis in part 1 of this book (the *exitus*), I will present a discussion of the various theological areas that the *nouvelle* theologians believed were in need of renewal (the *reditus*) in part 2. Accordingly, the structure of this book is meant to be an allusion to the Platonist-Christian synthesis that I believe we need to reengage. It is my conviction that evangelicals (as well as Catholics) do well to join *nouvelle théologie* in this journey of rediscovery. At stake is nothing less than participation in the heavenly reality of Jesus Christ.

Exitus: The Fraying Tapestry

The rise of modernity corresponded with the decline of an approach that regarded the created order as sacramental in character. The patristic and medieval mind recognized that the heavenly reality of the Word of God constituted an eternal mystery; the observable appearances of creation pointed to and participated in this mystery. I begin part 1 by sketching the contours of this sacramental tapestry of the fathers and the Middle Ages, a tapestry that took the form of a Platonist-Christian synthesis (chapters 1 and 2). Next, I describe the fraying of this tapestry of the Great Tradition through several late-medieval theological developments (chapters 3 and 4). The final chapter of part 1 explains that, while the Reformation reconfigured the nature-supernatural relationship, the movement was unable to restore the earlier sacramental tapestry. Today's uncritical acceptance of postmodernity among younger evangelicals unfortunately represents a turn toward skepticism rather than an embrace of sacramental mystery.

CHAPTER 1

The Shape of the Tapestry:
A Sacramental Ontology

It is difficult for Christians — whether Catholic or evangelical — to imagine a time when theology was regarded as the most important discipline.[1] The modern period has taught us to look to other sources as the main guides for establishing our life together. The argument that theology is *the* most authoritative guide for our common (public) life seems profoundly presumptuous to many who have grown up in modern liberal democracies. In fact, many will claim that such a high view of theology strikes at the very root of our cultural arrangement. I will not dispute this claim. It seems to me unsurprising and even logical, considering that modernity takes its cue from earthly rather than heavenly realities. Its basic, dissident choice has been to take temporal goods for ultimate ends. I find myself in agreement with John Milbank's oft-quoted statement: "The pathos of modern theology is its false humility. For theology, this must be a fatal disease. . . . If theology no longer seeks to position, qualify or criticize other discourses, then it is inevitable that these discourses will position theology."[2] Furthermore, if the political and economic establishment of modern liberal democracies feels threatened by the view that theology should be our primary disciplinary practice, perhaps this is simply an indication of the ultimate incompatibility between modernity and the theological

---

1. I will look at various meanings of the word "discipline" in chap. 10. I am not using the word simply in the sense of one academic discipline among others, but more in the sense of initiation into the Christian life.

2. John Milbank, *Theology and Social Theory: Beyond Secular Reason* (Oxford: Blackwell, 1990), 1.

convictions of the Great Tradition. None of this is to suggest that this book sets out to do battle with "outside" economic and political forces. Rather, I am taking aim at historical developments *within* theology, which I believe lie at the root of our contemporary cultural problems. As a result, I am calling for a resacramentalized Christian ontology (or outlook on reality).

The word "ontology" may put some people on edge. The expression places us, so it seems at least, in the area of abstract, metaphysical thought. Should Christians really concern themselves with ontology? Isn't the danger of looking at the world through an ontological lens that we may lose sight of the particularities of the Christian faith: God's creation of the world, the Incarnation, the Crucifixion, the outpouring of the Holy Spirit, the particular ecclesial community, and Scripture itself? I understand these fears, and I appreciate the word of caution as an important one.[3] Nonetheless, the objections do not make me abandon the search for an ontology that is compatible with the Christian faith. As I hope to make clear throughout this book, I believe that the Great Tradition of the church — most of the Christian era until the late Middle Ages — did have an ontology. The call for a purely "biblical" theology seems to me terribly naïve. Whether consciously or subconsciously, we all work with a particular ontology; unfortunately, usually the ontology of those who plead for the abolition of ontology turns out to be the nominalist ontology of modernity (something I will unpack in more detail in chapter 4). However, I do agree with the cau-

---

3. One of the common objections to Radical Orthodoxy has been that its focus on ontology attempts to establish the relationship between nature and the supernatural in cosmic, abstract categories, while it loses sight of the particular character of the historic Christ. In other words, with ontology in place, there hardly seems room left for reflection on Christology. A related objection is that the (rather postmodern) Neo-Platonic character of Radical Orthodoxy's ontology seems to blur the boundaries between the divine and the human, and as a result Radical Orthodoxy finds it difficult to retain appropriate boundaries, leading to a rather nebulous view of the church and to a sexual ethic that loses much of the particularity of traditional Christian morality. All of this, so the argument goes, is hardly surprising when ontology replaces biblically informed theology. I actually echo much of this criticism. See Hans Boersma, "Being Reconciled: Atonement as the Ecclesio-Christological Practice of Forgiveness in John Milbank," in *Radical Orthodoxy and the Reformed Tradition: Creation, Covenant, and Participation,* ed. James K. A. Smith and James H. Olthuis (Grand Rapids: Baker Academic, 2005), 183-202; see also Boersma, "On the Rejection of Boundaries: Radical Orthodoxy's Appropriation of St. Augustine," *Pro Ecclesia* 15 (2006): 418-47.

tionary comment that a Christian ontology must be centered on Christ, that it dare not avoid the particularity of the visible church, and that it needs to take seriously the church's engagement with divine revelation in Scripture.[4] These concerns, I believe, were carefully safeguarded in the Platonist-Christian synthesis of the Great Tradition. This tradition was quite conscious of the fact that there is no such thing as a universally accessible, neutral "ontology" separate from the very particular convictions of the Christian faith.

Sacramental Ontology as Real Presence

Before going any further into this discussion, I think it is necessary to define some of my terms. What do I mean by "sacramental ontology," and by the "Platonist-Christian synthesis" on which it relies? I devote this first chapter to answering this question — or, at least, to providing the basic contours of an answer. The argument of part 1 of this book is that until the late Middle Ages (say, the fourteenth and fifteenth centuries), people looked at the world as a mystery. The word "mystery" did not have quite the same connotations that it has for us today. Certainly, it did not refer to a puzzling issue whose secret one can uncover by means of clever investigation. Our understanding of "mystery novels," for example, carries that kind of connotation. For the patristic and medieval mindset, the word "mystery" meant something slightly — but significantly — different. "Mystery" referred to realities behind the appearances that one could observe by means of the senses. That is to say, though our hands, eyes, ears, nose, and tongue are able to access reality, they cannot *fully* grasp this reality. They cannot *comprehend* it. The reason for this basic incomprehensibility of the universe was that the world was, as the poet Gerard Manley Hopkins famously put it, "charged with the grandeur of God." Even the most basic created realities that we observe as human beings carry an extra dimension, as it were. The created world cannot be reduced to measurable, manageable dimensions.[5]

---

4. Bryan C. Hollon has rightly argued that one of the most significant differences between Radical Orthodoxy and premodern theology is the former's lack of engagement with the biblical text (*Everything Is Sacred: Spiritual Exegesis in the Political Theology of Henri de Lubac* [Eugene, OR: Cascade/Wipf and Stock, 2009], 7-8, 141-42, 164-65).

5. Flannery O'Connor puts it well: "The fiction writer presents mystery through

Up to this point, my explanation is probably relatively uncontroversial. Most of us, when we think about the ability of the senses to comprehend reality, realize that they are inadequate to the task. And I suspect that we generally recognize that the reason for this does not lie mainly in faulty hearing, poor vision, or worn-out taste buds, but in the fact that reality truly *is* mysterious. It carries a dimension that we are unable to fully express. But let me take the next step, and I suspect that in doing so, I may encounter some naysayers. Throughout the Great Tradition, when people spoke of the mysterious quality of the created order, what they meant was that this created order — along with all other temporary and provisional gifts of God — was a sacrament. This sacrament was the sign of a mystery that, though present in the created order, nonetheless far transcended human comprehension. The sacramental character of reality was the reason it so often appeared mysterious and beyond human comprehension. So, when I speak of my desire to recover a "sacramental ontology" in this book, I am speaking of an ontology (an understanding of reality) that is sacramental in character. The perhaps controversial, but nonetheless important, point that I want to make is that the mysterious character of all created reality lies in its sacramental nature. In fact, we would not go wrong by simply equating mystery and sacrament.

What, then, is so distinct about the sacramental ontology that characterized much of the history of the church? Perhaps the best way to explain this is to distinguish between symbols and sacraments. A road sign with the silhouette of a deer symbolizes the presence of deer in the area, and its purpose is to induce drivers to slow down. Drivers will not be so foolish as to veer away from the road sign for fear of hitting the deer that is symbolized on the road sign. The reason is obvious: the symbol of the deer and the deer in the woods are two completely separate realities. The former is a sign referring to the latter, but in no way do the two co-inhere. It is not as though the road sign carries a mysterious quality, participating somehow in the stags that roam the forests. In diagram 1, symbol X and reality Y merely have an external or nominal relationship. The distance between the two makes clear that there is

---

manners, grace through nature, but when he finishes there always has to be left over that sense of Mystery which cannot be accounted for by any human formula" (*Mystery and Manners: Occasional Prose,* ed. Sally and Robert Fitzgerald [1957; reprint, New York: Farrar, Straus and Giroux, 1970], 153).

no real connection between them. Things are different with sacraments. Unlike mere symbols, sacraments actually *participate* in the mysterious reality to which they point. Sacrament *X* and reality *Y* co-inhere: the sacrament participates in the reality to which it points.

Diagram 1. Symbols vs. Sacraments

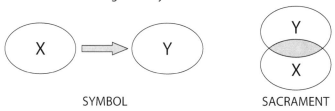

SYMBOL   SACRAMENT

In his essay "Transposition," C. S. Lewis makes this same point when he distinguishes between symbolism and sacramentalism. The relationship between speech and writing, Lewis argues, "is one of symbolism. The written characters exist solely for the eye, the spoken words solely for the ear. There is complete discontinuity between them. They are not like one another, nor does the one cause the other to be."[6] By contrast, when we look at how a picture represents the visible world, we find a rather different kind of relationship. Lewis explains:

> Pictures are part of the visible world themselves and represent it only by being part of it. Their visibility has the same source as its. The suns and lamps in pictures seem to shine only because real suns or lamps shine on them; that is, they seem to shine a great deal because they really shine a little in reflecting their archetypes. The sunlight in a picture is therefore not related to real sunlight simply as written words are to spoken. It is a sign, but also something more than a sign, because in it the thing signified is really in a certain mode present. If I had to name the relation I should call it not symbolical but sacramental.[7]

For Lewis, a sacramental relationship implies real presence. This understanding of sacramentality is part of a long lineage. According to the sacramental ontology of much of the Christian tradition, the created

6. C. S. Lewis, "Transposition," in *The Weight of Glory, and Other Addresses* (1949; reprint, San Francisco: HarperSanFrancisco, 2001), 102.

7. Lewis, "Transposition," 102.

order was more than an external or nominal symbol. Instead, it was a sign *(signum)* that pointed to *and* participated in a greater reality *(res)*. It seems to me that the shape of the cosmic tapestry is one in which earthly signs and heavenly realities are intimately woven together, so much so that we cannot have the former without the latter. Later on, I will need to say more about what this reality is in which our sacramental world participates. For now, it is enough to observe that the reason for the mysterious character of the world — on the understanding of the Great Tradition, at least — is that it participates in some greater reality, from which it derives its being and its value. Hence, instead of speaking of a sacramental ontology, we may also speak of a participatory ontology.

Of course, any theist position assumes a relationship between God and this world. And many evangelicals will, in addition, agree that this link between God and the world takes on a covenantal shape. God makes covenants both with the created world as a whole (Gen. 9:8-17; Jer. 33:19-26) and with human beings (Gen. 15:1-21; 17:1-27; Exod. 24:1-18; 2 Sam. 7:1-17; Jer. 31:31-33; Heb. 8:1-13). There is, I believe, a great deal of value in highlighting this covenantal relationship. But the insistence on a *sacramental* link between God and the world goes well beyond the mere insistence that God has created the world and by creating it has declared it to be good. It also goes beyond positing an agreed-on (covenantal) relationship between two completely separate beings. A sacramental ontology insists that not only does the created world point to God as its source and "point of reference," but that it also subsists or participates in God. A participatory or sacramental ontology will look to passages such as Acts 17:28 ("For in him we live and move and have our being. As some of your own poets have said, 'We are his offspring'"), and will conclude that our being participates in the being of God. Such an outlook on reality will turn to Colossians 1:17 ("He [Christ] is before all things, and in him all things hold together"), and will argue that the truth, goodness, and beauty of all created things is grounded in Christ, the eternal Logos of God.[8] In other words, because creation is a sharing in the being of God, our connection with God is a *participatory,* or real, connection — not just an *external,* or nominal, connection.

8. See also the angelic hymn of Isa. 6:3, which proclaims that "the whole earth is full of his glory"; and Eph. 1:23, which speaks of the church as Christ's body, "the fullness of him who fills everything in every way."

Few people have expressed this distinction better than C. S. Lewis has: "We do not want merely to *see* beauty, though, God knows, even that is bounty enough. We want something else which can hardly be put into words — to be united with the beauty we see, to pass into it, to receive it into ourselves, to bathe in it, to become part of it."[9] We do not want merely a nominal relationship; we desire a participatory relationship. In fact, a sacramental ontology maintains that the former is possible only because of the latter: a genuinely covenantal bond is possible only because the covenanting partners are not separate or fragmented individuals. The real connection that God has graciously posited between himself and the created order forms the underlying ontological basis that makes it possible for a covenant relationship to flourish.

When we talk about "real presence," we tend to think in terms of eucharistic theology, and we ask the question: Is Christ really present in the Eucharist (the sacramentalist position), or is the celebration of the Lord's Supper an ordinance in which we remember what Christ did by offering himself for us on the Cross (the memorialist position)? Of course, there are all kinds of shades and nuances in the various positions, but this is nonetheless a fair description of the issue at stake in the differing approaches to the Eucharist. On the one side, we have those who insist on a participatory or real connection between the elements and the heavenly body of Christ itself; on the other side, people argue for an external or nominal connection between the elements and the ascended Lord.[10]

Understandably, debates surrounding a participatory or real link between Christ and creation came to a head in connection with the issue of the ecclesiastical sacrament of the Eucharist. This was, after all, the central sacrament in the church's life. Eucharistic debates, important for their own sake, had wide-ranging implications. So, for good reason, by the time the sixteenth-century Reformation came around, the church had been debating the nature of Christ's presence in the Eucharist for centuries. Accordingly, I will devote special attention to the im-

9. C. S. Lewis, "The Weight of Glory," in *Weight of Glory,* 42.

10. As I mentioned, we do need to take account of nuances. For example, the way I have described the alternatives, it may be difficult to slot in Calvin's understanding of spiritual presence. On the one hand, clearly, Calvin is not a memorialist; on the other hand, he never describes Christ's presence in the Lord's Supper as "real" presence. For an interpretation of Calvin's views as in sync with "real presence," see William R. Crockett, *Eucharist: Symbol of Transformation* (Collegeville, MN: Liturgical, 1999), 149-52.

plications of medieval developments surrounding the Eucharist in chapter 6. For now, I simply wish to draw attention to the fact that the debates surrounding the real presence (or, we might say, participation) in the Eucharist were but the particular instantiation of a much broader discussion about real presence. While the church fathers and medieval theologians did look to the bread and wine of the Eucharist as the sacrament in which Christ was really present, in making this point they simultaneously conveyed their conviction that Christ was mysteriously present in the entire created order. Christ's sacramental presence in the Eucharist was, we might say, an intensification of his sacramental presence in the world.

The Celebration of Creation: Use or Enjoyment?

Why is this sacramental presence important? What does it have to do with life in our (post-)modern Western world? Let me explain by briefly mentioning some of the main factors that inform my theology. The basic motivation that drives much of my theologizing is twofold. First, I believe that, face to face with mystery of the triune God, theology needs a great deal of modesty. Theology, as Saint Anselm recognized, is a seeking of the face of God. Quoting Psalm 27:8 at crucial junctures of his "Proslogium," the great eleventh-century theologian pleaded with the God whom he knew as a humble believer:

> Do thou help me for thy goodness' sake! Lord, I sought thy face; thy face, Lord, will I seek; hide not thy face far from me (Psalms xxvii.8). Free me from myself toward thee. Cleanse, heal, sharpen, enlighten the eye of my mind, that it may behold thee. Let my soul recover its strength, and with all its understanding let it strive toward thee, O Lord. What art thou, Lord, what art thou? What shall my heart conceive thee to be?[11]

St. Anselm, often unjustly reproached for being a rationalist, had a deep appreciation for the mystery of God and was keenly aware that theology was not there to explain God but to draw us into the very mystery of his life. The modesty that theology needs is the recognition

---

11. St. Anselm, "Proslogium," in *St. Anselm: Basic Writings,* trans. S. N. Deane, 2nd ed. (La Salle, IL: Open Court, 1968), XVIII; see also *St. Anselm: Basic Writings,* "Proslogium," I.

that we cannot rationally comprehend God. Theology is based on mystery and enters into mystery. Not only can we not grasp God, but, adds the fourth-century mystical theologian Gregory of Nyssa: "I also ask: Who has known his own mind? Those who think themselves capable of grasping the nature of God would do well to consider whether they have looked into themselves. . . ."[12] For Gregory, not only is the nature of God himself a mystery to us, but as human beings created in God's image, we also remain a mystery to ourselves. My concern with much modern theology is precisely that it has lost a great deal of this sense of mystery. Modern theology's problem is its rational confidence — and thus, ultimately, its pride.

This is an important point, because many younger evangelicals are reacting against the propositionalism and intellectualism of their forebears.[13] They have found some of the theological handbooks from which they learned their theology to be dry and lifeless. Theology, younger evangelicals rightly sense, must be about more than just providing true propositional statements about God and our relationship with him. More importantly, many of today's evangelicals sense that these theological handbooks wrongly give the impression that we can fully and adequately grasp the truth to which our theological statements refer. Therefore, there is a growing sense that we need a healthy dose of mystery to counter sterile intellectualism. And to the degree that younger evangelicals sense the hubris of a good deal of modern theologizing, I can only echo their sentiments. But, of course, a return to mystery may take on different forms. Some of our younger evangelicals, it seems to me, run the danger of confusing postmodern skepticism with mystery. As we attempt to recover mystery in theology, it is critical that we recognize that the premodern notion of mystery owed nothing to skepticism or relativism. It had everything to do with acknowledging that the mystery of God's being had suffused the created world. Theology's genuine humility has less to do with skepticism than it does with mysticism.

My concern about the rational self-confidence of modernity leads to the second factor that drives much of my theologizing: a concern

---

12. St. Gregory of Nyssa, *De hominis opificio,* chap. 11, as quoted in de Lubac, *The Mystery of the Supernatural* (New York: Crossroad, 1998), 210.

13. Cf. Robert E. Webber, *The Younger Evangelicals: Facing the Challenges of the New World* (Grand Rapids: Baker, 2002), 83-106.

about our often uncritical acceptance of contemporary culture.[14] It seems to me that we too easily give in to the temptation of accommodation to the latest trends and fads of the culture around us, often naively and uncritically accepting the dictates of a society that is largely post-Christian. Whether it is secular criticism of our Christian past, politically correct agendas that we are massaged into accepting, or the backbone of our moral commitments, as evangelicals we look askance far too readily at countercultural Christianity and instead opt for accommodation to our surrounding culture.

For those with an inclination to pigeonhole, let me clarify that by no means do I locate myself theologically in the Anabaptist countercultural tradition. By opposing itself sharply to the evils of the world, this tradition insufficiently recognizes the many commonalities that believers and unbelievers share as a result of the goodness of God's created order in Christ. A shared humanity implies that Christians and non-Christians have some degree of a common participation in being. But this shared participation in being is not the only thing that needs to be affirmed. We also need to recognize that participation in being and goodness comes in degrees of intensity. The alien intrusion of evil in the world diminishes this participation. As Augustine recognizes, because created things "are not, like their Creator, supremely and unchangeably good, their good may be diminished and increased."[15] Evil sucks the life out of us and thus diminishes our existence and goodness. Wherever evil rears its head against the goodness of being, Christians have the calling to oppose it. Thus, as evangelicals, we need to recognize that accommodation (often masked theologically with claims that the goodness of creation means we should avoid escapism, that the gospel "redeems" every sphere of life, that the gospel needs to be "incarnated" in people's everyday existence, and so on) comes at a price when practiced in a culture that prizes human autonomy as the basic building block of our common life together. Such radical autonomy diminishes the goodness of being and must be resisted.

To my mind, there is deep irony in such an evangelical posture of accommodation. Let me illustrate the irony with an example from per-

14. See Hans Boersma, "Accommodation to What? Univocity of Being, Pure Nature, and the Anthropology of St. Irenaeus," *International Journal of Systematic Theology* 8 (2006): 266-93.

15. St. Augustine, *The Enchiridion on Faith, Hope and Love,* intro. Thomas S. Hibbs, ed. Henry Paolucci (1961; reprint, Washington, DC: Regnery, 1995), XII.

sonal experience. A few years ago, our local Christian high school organized a school trip to a "Body Worlds" exhibit set up at the well-known Science World (a hands-on science center and museum) in Vancouver. "Body Worlds" turned out to be an exhibit of plasticized human bodies that was organized by Gunther von Hagens, a German anatomist whose exhibitions and public autopsies (which he performs while wearing a black fedora) have elicited protests and legal controversies throughout the world. Von Hagens's displays reduce the human body to simply an object, one that we can purchase, plasticize, display, and analyze for the sake of education and entertainment. Objections to von Hagens's exhibits, especially among Catholics, have been quite pronounced. To my surprise, there was little or no concern within our evangelical school community about the exhibit's objectification and exploitation of the human body; instead, they regarded the exhibit as an opportunity for the students to see how the body was "fearfully and wonderfully made." I found that, more troubling perhaps than von Hagens's display, was the broad evangelical acceptance of it — with an appeal to the goodness of the created order. As this book will make clear, my argument is not with the goodness of the created order. Rather, I have become convinced that a certain kind of appeal to the goodness of creation, such as the one I just described, lapses into its opposite: that is, a denigration and commodification of the created order, in this case of the human body.

We certainly should celebrate the goodness of the created order along with Saint Irenaeus, that untiring second-century opponent of Gnostic escapism. But we can only truly celebrate it (and prevent its denigration) when we keep in mind two caveats. First, the created order (and this counts also for our time-bound history and for the Old Testament economy) does not exist in itself and for itself. Created truth, goodness, and beauty are merely borrowed by way of a loan given through the infinite mercy of the one who is truth, goodness, and beauty himself (see 1 Cor. 4:7). Over the past several decades, evangelicals have made up for lost time in affirming the goodness of the created order. But the Christian twist on things is that we dare not assign it ultimate significance. C. S. Lewis puts it this way:

> The books or the music in which we thought the beauty was located will betray us if we trust to them; it was not *in* them, it only came *through* them, and what came through them was longing.

These things — the beauty, the memory of our own past — are good images of what we really desire; but if they are mistaken for the thing itself, they turn into dumb idols, breaking the hearts of their worshippers. For they are not the thing itself; they are only the scent of a flower we have not found, the echo of a tune we have not heard, news from a country we have never yet visited.[16]

Created objects, as Lewis explains, turn into idols when we mistake them for ultimate realities. Or, as he memorably expresses it elsewhere: "You can't get second things by putting them first; you can get second things only by putting first things first."[17]

The temporal, created order has its ultimate end not in itself but in the mysterious reality that transcends it. The end of created being lies beyond itself. "I was created to see thee," confesses St. Anselm, "and not yet have I done that for which I was made."[18] For Augustine, the difference between enjoying *(frui)* something and using *(uti)* it is that "[t]o enjoy something is to hold fast to it in love *for its own sake.*" Accordingly, while we may use this good created order, only the triune God — Father, Son, and Holy Spirit — is to be enjoyed. Only he can be loved strictly *for his own sake.*[19] The temporal, created order may only be used with an eye to the eternal purpose of the enjoyment of God. (Needless to say, for Augustine, the word "use" did not have the negative connotation of "abuse," which our word "use" often does carry.) This point is important because it is precisely by celebrating created realities for their own sake *(frui)* that we unhinge them from their grounding in the eternal Word or Logos of God. Unhinged from their transcendent source, created objects lose their source of meaning; they become the unsuspecting victims of the objectifying human gaze and turn into the manageable playthings of the totalizing human grasp. The irony of a misunderstood focus on the goodness of creation is that it results in its mirror image: a Gnostic-type of devaluation of created life.

Second, the recognition of the goodness of the created order is al-

---

16. Lewis, "Weight of Glory," 30-31.

17. C. S. Lewis, "First and Second Things," in *God in the Dock: Essays on Theology and Ethics,* ed. Walter Hooper (Grand Rapids: Eerdmans, 1970), 280.

18. Anselm, "Proslogium," I.

19. Augustine, *On Christian Teaching,* trans. and intro. by R. P. H. Green, Oxford World's Classics (1997; reprint, Oxford: Oxford University Press, 2008), I.8, 10 (italics added).

ways predicated on its participatory status: that is, its goodness is not its own.[20] When we separate creation from the Creator, "from whom, through whom, and in whom everything is" (Rom. 11:36), we are forced to locate the creature's significance — its truth, goodness, and beauty — in itself.[21] In the process, we tear apart the beautifully woven cosmic tapestry. We forget that the creation is no more than a sacramental sharing or participating in the life of God. So, when I speak in this book about sacramental ontology or about creation's participation in God, this in no way erases the distinction between the Creator and the creature. Quite the opposite: to say that creation participates sacramentally in the life of God is to limit the status of the created order. By contrast, the modern notion of a separate creation does erase the Creator-creature distinction: by insisting that the created order carries its own truth, its own goodness, and its own beauty, modernity has made the created order into an idol.[22]

Maximus the Confessor (c. 580-662), the Platonist-Christian monk who famously had his tongue and right hand cut off for defending the orthodox Christian faith, recognized the importance of the participatory link between creation and the eternal Word of God.[23] He maintained that from eternity, the eternal Logos, or Word of God, held together in himself the many eternal *logoi* (words) of the created order. He argued that, when God created the world, he did this by first creating earthly *logoi,* which were based on eternal *logoi* (pp. 105-6). We need not go into the intricacies of Maximus's approach; the important thing is

20. See the delightful Platonist-Christian insight of John Calvin, who, at the very beginning of his *Institutes,* quotes Acts 17:28 and then comments: "For, quite clearly, the mighty gifts with which we are endowed are hardly from ourselves; indeed, our very being is nothing but subsistence in the one God" (*Institutes of the Christian Religion,* ed. John T. McNeill, trans. Ford Lewis Battles, vol. 1, Library of Christian Classics, no. 20 [Philadelphia: Westminster, 1960], I.i.1).

21. For Augustine's use of this biblical text, see *On Christian Teaching,* I.10; see also Acts 17:28; Col. 1:17.

22. See Job 31:26-28: "Or has the sight of the sun in its glory, or the glow of the moon as it walked the sky, secretly stolen my heart, so that I blew them a kiss? That too would be a criminal offence, to have denied the supreme God" (New Jerusalem Bible).

23. This paragraph is based on Radu Bordeianu, "Maximus and Ecology: The Relevance of Maximus the Confessor's Theology of Creation for the Present Ecological Crisis," *Downside Review* 127 (2009): 103-26. Hereafter, page references to this essay appear in parentheses in the text. I am indebted to Fr. Placidus Sander, O.S.B., for drawing my attention to this essay.

that he held to a participatory relationship between creation and the eternal Word of God. This created order was important, he believed, precisely because it participated in the eternal Logos of God. According to Maximus, this harmonious relationship was torn through Adam's fall: Adam, he explained, had failed to regard creation spiritually so as to discover the divine *logoi* in it. Instead, he had looked at nature in line with his passions, thereby reducing creation to a purely material reality.

Radu Bordeianu draws out the implications of Maximus's cosmology for our treatment of creation: "Maximus's insight is relevant to ecology because he specifies what happens when we look at the environment from the perspective of our selfish passions. Humans see it simply as a material reality, without any trace of the divine *logoi* in it" (p. 113). Maximus's participatory view of creation — for which he borrowed from the Platonic tradition — enabled him to regard creation as a sacramental offering to God. In contrast, by treating creation as an end in itself, Adam had lost sight of creation's sacramental purpose as a eucharistic offering to God. It was our task in Christ, Maximus was convinced, to offer back to God the divine *logoi* of the visible world. "The world," says Bordeianu, "thus becomes transparent to God's presence in it. God becomes all in all, even if not with the same sacramental fullness as in the Eucharist. However, our attitude toward creation should be as toward the Eucharist, to which we show much attention and care, so that no minuscule crumb will fall and be trampled upon or wasted" (p. 119). We sometimes tend to think that the "otherworldly" view of the church fathers lies at the root of our ecological problems. In actual fact, the opposite is the case. Their participatory or sacramental ontology allowed them to treat the material creation as a sacred eucharistic offering to God.

Only God is to be enjoyed for his own sake, and creation has no more than a sacramental participation in the life of God. It seems crucially important to me that we recapture these two caveats to the celebration of creation. As Christians, whenever we forget or ignore them, the result is that we tend to accommodate our contemporary desacralized culture in all sorts of unhelpful ways. If, however, we take our starting point in a participatory appreciation of creation, we can avoid our culture's denigration of the human body and of the environment. Furthermore, such an approach will give the highest possible (because it is eucharistic) value to creation. In this way we recognize the sacramental aim or purpose of the material creation in the eternal Word of God.

Christianity and the Platonic Heritage

How did the Great Tradition of the church argue for a sacramental on-tology? The best way to make this point in a satisfactory way is to ac-knowledge that nearly the entire Christian tradition, at least until the High Middle Ages, took the shape of a Platonist-Christian synthesis. The impact of Platonism (and especially Neo-Platonism) on the Chris-tian tradition is much lampooned today.[24] Nonetheless, in this book my argument is an extended one in favor of the traditional Platonist-Christian synthesis. This is not to say that any and all Christian use of the Platonic tradition has been appropriate; at times the relationship was so close that it became rather unhealthy. But the church fathers were, by and large, not naïve about what to accept and what to reject from the Platonic heritage; and there were at least three elements in the Christian faith that radically countered the Platonic tradition.[25]

First, and most importantly, the Christian faith inherited from the Old Testament and from Judaism the belief that God did not *have* to create but was *free* to create. For Christians, the Creation was not an au-tomatic or necessary emanation flowing from the being of God with-out an intervening act of his will.[26] Creation was not simply an excre-tion from preexisting matter or spirit. Rather, God created the world freely — *ex nihilo* (out of nothing). While creating the world was cer-

24. N. T. Wright associates Platonism with Gnosticism without wondering why it is that the Christian tradition carefully distinguished positive and negative elements in the former, while vehemently opposing the latter (*Surprised by Hope: Rethinking Heaven, the Resurrection, and the Mission of the Church* [New York: HarperOne, 2008], 88-91). North-American evangelical criticism of the Platonist-Christian synthesis owes much to the impact of the Dutch Neo-Calvinist tradition stemming from Abraham Kuyper and Herman Dooyeweerd, particularly through influential popular accounts such as Brian J. Walsh and J. Richard Middleton, *The Transforming Vision: Shaping a Christian Worldview* (Downers Grove, IL: InterVarsity, 1984), 107-16.

25. For the following three elements, I am taking my starting point in Louis Dupré, *Passage to Modernity: An Essay in the Hermeneutics of Nature and Culture* (New Haven: Yale University Press, 1993), 168.

26. The theory of emanation was a Neo-Platonic development entering the Platonic tradition through Plotinus. While Philo's Middle Platonism strongly impacted Origen and Gregory of Nyssa, Neo-Platonism impacted both Denys and Augustine, and thus much of the Western theological tradition. For further discussion, see Andrew Louth, *The Origins of the Christian Mystical Tradition: From Plato to Denys* (Oxford: Oxford Univer-sity Press, 1981); Norman Russell, *The Doctrine of Deification in the Greek Patristic Tradition* (Oxford: Oxford University Press, 2004).

tainly a fitting or congruous thing for God to do, it was not a necessary act. Creation did not simply emanate from the being of God.[27]

Second, Christians had a much higher regard for matter than did the Platonists. Platonists could not possibly see matter as inherently good. After all, matter was the involuntary result of divine emanation and was thus located at the very bottom of the hierarchy of being. And so, nothing was better for the divine and immortal soul than to be freed from the material, mortal body. The Christian doctrine of creation, along with a strong belief in the Incarnation and in the resurrection of the body, countered this Platonic suspicion of the material order.[28] Christians, throughout the church's tradition, celebrated matter and particularly celebrated the body, as good gifts of the Creator God.[29]

Third, both of these first two principles — creation as a free act *ex nihilo* and the acceptance of the goodness of creation — were based on a different understanding of the divine. The Neo-Platonic doctrine of emanation implied a hierarchy of being that posited at the top of the hierarchy the perfection of a simple monad, followed by various divine *Forms* or *Ideas,* which in turn led to the lowest realm, the imperfect world of multiplicity and matter — a world mirroring the realm of Forms or Ideas. In other words, Neo-Platonism functioned on the basis of a principle of absolute oneness: the one was the perfect, the many were the imperfect. Christians clashed sharply with the Platonic tradition on this point. They agreed that Scripture reflects the principle of hierarchy;

27. Cf. Louth's comment: "The clear assertion of the doctrine of *creatio ex nihilo* which, from Athanasius onwards becomes an accepted premise in patristic theology, has disclosed an ontological gulf between God and the creature and, *a fortiori,* between God and the soul. . . . So [Athanasius] has, at one level at any rate, made a complete break with the Platonist tradition" (*Origins of the Christian Mystical Tradition,* 78).

28. Augustine's *Confessions* waxes eloquent about the positive impact of "the Platonists" in effecting his conversion to Christianity. Augustine goes so far as to suggest that the Platonists, too, knew about the eternal Word being with God in the beginning. "But," Augustine then adds, "that 'the word was made flesh and dwelt among us' (John 1:13-14), I did not read there" (*Confessions,* trans. Henry Chadwick [Oxford: Oxford University Press, 1991], 121 [VII.9]).

29. Again, this is not to say that the fathers' borrowings from the Platonic tradition never inhibited their appreciation of the goodness of the body and of sexuality. Nonetheless, even a thinker as Platonic as Gregory of Nyssa went to great lengths defending the resurrection of the body, even if at times his Platonic convictions made it difficult for him to do so. See Gregory of Nyssa, *On the Soul and the Resurrection,* trans. Catharine Roth (Crestwood, NY: St. Vladimir's Seminary Press, 1980).

thus were they ready to ally themselves with Neo-Platonism on that point. But they did not accept that the one implied perfection while the many implied imperfection. The doctrine of the Trinity provided a strong counterbalance to an unhealthy form of divine monarchy: Father, Son, and Spirit were consubstantial, Christian orthodoxy insisted. The one and the many both went back to the heart of who God is.

All of this is simply to say that Christians generally knew when to say no to the Platonic worldview. They knew what to accept from Middle Platonists such as Philo (c. 20 BC–AD 50) and from Neo-Platonists such as Plotinus (c. AD 204-270) and Proclus (AD 411-485) and what to reject in them. There's a fairly common story going around among evangelicals that blames most of the history of Christianity for uncritically accepting Platonism. Sometimes one almost gets the impression that it's only recently that some evangelicals have managed to recover the importance of the human body, and thus have finally overcome the evils of the Platonic tradition. That story says a great deal more about contemporary evangelicalism than it does about the history of Christian thought. While such evangelical accounts purport to be simply "biblical," they in fact often work with a philosophical framework in which it is assumed that the relational language of Scripture exhausts the character of God.[30] The result is a radical historicizing of our understanding of God and thus a loss of transcendence.[31] This approach ignores the fact that, by and large, Christians did reject the excesses of Platonism. They were keen to assert divine freedom, as shown particularly in the Creation and in the Incarnation. They largely agreed on the goodness of the material order and thus celebrated their belief in the resurrection of the body and in an eschatological future of a new heaven *and* a new earth. And, most important, they were eager to affirm the Trinitarian character of God.[32]

---

30. Both advocates of a nonreductive physicalist anthropology and open theists often regard the Christian tradition as having fallen from its purely "biblical" origins by being amalgamated with Platonism.

31. David Bradshaw, in his excellent book *Aristotle East and West: Metaphysics and the Division of Christendom* (Cambridge: Cambridge University Press, 2004), traces the pre-Christian and Christian distinction between *ousia* (essence) and *energeia* (energy), with the church fathers regarding the former as always remaining out of human reach. Some kind of distinction along these lines seems necessary to avoid the danger of collapsing the divine into the natural order.

32. See Robert Louis Wilken, *The Spirit of Early Christian Thought: Seeking the Face of God* (New Haven: Yale University Press, 2003), 136-61.

But Christians were also careful not to overreact and simply de-
nounce everything Platonic as incompatible with the gospel. Despite
the strong reservations that I have just listed, Christian theology did
look to the Platonic tradition as in many ways an ally rather than an
opponent. The resulting synthesis with Platonism lasted well into the
High Middle Ages. Some scholars locate the demise of this Platonist-
Christian synthesis in the theology of Thomas Aquinas: his rational
approach to theology, his borrowing from Aristotle and his commentators, the clear distinction he made between nature and the supernatural, and the related focus on the autonomy of the natural realm may
appear to have introduced a theological shift in thirteenth-century
Scholasticism. Without denying that Thomas's (this-worldly) Aristotelianism did bring about a change in theological ethos, I want to emphasize that, in many ways, the angelic doctor still continued the synthesis between Christianity and (other-worldly) Platonism.

One of the authors quoted most often by Thomas was Denys, a
sixth-century Syrian monk, for whom the entire universe was one
beautiful, harmonious whole, predicated on a hierarchy of being, and
for whom the universe had not only come from God but would also return to him — by means of the deification of human beings. God had
become human so that humans might become divine. God opened his
divine life for the participation of human beings. Denys introduced to
Thomas an approach to theology that was by no means a discipline establishing objective propositional truths; instead, it was intent on
drawing human beings into mystical union with God and ultimately
into the divine life itself.[33] Already as a student of Albert the Great
(c. 1206-1280), Thomas acquainted himself with Denys's *On the Celestial
Hierarchy.*[34] As a mature theologian, Thomas wrote his commentary on
Denys's *Divine Names,* which shows beyond any doubt his deep indebtedness to this mystical monk's Neo-Platonic worldview. We see the im-

---

33. For Aquinas, in the hereafter, the illumination of the intellect by divine grace
would allow the created intellect to see the essence of God: "By this light the blessed are
made *deiform* — that is, like to God, according to the saying: *When He shall appear we shall
be like to Him, and* [Vulgate: *because*] *we shall see Him as He is* (1 John, ii.2)" (Thomas Aquinas, *Summa Theologica* [*ST*], trans. Fathers of the English Dominican Province [1948; reprint, Westminster, MD: Christian Classics, 1981], I, q.12, a.5); cf. *ST* I-II, q.2, a.7; I-II, q.2,
a.8; I-II, q.3, a.8.

34. Aidan Nichols, *Discovering Aquinas: An Introduction to His Life, Work, and Influence*
(Grand Rapids: Eerdmans, 2002), 5.

pact of Denys in Thomas's acknowledgment that there are limits to the human knowledge of God: God's essence was inaccessible to us in our current condition, and he remained the Wholly Other one.[35] We see this same impact in Thomas's insistence that all true being participated in God's being.[36] We see it also in his understanding of salvation as a sharing by grace in the divine life — deification.[37] And, of course, we see it especially in the way he structured the entire *Summa* around the scheme of life both originating in God and returning to him.[38] For Thomas, all of life — and Christian theology particularly — served the ultimate end of eternal happiness in the beatific vision of God (1 Cor. 13:12). St. Thomas's thought still retained these Platonic proclivities.[39] The Platonist-Christian synthesis dominated the Great Tradition for an entire millennium.

In subsequent chapters, I will outline what happened to this Platonist-Christian synthesis. At this point, I simply wish to highlight its central characteristic: the doctrine of participation or, we might say, its sacramental ontology. One of the main objections that many evangelicals have against the Platonic notion of a world of eternal Forms, or Ideas, of which our terrestrial life is a mere copy or shadow, is that it appears to undermine the goodness of the created order, whose value is much greater than that of a mere shadow or copy. Add to this the fact

35. See Karen Kilby, "Aquinas, the Trinity and the Limits of Understanding," *International Journal of Systematic Theology* 7 (2005): 414-27.

36. For St. Thomas, God was being *per essentiam,* while humans merely shared or participated in God's being analogically (*ST* I, q.3, a.4; I, q.6, a.4; I, q.13, a.5; I, q.45, a.5). See Rudi A. te Velde, *Participation and Substantiality in Thomas Aquinas* (Leiden: Brill, 1995), 99-100.

37. See A. N. Williams, *The Ground of Union: Deification in Aquinas and Palamas* (Oxford: Oxford University Press, 1999); Fergus Kerr, *After Aquinas: Versions of Thomism* (Malden, MA: Blackwell, 2002), 149-61.

38. The *Summa* is structured according to an *exitus-reditus* schema in which the universe originates in God and returns to him. The *Prima Pars* deals with the doctrine of God and creation; the *Prima Secundae* explains human happiness and beatific bliss as the purpose of morality; the *Secunda Secundae* discusses the Christian virtues — faith, hope, and love — as the pathway of the human return to God; and the *Tertia Pars* presents an exposition of salvation in Christ, i.e., Christology proper and the sacraments.

39. It is important to keep in mind that Denys's mysticism was not individualist in character. See Denys Turner, "How to Read the Pseudo-Denys Today," *International Journal of Systematic Theology* 7 (2005): 428-40. As Turner shows, Thomas's appropriation of Denys was judicious in that it did not undermine the centrality of the church and the sacraments.

that we can easily (and perhaps, better) conceive of a relationship between creation and Creator without the seemingly speculative notion of eternal Forms, and we get a sense of why many consider the early church's appropriation of Platonic thought an unhelpful "hellenization" of Christianity. Let's just discard the unhelpful philosophical accretions of Platonism and simply accept the pure gold of the biblical Christian faith.

Before jumping to the defense of Tertullian by insisting that Jerusalem has nothing to do with Athens, however, let us listen to a voice that disagrees. Robert Louis Wilken, in his beautiful book *The Spirit of Early Christian Thought,* makes the following observation:

> The notion that the development of early Christian thought represented a hellenization of Christianity has outlived its usefulness. The time has come to bid a fond farewell to the ideas of Adolf von Harnack, the nineteenth-century historian of dogma whose thinking has influenced the interpretation of early Christian thought for more than a century. It will become clear in the course of this book that a more apt expression would be the Christianization of Hellenism, though that phrase does not capture the originality of Christian thought nor the debt owed to Jewish ways of thinking and to the Jewish Bible.[40]

Wilken makes clear that the so-called hellenization of the gospel simply does not do justice to the judicious, careful use that the fathers made of the Platonic tradition. Furthermore, his mention of Adolf von Harnack — one of the stalwarts of the German liberal school — should give evangelicals pause. If Harnack, as a liberal theologian, thought it prudent to remove Platonic notions (such as creation's participation in eternal forms) from Christian theology, evangelicals should perhaps consider the consequences of the "hellenization" thesis before simply adopting it.

While I understand that evangelical anti-Platonic tendencies are generally meant to defend the Bible, it is ironic that Scripture itself suffers the most serious consequences. The Platonist-Christian synthesis made it possible to regard creation, history, and Old Testament as sacramental carriers of a greater reality. Creation, history, and Old Testament had significance throughout most of the Christian tradition pre-

40. Wilken, *Spirit of Early Christian Thought,* xvi.

cisely because they pointed to and participated in a greater reality: what the Platonists called "Forms" or "Ideas," and what Christians insisted was the Word of God himself. This meant that the church fathers worked on the assumption that Old Testament events were sacraments of the christological reality of the New Testament, something I will discuss in more detail in chapter 8 below. The fourth-century theologian Rufinus of Aquileia, for example, maintained: "In his Revelation, John reads the things that have been written in the Law according to the history of the divine mysteries and teaches that certain sacraments are contained within them. These truths are both useful and divine but . . . have been covered over with sacraments and wound up in mysteries."[41]

Time and time again, the church fathers and medieval theologians explained the events reported in the Old Testament as "future mysteries" *(futura mysteria)* or "future sacraments" *(futura sacramenta),* referring to Jesus Christ and to the church.[42] Thus the Great Tradition did not just interpret created realities sacramentally. History, too — including the biblical history of redemption — was sacramental in character. For the Great Tradition, the only way to make sense of the world was by means of a sacramental ontology: God had graciously provided a sacramental link between his own divine life and the time-bound order of creation. It was this sacramental participation that gave the temporal order eternal significance.

---

41. Quoted in Henri de Lubac, *Medieval Exegesis: The Four Senses of Scripture,* vol. 2, trans. E. M. Macierowski (Grand Rapids: Eerdmans, 2000), 20. The two sentences of Rufinus are from *In Num.,* h. 20 n. 1, and *In Jos.,* h. 20 n. 4, respectively.

42. De Lubac, *Medieval Exegesis,* 2:94-96.

CHAPTER 2

Weaving the Tapestry:
The Fathers' Christological Anchor

Christ is the origin, stability, and end of the Christian narrative. In him lies our hope, for in him all things heavenly and earthly will be summed up or recapitulated (Eph. 1:1-14). The Word (or Logos) of God is the key that unlocks the entire Christian message (John 1:1-5): he is both the firstborn of all creation and the firstborn from among the dead (Col. 1:15, 18), both Creator and Redeemer. Hence Paul "resolved to know nothing . . . except Jesus Christ and him crucified" (1 Cor. 2:2). The centrality of Christology to the biblical message is obvious. A point on which evangelicals do not show consensus, however, is how to make sense of this centrality of Christ theologically. While it may be clear to all that Christ is the climax of the history of redemption, not all agree on what its implications might be.

I confess that I am a maximalist when it comes to this. As I see it, Christ is not just the climax of the covenant — though he certainly is that — but he is also the eternal anchor for all of created existence. In this chapter I will outline the implications of this claim. To do so, I first have to return to the theme of the Platonist-Christian synthesis to which I have already alluded in the previous chapter. I will make clear that the christological focus of the Christian tradition meant that it was truly a Platonist-*Christian* synthesis. By looking at some of the church fathers, I will illustrate the fact that when the early church began to weave her cosmic tapestry — a sacramental ontology — she acknowledged Christ as central to the process. The church recognized Christ, we might say, as the central thread of the cosmic tapestry. I will then go beyond this claim to insist that this traditional synthesis is indispensable if we are to retain anything resembling the ecumenical consensus that we have inherited from the early church.

Irenaeus: Salvation through Recapitulation

The church fathers were by no means naïve. As we have seen, they recognized the problems inherent in the Platonic tradition. Why, then, were they willing to ally themselves with this tradition to the extent that, in retrospect, we may speak of the birth of a Platonist-Christian synthesis? The basic reason is that the church fathers saw in the Platonic tradition tools with which to defend and advance their christological claims. It is perhaps easiest to explain this by referring to three of the church fathers: Irenaeus (c. 115–c. 202), Athanasius (c. 296–373), and Gregory of Nyssa (c. 335–c. 394). For all three theologians, Christology was central; and, though there are differences in how much the Platonic tradition influenced each of them, we do see the alliance with (Neo-) Platonism take concrete shape, especially in Athanasius and Gregory.[1] It is this alliance that allowed them to articulate the common christological confession of the church.

The second-century father Saint Irenaeus was the theologian of unity.[2] Over against the polytheism of the Gnostics, he asserts the unity of the one, triune God; over against the Gnostic separation between the human Jesus and the divine Christ, Irenaeus confesses that Jesus Christ, sent by the Father, has suffered for us; over against the Gnostic division of Old and New Testaments, he maintains the unity of the economy of salvation; over against the Gnostic partition of humanity into earthly, natural, and spiritual beings, Irenaeus argues that God reveals himself publicly to all alike, and that all have the freedom and obligation to answer God's call in Jesus Christ. And finally, over against the Gnostic view of salvation as escape from the material world, Irenaeus points to the Incarnation as providing the possibility of salva-

---

1. See E. P. Meijering, *Orthodoxy and Platonism in Athanasius: Synthesis or Antithesis?* (1968; reprint, Leiden: Brill, 1974); Harold F. Cherniss, *The Platonism of Gregory of Nyssa,* Philosophy Monograph Series, no. 81 (1930; reprint, New York: Franklin, 1971); Andrew Louth, *The Origins of the Christian Mystical Tradition: From Plato to Denys* (Oxford: Oxford University Press, 1981), 77-97.

2. See Hans Boersma, "Redemptive Hospitality in Irenaeus: A Model for Ecumenicity in a Violent World," *Pro Ecclesia* 11 (2002): 207-26.

tion. God became human that we might become divine. Irenaeus puts it this way: "[H]ow could we be joined to incorruptibility and immortality, unless, first, incorruptibility and immortality had become that which we also are, so that the corruptible might be swallowed up by incorruptibility, and the mortal by immortality, that we might receive the adoption of sons?"[3] For church fathers such as Irenaeus, deification resulted when God's immortality swallowed up our mortality.

Irenaeus uses the notion of "recapitulation" to articulate *how* he believes God made possible our deification or adoption. The Bishop of Lyons took the term "recapitulation" from Ephesians 1:10, where Paul says that the mystery of God's will be "put into effect when the times will have reached their fulfillment — to bring all things in heaven and on earth together under one head, even Christ." The expression "bring together under one head" is actually only one word: in Greek the verb is *anakephalaioō;* in Latin it has sometimes been rendered *recapitulare.* In both languages, Christ is identified as the "head" (Greek: *kephalē;* Latin: *caput*). Irenaeus presents this notion of recapitulation in some intriguing and beautiful statements. Christ, he explains,

> came to save all through means of Himself — all, I say, who through Him are born again to God — infants, and children, and boys, and youths, and old men. He therefore passed through every age, becoming an infant for infants, thus sanctifying infants; a child for children, thus sanctifying those who are of this age, being at the same time made to them an example of piety, righteousness and submission; a youth for youths, becoming an example to youths, and thus sanctifying them for the Lord. Likewise, He was an old man for old men, that He might be a perfect Master for all, not merely as respects the setting forth of the truth, but also as regards age, sanctifying at the same time the aged also, and becoming an example to them likewise. Then, at last, He came on to death itself, that He might be "the first-born from the dead, that in all things He might have the pre-eminence," the Prince of Life, existing before all, and going before all.[4]

3. Irenaeus, *Against Heresies,* in *Ante-Nicene Fathers,* vol. 1, ed. Alexander Roberts and James Donaldson (1885; reprint, Peabody, MA: Hendrickson, 1994), III.19.1.

4. Irenaeus, *Against Heresies,* II.22.4. With an appeal to tradition and John 8:56-57, Irenaeus argues that Jesus reached the age of 50 (II.22.5-6); cf. George Ogg, "The Age of Jesus When He Taught," *New Testament Studies* 5 (1958-59): 291-98.

Notice how, according to Irenaeus, Christ had to go through every stage of human life, from the very young to the very old. The incarnate Son of God had to become truly the head — the *caput* — of every human being, and the only way to recapitulate all humanity was to share the life of all humanity.

This process of recapitulation was, for Irenaeus, also the explanation of the virgin birth: "For as by the disobedience of the one man who was originally molded from virgin soil, the many were made sinners, and forfeited life; so was it necessary that, by the obedience of one man, who was originally born from a virgin, many should be justified and receive salvation."[5] It may appear as though Irenaeus was simply looking for arbitrary (though perhaps interesting) parallels between Adam and Christ, between the virgin soil and the virgin birth, and, in other places, between Eve and Mary. But Irenaeus was not an abstract or speculative theologian looking for parallels. Instead, what we see here is a theological attempt to ground our salvation in the Incarnation itself. The Incarnation could only save us if somehow Christ swallowed up our mortal and corruptible existence. And he could only do so if, without any moral failure whatsoever, he was able to retrace human existence. The virgin birth was necessary because Adam was made from virgin soil. Mary had to give her obedient consent to the angel because Eve had been disobedient to an angel. Christ had to withstand satanic temptation in the desert because Adam had failed the test in paradise.

Today we are witnessing a fascinating resurgence in Irenaeus scholarship, and this is a most welcome development for a number of reasons. One of the reasons is the fact that Irenaeus was a theologian of unity, celebrating the unity of God, the unity of Jesus Christ, the unity of history, the unity of humanity, and — above all — the unity of salvation. Moreover, Irenaeus managed to weave this unified tapestry in such a way that he did not fall into the opposite extreme of a totalizing imposition of sameness that quashed all difference. Many today are wondering whether to embrace modernity's violent imposition of sameness or to instead opt for postmodernity's funky celebration of carnivalesque difference. In this context, Irenaeus's theology provides us with a sane word of wisdom: the wisdom of the gospel, the wisdom that pleads for a unity that does not obliterate differences. Irenaeus's theology offers a true alternative to both ancient and contemporary

5. Irenaeus, *Against Heresies*, III.18.7.

forms of Gnosticism. In particular, his theology of salvation, centered on recapitulation, continues to provide us with a christological anchor for the salvation of humanity. Recapitulation in Christ is, for Irenaeus, the central thread that allows for a harmonious cosmic tapestry.

Athanasius: Unity in the Incarnate Logos

When we turn to *De incarnatione (On the Incarnation),* a brief but probing theological exposition written by Saint Athanasius, the fourth-century defender of the Council of Nicaea (325), we get a clear picture of how this defender of Trinitarian orthodoxy argued for the possibility of salvation in Christ. For Athanasius, if human beings are to be saved in and through Jesus Christ, there *has* to be a common humanity in which they all participate. Athanasius wrote *On the Incarnation* in about 318, and in the booklet he sets out to deal with the question of why God took on human flesh. The first reason is so that God could die in our place in human form.[6] Or, as Athanasius expresses it, the Word died "in the stead of all" (§§8-9). The Alexandrian father then offers an intriguing analogy:

> And like as when a great king has entered into some large city and taken up his abode in one of the houses there, such city is at all events held worthy of high honour, nor does any enemy or bandit any longer descend upon it and subject it; but, on the contrary, it is thought entitled to all care, because of the king's having taken up his residence in a single house there: so, too, has it been with the Monarch of all (§9).

The eternal Logos of God, who was incorruptible, took on a body like ours, came as king to live in our city, and, it seemed, by his mere presence (by the mere fact of the Incarnation, one could say) bestowed incredible honor on the human race and held at bay the enemy, who no longer dared attack the people in whose midst the Logos had taken up his living quarters. Athanasius's analogy sounds remarkably similar to Irenaeus's recapitulation, according to which Christ was the head of hu-

---

6. Athanasius, *On the Incarnation of the Word,* in *Nicene and Post-Nicene Fathers,* 2nd ser., vol. 4, ed. Archibald Robertson (1892; reprint, Peabody, MA: Hendrickson, 1994), §§7-10. Hereafter, references to this work appear in parentheses in the text.

manity. Athanasius agrees that the one residence that houses the Logos represents every house of the entire city that the king has entered.

The second reason for the Incarnation, according to Athanasius, was so that the Logos, as the image of God, might teach us the knowledge of the Father (§§11-19). Since, for Athanasius, to be made in the image of God means to be rational, Christ has to teach us in order to restore us in God's image and likeness. We are only truly rational if we know the Word (and reason) of the Father. The only way we can have access to the Logos is through God's own image, through Jesus Christ, for that is where we get to see what the Father is like (§11). Therefore, Athanasius traces God's teaching program in the Law and the Prophets, as well as in what he calls the "harmony of creation" (§12). Sadly, however, neither the Jews nor the rest of the world listened to God's teaching. "What then was God to do?" Athanasius asks (§13). The solution he presents is the Incarnation of the Logos: "Whence the Word of God came in His own person, that, as He was the Image of the Father, He might be able to create afresh the man after the image" (§13). Athanasius again uses an analogy to make his point:

> For as, when the likeness painted on a panel has been effaced by stains from without, he whose likeness it is must needs come once more to enable the portrait to be renewed on the same wood: for, for the sake of his picture, even the mere wood on which it is painted is not thrown away, but the outline is renewed upon it; . . . in the same way also the most holy Son of the Father, being the Image of the Father, came to our region to renew man once made in His likeness, and find him, as one lost, by the remission of sins. . . . (§14)

The image of God (the picture) is going to be restored in humanity (the wood) by means of teaching, Athanasius insists. The Word of God "sojourns here as man, taking to Himself a body like the others, and from things of earth, that is by the works of His body [He teaches them], so that they who would not know Him from His Providence and rule over all things, may even from the works done by His actual body know the Word of God which is in the body, and through Him the Father" (§14). Christ's teaching restores in human beings the likeness of God.

The Egyptian church father next explains why God did not merely save mankind by way of a simple declaration of a clean bill of health.

Our cure, Athanasius declares, requires more than merely a spoken word. Salvation, for Athanasius, is not just an external or nominal matter; it is a participatory — or real — event. Therefore, God became man and used a human body as his instrument: "[I]f death was wound closely to the body . . . it was required that life also should be wound closely to the body" (§44). For the third time in a row, Athanasius uses an analogy:

> And just as, whereas stubble is naturally destructible by fire, supposing (firstly) a man keeps fire away from the stubble, though it is not burned, yet the stubble remains, for all that, merely stubble, fearing the threat of the fire — for fire has the natural property of consuming it; while if a man (secondly) encloses it with a quantity of asbestos, the substance said to be an antidote to fire, the stubble no longer dreads the fire, being secured by its enclosure in incombustible matter. (§44)

A simple declaration from God would not make human beings immortal. What they need is for their natural bodies to "put on the incorporeal Word of God," so that they may become incorruptible (§44). The similarity to Athanasius's other two analogies, as well as to Irenaeus's recapitulation theory, will be obvious. Whether we're using the simile of a king entering a city, of a painting that is being restored, or of asbestos securing the stubble, in each case protection or salvation is only possible because, through his identification with human nature, Christ secures the salvation of humanity. For the church fathers, salvation is possible because, in a real sense, Christ *is* the new humanity.

The underlying assumption throughout Athanasius's *De incarnatione* is that human beings are not separate, fragmented individuals; rather, they participate in a common humanity. This principle of a common, essential unity of all human beings, underlying whatever differences they might have, was clearly central to the early Christian understanding of salvation. When the eternal Word took on human flesh, he took on our common humanity and by doing so redeemed it. Salvation in Christ is possible because he truly recapitulated all of humanity in his person, because humanity really does find its common identity in the one person of Jesus Christ. This Irenaean and Athanasian principle of human unity in the incarnate Logos would lead the Eastern tradition to emphasize that salvation came not just through Christ's death, but that the Incarnation itself was redemptive in its effects. The hinge of our salvation, in this scheme, was the Incarnation itself. The Incarnation is the restoration of our incorruptibility and immortality, and it allows us to become like God — that is, deification. Thus does Athanasius explicitly bring out the element of deification: "For He was made man that we might be made God; and He manifested Himself by a body that we might receive the idea of the unseen Father; and He endured the insolence of men that we might inherit immortality" (§54). The unity of humanity lies anchored in the one Word — the Incarnation — and it is this christological anchor that allows for the saving deification of human beings.

Gregory of Nyssa: Universals and Particulars

We find much the same in Saint Gregory of Nyssa, though the fourth-century Cappadocian father worked more explicitly with a Neo-Platonic philosophical framework than did Athanasius. When Gregory wrote his well-known *Letter to Ablabius,* also known as *On "Not Three Gods,"* he explained how he could affirm the threeness of God without falling into tritheism or polytheism. In other words, what Gregory sets out to do is affirm the unity of God despite the assertion that diversity also lies at the heart of who God is. Gregory immediately goes to the heart of the matter, the issue that lies at the basis of much of our contemporary nervousness with regard to the Platonist-Christian synthesis. He presents an intricate discussion about what in philosophy are called "universals" and "particulars." Gregory faces the objection, likely from people denying the divinity of the Holy Spirit (the so-called pneumatomachians), that if there is a Father, a Son, and a Holy Spirit, and if all three are coequal, fully divine, don't we have three gods? Isn't this straightforward polytheism? Gregory opened himself up to this particular criticism because he made the point that one could compare the persons of the Trinity to three human persons, such as Peter, James, and John. He argues that, just as these human persons participate in one humanity, while they are nonetheless distinct, so also is there in the Trinity a common divinity, and yet three divine persons. This raises the understandable question: How is this not tritheism?

In response, Gregory makes use of his Neo-Platonic training, insisting that we must distinguish between what is common within a group and what is unique to any particular subject. He goes back to the general term "man," or "humanity," and he makes the point that people use the word "man" both in a general sense for all people (just like our word "humanity") *and* for individual human beings, such as Luke and Stephen. At this point, Gregory makes an interesting move. He insists that, properly speaking, we really should only use the word "man" to refer to our common humanity. It is only by an "abuse of language" that we talk about "many men." Talking about "many men" is like saying that there are "many human natures." And while Gregory does not get hot and bothered about the confusion between "man" and "man," he does believe that something crucial is at stake if we are to apply the word "god" not just to the common divinity of the three, but also to each of the three persons individually. Talking about three men is, strictly speaking, erroneous, but nonetheless acceptable. But talking about three gods is not merely erroneous; it is, in addition, absolutely unacceptable and blasphemous.[7]

What Gregory does here is distinguish between what is "common" to all people and what is particular to individuals. He applies the Platonic distinction between universals (which were common) and their particular, distinct instantiations to insist that with God we can speak of one God and of one nature *(ousia)*, while maintaining that there are three persons *(hypostases)*. Just as it is quite logical to say that three human persons participate in a common nature, so it is in no way irrational to say that three divine *hypostases* participate in a common *ousia*. In other words, Gregory uses his Platonic background to argue that universals provide an anchor for the particular instantiations. And he uses this philosophical distinction in order to shore up a defense of orthodox Trinitarian theology.

We may well ask: Is this distinction between universals and particulars really so helpful? Don't we still end up with three individual gods, just as we still have Peter, James, and John as three individuals? The three divine persons — the three *hypostases* — may share a common nature *(ousia)*, but don't we say of each of them that they are divine? Isn't this still tritheism? This is where Gregory's second theological argument comes in: the analogy between the common humanity of Peter,

---

7. Gregory of Nyssa, *On "Not Three Gods": To Ablabius,* in *Nicene and Post-Nicene Fathers,* 2nd ser., vol. 5, ed. William Moore and Henry Austin Wilson (1893; reprint, Peabody, MA: Hendrickson, 1994), 332.

James, and John, on the one hand, and the common divinity of Father, Son, and Spirit, on the other hand, breaks down, he argues, at a crucial point. Peter, James, and John, were distinct centers of consciousness (my term, not Gregory's). Each made his own decisions and undertook his own actions. When Peter did something, it was his action alone, and the same was the case when James or John decided to do something. One cannot apply this kind of distinctiveness to the Trinity, Gregory insists. The deity in which Father, Son, and Spirit participate implies a common activity. It is impossible to say that the Father does one thing, the Son something else, and the Spirit something else. Rather, Gregory explains, "every operation which extends from God to the Creation, and is named according to our variable conceptions of it, has its origin from the Father, and proceeds through the Son, and is perfected in the Holy Spirit."[8]

This theological principle later became known as the idea that "the external activities of the Trinity are indivisible" *(opera trinitatis ad extra indivisa sunt)*. Therefore, when Gregory's analogy of three particular human beings (Peter, James, and John) participating in a common humanity made people wonder whether he was surreptitiously introducing tritheism, Gregory vehemently rejected the accusation: the unity among the divine persons is far more intimate than that among human persons. The common deity of the three divine persons implies a common will and activity toward the outside world. One cannot possibly talk of such a common will and activity among human persons.[9]

Thus, just as Athanasius did in developing his Christology and his doctrine of salvation, so Gregory of Nyssa, in developing his Trinitarian theology, regarded Platonism as a significant philosophical ally rather than simply as an opponent. For both theologians, the reason lay in the Platonic affirmation of unity. To be sure, for pagan Platonists, cosmo-

---

8. Gregory, *On "Not Three Gods,"* 334.

9. Those familiar with Trinitarian theology will recognize the significance of the above discussion. The common appeal among social Trinitarians to Gregory's letter to Ablabius completely misses the point that Gregory's letter was not arguing for a greater differentiation among the divine persons (as does social Trinitarian theology), but that it was making the very opposite point. See the helpful discussions of Lewis Ayres, *Nicaea and Its Legacy: An Approach to Fourth-Century Trinitarian Theology* (Oxford: Oxford University Press, 2004), 344-63; Mark Husbands, "The Trinity Is *Not* Our Social Program," in *Trinitarian Theology for the Church: Scripture, Community, Worship,* ed. Daniel J. Treier and David Lauber (Downers Grove, IL: InterVarsity, 2009), 120-41.

logical unity does not allow for a creation that is distinct from the Creator; nor does it allow for the Incarnation of God into a good material order. Despite the distinctly non-Christian aspects of this pagan view of the cosmos, Gregory's convictions nonetheless drew him toward certain aspects of the Neo-Platonist tradition, because he discerned in universals (Plato's Forms or Ideas) a distant echo of the Christian understanding of the eternal Logos. The created order, for Gregory, receives its being and significance from its participation in the eternal Word. Therefore, for Gregory, the created order does not have its being from itself but exists by way of participation in the divine Word.

Even if, at times, we might wish that Gregory had put up a stronger defense against some of the more problematic aspects of Neo-Platonism, there is an important point to be learned from his Platonist-Christian synthesis: the material order and the historical progress of time may be valued, but they find their significance precisely because they are part of a larger tapestry: they point *beyond* themselves and participate in the eternal Word of God.

Precisely this sacramental tapestry allowed Gregory — unlike the Neo-Platonists — to insist that change could be a positive good. While Neo-Platonism has an engrained suspicion about all change (since everything lies anchored in eternal, static Forms), for Gregory change was not something inherently negative. "For," Gregory declares,

> man does not merely have an inclination to evil; were this so, it would be impossible for him to grow in good, if his nature possessed only an inclination towards the contrary. But in truth the *finest aspect of our mutability* is the possibility of growth in good; and this capacity for improvement transforms the soul, as it changes, more and more into the divine. And so . . . what appears so terrifying (I mean the mutability of our nature) can really be as a pinion in our flight towards higher things, and indeed it would be a hardship if we were not susceptible of the sort of change which is towards the better.[10]

Along with the Platonic tradition, Gregory held that the ultimate Good, God himself, was unchangeable. But unlike the Neo-Platonists,

---

10. Gregory of Nyssa, *From Glory to Glory: Texts from Gregory of Nyssa's Mystical Writings,* intro. Jean Daniélou, ed. and trans. Herbert Musurillo (1961; reprint, Crestwood, NY: St. Vladimir's Seminary Press, 2001), 83-84 (italics added).

Gregory argued that in our created order, mutability was a good gift, since it allowed the increasing perfection of human beings, as they were being drawn into the divine life of truth, goodness, and beauty.

It will be clear at this point why I hold to the Platonist-Christian synthesis, and why I believe we need a *ressourcement* of this premodern consensus. We have already seen that Gregory of Nyssa defends Trinitarian theology with an appeal to the Platonic distinction between universals and particulars. This means that the articulation of the unity of God, as defended by Nicene Christianity, depended on the context of the Platonist-Christian synthesis. Much the same can be said about other Christian doctrines. In terms of redemption, the patristic basis for our salvation was given with the fact that all "men" shared in Christ as the one "man." In other words, the Christian doctrine of salvation arose from the conviction that the destiny of our particular human natures depends on their participation in the one humanity of Christ. In much the same way, the later doctrine of original sin developed on the assumption of the reality of a common human nature. And in terms of eucharistic theology, the very term "real presence" is an indication of the deep impact that the Platonist-Christian synthesis exerted on the church's worship. The eucharistic body "really" participated in the mystery of the unity of Christ himself. Therefore, a radical jettisoning of the Platonic elements that entered into the Christian faith may carry significant (and troubling) theological consequences.

Most importantly, perhaps, it seems to me that Platonic philosophy allowed the church fathers (as well as the subsequent medieval tradition) to argue for a christological anchor that is not caught up in the narrative flow of history and in the vicissitudes of human life. The Platonic connection allowed Christians to say that the eternal Logos — infinitely transcending the created order — provides the foundation and stability of the created order and of human history. The fragmentation of postmodernity witnesses to the fact that once we lose this christological foundation, natural realities end up drifting anchorless in the raging waves of history. To put it differently, the loss of the christological thread undermines the unity of the sacramental tapestry. Culturally, therefore, we are more than ever in need of a philosophical position that allows us to maintain that universals are real, as well as a theological position that argues that they find their reality in the eternal Word of God. In short, we are in need of a *ressourcement* of the Platonist-Christian synthesis.

CHAPTER 3

Unraveling the Tapestry:
The Medieval Revolt of Nature

The confession of Jesus Christ as Lord provided, so I have argued, the guiding principle for the early church and the Middle Ages in their appropriation — and, where necessary, critique — of Platonic philosophy. By insisting that the Platonic Forms or Ideas had real existence in the eternal Word of God, Christian theology was able to establish two foundational principles that otherwise would have been strikingly at odds with one another. First, for the sacramental ontology of the Great Tradition, the participatory anchoring of the created order in the eternal Logos immeasurably elevated the value of the terrestrial order. The acknowledgment that created objects themselves provided a glimpse into eternal mystery meant the recognition of a tremendous surplus value in created objects. If the cosmos was truly sacramental in character, it meant that matter was important: in mistreating it, one offended the mystery present within the sacramental, created order. This sacramentality of the material world was experienced most intensely in the Eucharist: the eating of bread and drinking of wine for the sake of their participation in Christ meant that the material world of the created order was infinitely precious.

Second, this same sacramental ontology prevented the Great Tradition from valuing the created order *for its own sake*. Since its being — as well as its goodness, truth, and beauty — was simply *derived* existence, one could not legitimately assign ultimate value to it. To be sure, one might often be tempted to do so by treating penultimate, created realities as if they were ultimate ends in themselves; but such an approach would immediately be recognized as idolatrous — worshiping the creature rather than the Creator.

If the church fathers and medieval theologians sometimes sound otherworldly to us, it is because that is exactly what they were: the source and grounding of the value of the created order was otherworldly, shrouded in mystery. And if they sometimes seem to us unable to acknowledge the goodness of the created order, we should probably first ask ourselves whether the problem might lie with ourselves: our (post-)modern point of view disposes us to insist on the value of creation in and of itself rather than to recognize that its goodness stems from its sacramental sharing in the mystery of Christ. Naturally, from such a radically different standpoint, any assertion of the *relative* value of terrestrial goods comes across as a devaluation of this-worldly existence. This is not to deny that the Neo-Platonic proclivities of theologians such as Gregory of Nyssa and Augustine did not at times entangle them in difficulties. It is simply to say that our own contemporary perspective tends to cloud our recognition of the fine-tuned balance of the sacramental significance of the created order.

This raises a question: What has happened in the history of Christian thought to make us look at the world so differently? How did we step away from the Platonist-Christian synthesis? At this point in the discussion, I want to introduce the movement of *nouvelle théologie,* the movement of mid-twentieth-century French Catholic theologians that pointed toward a number of factors leading to the disintegration of the Platonist-Christian synthesis — and, by extension, to the loss of a sacramental ontology. The rise of modernity, as *nouvelle théologie* understood it, can be traced to the High and late Middle Ages, and in this chapter I will marshal the various factors that the *nouvelle* theologians believed were responsible for the modern unraveling of the sacramental tapestry. (In the next chapter I will add to the account of the *nouvelle* theologians several related factors that I believe also contributed to a desacramentalizing of the universe in modernity.) By implication, these next two chapters are the most disheartening of the book: they describe the causes of our contemporary cultural malaise.

Juridicizing of the Church

In the introduction, I noted that *nouvelle théologie* regarded Neo-Thomist Scholasticism as a contributing factor to secularism. The Neo-Thomists, implacable enemies of secular modernity, were understandably irate with the suggestion that their sharp distinction between nature and the supernatural had somehow contributed to the growing apart of church and society. They were far from convinced that the Neo-Thomist tradition had itself to blame for the loss of Catholic influence. The *nouvelle* theologians nonetheless maintained that, at least in part, the unraveling of the Platonist-Christian tapestry had its origins in theological developments themselves. Modernity was by no means something that had simply burst in from the outside on an unsuspecting church. If the church had any hope of countering the secularizing tendencies of modernity, she would have to look back to a period in which the sacramental, cosmic tapestry had been more intact. Accordingly, at this point we need to trace the way *nouvelle* theologians themselves looked at the unraveling of the tapestry and at the concomitant rise of modern secularism. To my knowledge, none of these theologians undertook a systematic analysis of what happened in the history of Christian thought to cause the loss of the Platonist-Christian synthesis. After scouring their writings, however, I have come to the conclusion that these *ressourcement* theologians, throughout their writings, identified five developments that allowed Western society to step away from the earlier sacramental ontology that had characterized the Great Tradition.[1]

First, the *nouvelle* theologians — and Yves Congar in particular — looked to the Gregorian Reform of the late eleventh century as a cause of the desacramentalizing of the cosmos. Pope Gregory (1073-1085) had initiated a major program of reform in the Middle Ages, and as a result he had been embroiled in the Investiture Controversy, a major wrangle with Emperor Henry IV (1084-1105) over the right to appoint people to ecclesiastical office. Pope Gregory's reassertion of papal power (in relationship to the emperor's control) resulted in an enormous increase, over time, in the juridical authority of the pope, and it led to a tremendous centralizing and juridicizing of power in the human institution of the church.

Connecting this rise of ecclesiastical power in the eleventh century to the desacramentalizing of the cosmos may seem to be a stretch, perhaps even counterintuitive. After all, if the church's power increased, wouldn't one expect the church's Platonist-Christian synthesis to have gained in

---

1. See Hans Boersma, *Nouvelle Théologie and Sacramental Ontology: A Return to Mystery* (Oxford: Oxford University Press, 2009). Several sections of that book also deal with these historical developments, though nowhere in that book do I distinctly list them.

influence? Yves Congar, the Dominican Saulchoir theologian, was not convinced of such logic. He believed that it was not primarily the church's influence, but rather the *manner* in which authority functioned in the church, that was indicative of how well a sacramental ontology would be able to function in the church. Prior to the twelfth century, Congar maintained, people used to have little inclination to distinguish, let alone separate, divine and human actions in the church. He expresses it this way: "For the Fathers and the early Middle Ages, the sacred actions are performed *in* the Church, according to the forms of the Church, and are rigorously sacred as such. But their *subject is God,* in an actual and direct way. . . ."[2] In other words, during the period of the Platonist-Christian synthesis, people had believed that God was at work in the church in a rather direct fashion. God, according to this view, made his active presence felt in the church in a quite immediate way. There had been little need for careful reflection on the exact delimitations of the church's juridical powers, because people had regarded authority not so much as a bureaucratic or juridical structure, but more as God working actively in the life of the church.

Congar observes that as the church began to assert her power ever more strongly through the Investiture Controversy, people began to distinguish more and more clearly between divine and human authority — and between primary and secondary causality. From the twelfth century onward, secondary human causality began to take on a life of its own. As a result, it became necessary to delimit more precisely the exact parameters of the church's (human) authority. In the High and late Middle Ages, people became less inclined to view authority as something that God worked directly in and through the life of the church; instead, power now seemed to come from above, from the outside, by means of the carefully defined structures of the hierarchy. Whereas the earlier, sacramental ontology had regarded authority as intrinsically connected to the church's life, the new emphasis on secondary, human causality tempted people to regard authority as an external power, imposed from the outside. The move, we could also say, was from an intrinsic to an extrinsic understanding of authority.[3]

---

2. Yves M.-J. Congar, *Tradition and Traditions: The Biblical, Historical, and Theological Evidence for Catholic Teaching on Tradition,* trans. Michael Naseby and Thomas Rainborough (San Diego: Basilica, 1966), 135.

3. Congar pointed to several theologians in particular: "From the end of the thir-

Congar realized what was at stake: the survival of the Platonist-Christian synthesis, in which the natural and supernatural aspects of the church's life had been intricately connected. Because of the new emphasis on secondary causality and human powers, it became more difficult to regard human realities as sacramental in character. Or, we could say, the autonomy or independence of the natural, human realm began to assert itself. Congar connected the growth of juridical papal power to the loss of a sacramental ontology. Human realities, human powers, and human decisions, imposed from the outside, began to take center stage. The once-sacred cosmos, in which the world of nature had been suffused with supernatural presence, started to make room for a naturalized world, in which the sacramental, divine character of authority slowly disappeared from view. Congar describes the change as follows:

> We (partially) step out of a Platonizing world, dominated by a heavenly exemplarism, so as to enter into a world interested in the nature and consistency of things. A certain juridicizing of the notion of Church seems to us incontrovertible: for nearly two centuries, it was simply placed alongside a vision that was still very theological and very sacramental, but it ended up prevailing by the beginning of the fourteenth century.[4]

Perhaps most striking about this quotation is Congar's recognition that at the same time that people stepped out of a "Platonizing world," they also faced the loss of a "theological," or "sacramental," ontology.

The juridicizing of authority, according to Congar, had to do with human powers being imposed from the outside. In other words, the extrinsicism that I mentioned above implied the imposition of the (divine) supernatural on the (human) natural world. God only worked in the church's life by means of very carefully defined parameters of the ecclesiastical power structures. Although Congar was careful in how he expressed himself, it seems clear that he sensed a certain irony. At the very time that the church's hold on society grew beyond anything she had been in previous centuries, the sacramental tapestry that had

---

teenth century, with Henry of Ghent, Scotus, Ockham, and then under the pressure of the criticisms of Wycliffe and Huss, there emerges a clearer perception of the human and historical modalities" (Congar, *Tradition and Traditions*, 136).

4. Yves Congar, *L'Église: De saint Augustin à l'époque moderne*, Histoire des dogmes, no. 3 (Paris: Cerf, 1970), 153.

shaped her theological identity began its unraveling process. What is more, the two developments appeared to be directly connected to one another.

Discovery of Nature

Second, the eleventh century witnessed sharp debates about the nature of Christ's presence in the Eucharist. Henri de Lubac, the patristic scholar from Lyons, traced these developments in detail in his controversial book *Corpus mysticum* (1944). We have already observed that the general sacramental mindset of the Platonist-Christian synthesis came to its fullest expression in the ecclesiastical sacrament of the Eucharist. Everyone understood that God most truly and fully gives himself in the body of Christ in the eucharistic celebration. Thus, people experience participation in heavenly realities — in the eternal Son of God himself — nowhere as gloriously as in the Eucharist itself. Heaven and earth, nature and the supernatural come together in the real presence of Christ on the altar. In a very important sense, the general sacramental ontology — the participation of natural, created existence in the christological anchor — provides the basis for the real presence of Christ in the Eucharist.

Thus when, in the eleventh century, Berengar of Tours (d. 1088) seemed to deny the real presence of Christ in the Eucharist — focusing on spiritual rather than physical presence — it wasn't just the eucharistic participation of the elements in Christ that was at stake (even though that issue was important enough in itself). Also at risk was the underlying Platonist-Christian synthesis that supported traditional eucharistic teaching. (Or we might say, with equal justification, the traditional eucharistic teaching provided support for the overall Platonist-Christian ontology.) I will not, at this point, trace in detail de Lubac's description of the medieval developments surrounding the Berengarian controversy (which I will do in more detail in chap. 6 below). At this point I simply wish to draw attention to the fact that de Lubac regarded the developments as crucial for the shaping of modernity.

Although the church rejected Berengar by robustly reasserting the physical presence of Christ in the Eucharist, de Lubac was convinced that this reaction of the church actually adopted some of the underlying presuppositions that Berengar and others had introduced. The earlier sacramental or participatory view had upheld a link between the Eucharist as the sacrament *(sacramentum)* and the unity of the church as the mysterious reality *(res)* to which it pointed. Berengar had found it difficult to maintain this connection between sacrament and reality. De Lubac points out that when Berengar separated the two by focusing on a spiritual participation in the mysterious reality *(res)*, his opponents made the opposite error by focusing strictly on the physical participation in the sacrament *(sacramentum)*. Unfortunately, both took for granted the widening gap between sacrament and reality, between nature and the supernatural.

The ultraorthodox party, de Lubac explains, had "foolishly followed" Berengar "into his own territory, without realizing the danger that awaited them there," so that they "fell into the trap that had been set for them by the heretic." The false dichotomy, "whose hypothesis ought to have been refuted from the outset," was that of a universe in which sacrament no longer participated in its reality, in which nature became dislodged from the supernatural.[5] Whether the focus was on the former or the latter, both parties took for granted the underlying desacramentalized universe that would characterize modernity. The Platonist-Christian synthesis was about to unravel.

Third, the *nouvelle* theologians pointed to the overall "discovery of nature" in the twelfth and thirteenth centuries. Particularly did Marie-Dominique Chenu, the medievalist from Le Saulchoir, make a point of highlighting this discovery of nature and the loss of a sacramental ontology that went along with it.[6] Chenu believed the rediscovery of Aristotle in the High Middle Ages to be particularly significant in this regard. The translation of Aristotle, as well as of his Arabic commentators, proved hugely controversial, because these new ways of thinking highlighted the inherent goodness of the created order. The sudden repudiation of eternal Platonic Forms or Ideas as distinct from created objects; the new emphasis on natural law and human reason; and the notion that happiness could be obtained already in this life — all these were re-

5. Henri de Lubac, *Corpus Mysticum: The Eucharist and the Church in the Middle Ages: Historical Survey*, trans. Gemma Simmonds with Richard Price and Christopher Stephens, ed. Laurence Paul Hemming and Susan Frank Parsons (London: SCM, 2006), 223.

6. See esp. Marie-Dominique Chenu, *Nature, Man, and Society in the Twelfth Century: Essays on New Theological Perspectives in the Latin West*, pref. by Étienne Gilson, trans. and ed. Jerome Taylor and Lester Little, Medieval Academy Reprints for Teaching, no. 37 (1968; reprint, Toronto: University of Toronto Press, 1997), 1-48.

pugnant to many Christian theologians, as all of these ideas clashed with the inherited Platonist-Christian synthesis.[7]

Chenu's *ressourcement* of Thomas Aquinas depicted in detail the rise of the mendicant orders in the High Middle Ages, the decline of the feudal order, the burgeoning of the urban middle classes, and the replacement of the monastery schools with secular universities in Paris and other European cities. And the contemporary implications were never far from Chenu's mind.

> To vow "mendicancy" in the thirteenth century was to refuse the feudal system of the Church both institutionally and economically, including benefices and the collection of tithes, even when they were destined for apostolic and charitable purposes. It was also to dislodge the free proclamation of the word of God from the heavy apparatus of feudalism. . . . The mendicants renounced feudalism in the same way that liberation movements have separated themselves from capitalism, by gospel inspiration, not by ideological persuasion. The return to the gospel brings about a break with debilitating institutional structures as with inappropriate personal behaviour.[8]

Chenu portrays Aquinas as riding the crest of new, revolutionary developments in society, which the old feudalist powers were unable to stop.

However, these new developments meant a decline in the sacramental ontology of the Great Tradition, of which decline Chenu was quite aware. He depicts the thirteenth century as the century of crisis for what he regarded as otherworldly Platonism. The introduction of Aristotle, with his emphasis on this-worldly realities, meant a corresponding farewell to Plato. "St. Thomas," Chenu insists, "continually challenged the Platonic worldview with its dualism of matter and spirit, its split into two of human intelligence, its too easy contempt for sensible things, and its seduction by spiritual escapism."[9] These were harsh

---

7. For an excellent and quite accessible discussion of the rediscovery of Aristotle, see Richard E. Rubenstein, *Aristotle's Children: How Christians, Muslims, and Jews Rediscovered Ancient Wisdom and Illuminated the Dark Ages* (Orlando, FL: Harcourt, 2003).

8. Marie-Dominique Chenu, *Aquinas and His Role in Theology,* trans. Paul Philibert (Collegeville, MN: Glazier/Liturgical, 2002), 8-9. The original speaks of the controversial worker-priest movement "Mission de France" rather than of liberation movements.

9. Chenu, *Aquinas and His Role,* 89-90; cf. 116-17.

words directed at medieval Platonism and in favor of the newly introduced Aristotelianism.[10] Chenu's sometimes sharp attacks on the
Platonist-Christian synthesis set him apart from some of the other *nouvelle* theologians. Chenu's interest in following what he called the "law
of the Incarnation" and in upholding the autonomy of the natural
world drew him away from the sacramentalism of medieval feudalism
and attracted him to the naturalism that arose in the High Middle
Ages. Describing thirteenth-century Gothic art, Chenu waxes eloquent:

> Observe the developments in both landscape and portrait painting.
> Nature and human beings find a place for themselves for their own
> sake, no longer merely as symbols. The folds of garments and the
> gestures of personalities cease being hieratic and become ordinary.
> Trees, fields, and rivers are portrayed with a palpable existence as
> concrete and solid — and along with these, so also the work of men
> and women. Their naturalistic realism and their secular social life
> apparently disconnect them from sacral significance; but then, in a
> stroke, they enter within the concrete unfolding of Providence and
> into the economy of an incarnate God.[11]

Chenu contrasts the Aristotelian "economy of an incarnate God" with
the Platonic "hieratic" universe, and decidedly opts for the "naturalistic
realism" of the former.

Chenu's choice seems unfortunate to me. He realized that the decline of the Platonist-Christian synthesis led over time to the
desacralizing or desacramentalizing of Western culture. Sounding typically modern, Chenu describes the twelfth-century revolt of nature
with a degree of bravura: "Henceforth, the new *homo artifex*, maker of
shapes and forms, distinguished between the animate and the mechan-
ical, rid himself of the childish fancies of animism and of the habit of
seeing divinity in the marvels of nature. The shared realm which he sec-
ularized by this process no longer possessed any properly religious
value for him."[12] Chenu applauds the new inability to see divinity in
nature. The "desacralizing," or "desacramentalizing," of nature, which

---

10. To be sure, Chenu did recognize that Thomas had also been deeply influenced by
Neo-Platonism, particularly by way of the sixth-century monk Denys (Chenu, *Aquinas
and His Role*, 53-54).

11. Chenu, *Aquinas and His Role*, 99-100.

12. Chenu, *Nature, Man, and Society*, 44-45.

coincided with the abandonment of the Platonist-Christian synthesis, was, to Chenu, a laudable development. As I have mentioned, Chenu was alone among the *nouvelle* theologians in his rather straightforward rejection of the medieval synthesis.[13]

However, what is more important than Chenu's personal evaluation is his recognition that the twelfth and thirteenth centuries brought about a fairly radical change: the Platonist-Christian sacramental ontology had to make room for the naturalism of modernity. Thus is his analysis of a piece with Congar's description of the juridicizing of ecclesial power around this same time, and with de Lubac's depiction of the church's focus on the eucharistic elements themselves. Each of these developments was the result of a widening gap between nature and the supernatural and of an increasing inability to see the created order as participating in Christ as the eternal anchor of the sublunary world.

Scripture, Church, and Tradition

Fourth, Congar points out that the fourteenth and fifteenth centuries witnessed an ever-increasing separation between the authority of Scripture and that of the church. To a sacramental mindset, the supernatural presence of God, both in Scripture and in the church, was obvious. Therefore, medieval Christians would never have dreamed of opposing the one to the other. This changed in the late Middle Ages. Congar drew on an influential book by George Tavard on the relationship between Scripture and church. In *Holy Writ or Holy Church*, Tavard reports: "The fourteenth century witnessed a remarkable, if unfortunate, break with the hitherto conventional doctrine on Scripture and the Church. The Fathers and the great medieval Schoolmen assumed that Church and Scripture co-inhere. The fourteenth century introduced a cleavage between them."[14] According to Congar, this cleavage between church and Scripture tied in with the increasing juridicizing of the church in the High Middle Ages. The centrality of human power in the church meant

13. As we will see in chap. 10, even Chenu had a profoundly mystical side, which opened him up to some of the contemplative elements of Denys's Neo-Platonism.

14. George H. Tavard, *Holy Writ or Holy Church: The Crisis of the Protestant Reformation* (London: Burns and Oates, 1959), 22.

that the church's hierarchy made increasingly strong claims concerning her power to make decisive and binding interpretations of the Bible.

The trouble began, according to Congar, when the thirteenth-century theologian Henry of Ghent (c. 1217-1293) asked the audacious question: "Must we believe the *auctoritates* (= the *dicta,* the texts) of sacred Scripture rather than those of the Church, or *vice versa?*"[15] Henry seemed to raise the possibility that Scripture and church might find themselves on opposing sides of particular theological debates. More disturbingly, John Duns Scotus (c. 1265-1308) and William of Ockham (c. 1288-c. 1347) did not merely ask the question about which of the two authorities had priority; they also answered it: Scripture had priority over the church (p. 95). John Wycliffe (c. 1328-1384), John Hus (c. 1369-1415), and the later Reformers would be even more unambiguous on this score. However, while the Reformers favored Scripture over the church, the Catholic Counter Reformation reacted by adopting the opposite: ultimate authority was vested in the church (p. 98). Ironically, while some of the critics of the church appealed to Scripture itself over against ecclesial authority — something we can observe especially in Wycliffe — others countered by pitting church against Scripture. Congar puts it this way:

> [Wycliffe] prosecuted his demands for reform so radically that they constituted in effect the principle of *Scriptura sola* and the separation of Scripture from the Church. As a result, his orthodox critics felt obliged to defend the unwritten traditions *by arguing from the insufficiency of Scripture, and therefore, to a certain extent, by opposing them to it* — something which we can only regret, while recognizing that it was more or less inevitable. (p. 98)

Congar was obviously ill at ease with the "orthodox critics" of Wycliffe and the later Reformers. Just as de Lubac points out that Berengar and his critics both adopted the same separation between sacrament and reality, or between nature and the supernatural, Congar argues that Wycliffe and his critics both worked with an understanding of authority in which Scripture and church had been pitted against each other. In both historical controversies, the "orthodox critics" overreacted and did so precisely because they shared the underlying presuppositions of their opponents.

15. Congar, *Tradition and Traditions,* 99. Hereafter, references to this work appear in parentheses in the text.

Equally obviously, Congar is concerned with the common Catholic assertion that Scripture is insufficient. For Congar, the way to hold Scripture and church together is by insisting that Scripture and tradition are not two separate sources of authority. Holy Scripture, for Congar, contains everything necessary for faith: Scripture is materially sufficient. Therefore, there is no separate source of oral tradition that secretly passed on additional truths that the church is required to believe. I will unpack Congar's understanding of tradition in more detail in chapter 7; but at this point let me simply observe that Congar desired a return to the earlier sacramental ontology, in which neither Scripture nor church were regarded as authorities simply imposed from above.

The same extrinsicism that Congar opposes when he describes the rise of juridicism he also rejects when he discusses the relationship between Scripture and church. The earlier Platonist-Christian synthesis regarded the Spirit's revelation in Scripture as quite similar to his continued guidance of the church (pp. 119-37).[16] The sacramental ontology dominating the Great Tradition ensured that Scripture and church were kept together. Thus Congar speaks of the "period from the beginning of the patristic age until modern theology, where we find a conviction of a permanent action of the Spirit 'inspiring' Christians, churchmen, councils, sacred writers: for every right explanation or determination that occurs in the life of the Church comes from the Holy Spirit. The thought here is less historical than theological and sacramental" (p. 339). Congar pines for the days when the approach to the church was more "theological and sacramental." A return to a more sacramental understanding of God's direct presence and activity in the church will, to his mind, also solve the problem of Scripture and tradition as two separate, extraneously imposed authorities.[17]

---

16. Prior to the thirteenth century, Congar pointed out, the terminology of "inspiration," "revelation," and "illumination" had been applied both to Scripture and to the church.

17. To be sure, Congar acknowledges the validity of the modern distinction between the Spirit's "inspiration" of Scripture and the Spirit's "assistance" of the church (pp. 208-9, 302, 314); see also Yves Congar, *The Meaning of Tradition*, trans. A. N. Woodrow (San Francisco: Ignatius, 2004), 99-100. But this acknowledgment does not fit well with his criticisms of the church's juridicizing and of the elevation of church over Scripture. Congar's sacramental ontology really requires a reworking of the modern distinction between the Spirit's "inspiration" and "assistance."

Nature and the Supernatural

Fifth, and finally, the separation between nature and the supernatural became the direct object of controversy in the sixteenth century. According to *nouvelle théologie*, each of the four issues that we have looked at so far contributed to the loss of the Platonist-Christian consensus, while under the surface of each of them lurked the relationship between nature and the supernatural. As a result of the Gregorian Reform and the ensuing juridicizing of the church, people came to regard ecclesiastical authority as an extraneous power. This extrinsicism meant the imposition of the (divine) supernatural upon the (human) natural world. Underlying the Berengarian controversy lay a similar separation: both the Berengarians and their opponents took for granted the widening gap between sacrament and reality, and thus between nature and the supernatural.

The twelfth- and thirteenth-century discovery of nature, which depended a great deal on the reintroduction of Aristotle in Europe, was likewise predicated on the rejection of the Platonist-Christian synthesis of medieval feudalism. Aquinas and others celebrated the goodness and (at least relative) autonomy of the natural order vis-à-vis the supernatural, with the "desacralizing" of Western culture as the inevitable result. And the late medieval separation between Scripture and church resulted likewise from an increasing inability to see the Spirit directly at work in the human life of the church. In each of the issues, Western Christians found themselves at a loss about how to keep nature and the supernatural together. As the natural world gained autonomy, the supernatural was forced into an inevitable retreat. The *ressourcement* theologians maintained that the sacramental tapestry of the Great Tradition, in which nature participated in the supernatural, made way for a new — and ultimately secular — configuration.

Consequently, the sixteenth-century controversies concerning the nature-supernatural relationship came by no means like a thunderbolt from the blue sky. Furthermore, the *nouvelle* theologians argued, in these controversies Catholic theologians overreacted to their opponents and in so doing exacerbated the problems that I have already described in this chapter. Henri de Lubac's *Surnaturel* (1946) presents a detailed historical analysis of the relationship between nature and the supernatural in which he sharply criticizes the ever-widening gap between the two. As a result of that book, this Jesuit theologian bore the brunt of the wrath of the Neo-Scholastic establishment. However, it should be clear by now that, not just de Lubac, but most of the other *nouvelle* theologians as well, were interested in reconfiguring the nature-supernatural relationship. The extrinsicism of the Neo-Thomists had to give way, they argued, to a more intrinsic approach in which nature participated in the supernatural.

De Lubac was particularly dissatisfied with what he regarded as Catholic overreactions to the Protestant Reformation and to the theologies of Michael Baius (1513-1589) in the sixteenth century and Cornelius Jansenius (1585-1638) in the seventeenth century. Without going into detail, I will suggest that de Lubac was convinced that, in its reaction to these controversies, the Catholic Counter Reformation made two mistakes. First, its scholars introduced the notion of "pure nature" *(pura natura)*, by which they meant the state of human nature before the Fall, quite apart from any consideration of divine grace. The notion of "pure nature" served to highlight the autonomous character of the natural realm, and thus further separated that realm from the supernatural. Robert Bellarmine (1542-1621) had first introduced the notion in his battle against Baius. Bellarmine had spoken of "pure nature" in order to argue that grace was exactly that: gratuitous. God did not *have* to give anyone justifying grace. The notion of "pure nature" made clear that there was nothing in human beings that somehow merited the grace of God. In the light of aforementioned historical developments, it will be clear why de Lubac was rather concerned with the independence that this seemed to grant to the natural world.[18] While he recognized the polemical value of "pure nature," he was concerned with the autonomy of the natural realm that resulted from it.

Second, some Scholastic theologians, over time, began to deny that everyone had a "natural desire" *(desiderium naturale)* for supernatural communion in the Trinitarian life. This denial took root especially with Thomas Cajetan (1469-1534) and Francisco Suárez (1548-1617).[19] Since grace was supernatural, so they thought, the idea that people naturally desired the beatific vision placed too much trust in the human capacity

---

18. See, e.g., Henri de Lubac, *Augustinianism and Modern Theology,* intro. by Louis Dupré, trans. Lancelot Sheppard (New York: Crossroad/Herder and Herder, 2000), xxxv, 212, 240.

19. De Lubac, *Augustinianism and Modern Theology,* 163-69; see also Henri de Lubac, *The Mystery of the Supernatural,* trans. Rosemary Sheed (New York: Crossroad/Herder and Herder, 1998), 143-49.

to attain supernatural grace. In other words, natural desire seemed to them an assertion of the Pelagian error. However, de Lubac was not convinced of the charge of Pelagianism. The net effect of these two moves — the notion of "pure nature" and the denial of "natural desire" — was, according to de Lubac, a further desacramentalizing of the cosmos. Nature and the supernatural drifted further and further apart as the Platonist-Christian tapestry unraveled further.

As a result of its revolt, the natural realm managed quite well by itself, and the gift of supernatural grace had precious little to do with the hopes and dreams of people's everyday lives. As Tracey Rowland puts it, "The supernatural could subsequently be privatized and social life would then proceed on the basis of the common pursuit of goods associated solely with the 'natural' order."[20]

This meant, according to de Lubac, not only that he was falsely accused of Pelagianism for insisting on "natural desire," but that his accusers themselves were the ones who had actually fallen into that error. For them, autonomous nature was no longer in need of the supernatural and could manage its own affairs without supernatural aid.

Perhaps the most remarkable thing about these five developments, each of which we could see as a step away from the Platonist-Christian synthesis and its sacramental ontology, is that almost all of them took place long before the Protestant Reformation. The juridicizing of the church began with the eleventh-century Gregorian Reform. The loss of sacramental unity between Eucharist and church was also the result of an eleventh-century controversy. The "discovery of nature" must be located in the twelfth century. The disjunction between church and Scripture as potentially opposing authorities can be traced to the fourteenth and fifteenth centuries. Each of these developments predated the Reformation. Only the idea of "pure nature" and the repudiation of "natural desire" had to wait until the sixteenth and seventeenth centuries before they really became common fare. And the chronology of these developments was not lost on the *nouvelle* theologians. The not so subtle message that they were driving home in the 1930s and 1940s was that Catholicism and the Reformation shared a common problem. It was no longer quite as easy to point to the various branches of the Reformation and to accuse them of having abandoned the true faith. The

20. Tracey Rowland, *Culture and the Thomist Tradition after Vatican II* (London: Routledge, 2003), 94.

edges of the tapestry were showing clear signs of fraying long before the Reformation, and each of the developments caused a further desacramentalizing of the cosmos.

For *nouvelle théologie,* the loss of the Platonist-Christian synthesis was a problem that Catholics and Protestants had in common. This means that ecumenical dialogue can hardly proceed with an attitude of superiority — either on the part of Catholics or on the part of Protestants. The theological way forward, which I will sketch in part 2 of this book, is a task on which Catholics and evangelicals can only embark together.

CHAPTER 4

Cutting the Tapestry:
The Scissors of Modernity

The *ressourcement* theologians presented a compelling sketch of the developments that caused Western society to step away from the sacramental mindset of the Great Tradition. Contemporary historians, theologians, and philosophers of culture broadly confirm the conclusions of *nouvelle théologie*. At the same time, however, these scholars complicate the picture by focusing more directly on two additional related developments in the late Middle Ages. Sympathetic to the earlier Platonist-Christian synthesis, they point to two factors as contributing to the loss of a sacramental ontology and the origin of the autonomous natural realm of modernity: the rise of univocity and nominalism, two philosophical currents of thought that I will explain in greater detail. The contemporary scholars explaining modernity largely as the result of these two factors are, on the one hand, a group of theologians clustered around the so-called Radical Orthodoxy movement and, on the other hand, individual scholars such as Louis Dupré. Whereas I used the metaphor of an unraveling of the sacramental tapestry in the preceding chapter, I believe that we need the stronger metaphor of an actual cutting of the tapestry to describe the philosophical developments I will discuss in this chapter.

Scotus and Univocity of Being

It is not my purpose to provide a lengthy introduction to the thought of the various theologians (many of them high Anglican and Catholic) associated with Radical Orthodoxy.[1] In several ways, one could argue that theologians such as John Milbank and Graham Ward are neither radical nor orthodox. I do believe, however, that the movement's attempt to restore theology to the position of "queen of the sciences" involves a bold reassertion of the medieval approach to theology. Furthermore, the desire to reappropriate a Platonist-Christian synthesis is certainly laudable (even if the postmodern spin on Neo-Platonism sometimes makes it difficult for Radical Orthodoxy to appreciate the goodness of created boundaries).[2] Particularly commendable, I feel, is Radical Orthodoxy's rejection of materialism by insisting that creation participates in the life of God. As a result, the movement's critique of late medieval philosophical and theological developments deserves a serious hearing.

In what follows I will outline the critique that Radical Orthodoxy theologians — as well as other scholars — offer of late medieval developments, in particular of univocity and nominalism. These two concepts, we might say, serve as the two blades of a pair of scissors that cut the tapestry by severing the participatory link between earthly sacrament *(sacramentum)* and heavenly reality *(res)*. In order for us to understand how the incisive cuts of this scissors have resulted in the desacralizing or desacramentalizing of the universe, I need to begin by briefly returning to the Platonist-Christian synthesis. As I emphasized in chapter 1, for the Great Tradition, earthly realities existed not just for themselves but for the sake of a greater purpose.[3] Augustine, for example, maintained that only God should be enjoyed for his own sake. The life of the triune God was the only ultimate end. Since all other realities had their being only inasmuch as God graciously granted participation in his own being, those realities could never be ultimate in character. Created objects and earthly ends had never more than penultimate significance; they were always ordered to something greater — the life of God himself. Their anchoring in the eternal Word or Logos meant that their truth, goodness, and beauty both originated in and aimed at the truth, goodness, and beauty of the Son of God himself.

---

1. For an excellent overall introduction, see James K. A. Smith, *Introducing Radical Orthodoxy: Mapping a Post-Secular Theology* (Grand Rapids: Baker Academic, 2005). Radical Orthodoxy takes its name from the title of the book *Radical Orthodoxy: A New Theology,* ed. John Milbank, Catherine Pickstock, and Graham Ward (London: Routledge, 1999).

2. Cf. Hans Boersma, "On the Rejection of Boundaries: Radical Orthodoxy's Appropriation of St. Augustine," *Pro Ecclesia* 15 (2006): 418-47.

3. See chap. 1, under subheading "The Celebration of Creation: Use or Enjoyment?"

Some readers may continue to worry about elements of the Great Tradition's sacramental or participatory account of reality. It is one thing to charge modernity with being idolatrous for treating penultimate realities of this world as if they were ultimate in character; but slinging mud at the other party does not necessarily mean you are clean yourself. Doesn't a sacramental or participatory cosmology lapse into a pantheist divinizing of nature? If created being participates in the being of God (the eternal Word), does this not make created being divine? And isn't the problem with the Platonic tradition precisely that it cannot distinguish between Creator and creature — thus resulting in pantheism? These are important criticisms, and I believe we need to readily acknowledge that Platonism does court pantheism. As I made clear in the first chapter, the Platonist-Christian synthesis emphatically did not mean a wholesale adoption of Neo-Platonism.[4]

Although it is true (and unavoidable) that a certain "hellenization" of the gospel did take place in the early church, as well as in the church during the Middle Ages, the Great Tradition generally knew that at certain junctures it was important to say no to the Platonic tradition. This was true particularly with respect to the way "participation" functioned in Neo-Platonism. Its understanding of participation was based on the idea that creation emanated by necessity from eternal Ideas, and ultimately from an impersonal, unconcerned deity. Christians rejected these notions of a necessary emanation, as well as the pantheist worldview that it entailed. We could say that for the Great Tradition, creation was *merely* a sacramental sharing (or participating) in the life of God.

Let me try to articulate what I mean by my suggestion that creation was *merely* a sacramental participation in the divine life. The word "merely" alerts us to the infinitely great difference or dissimilarity that the Christian tradition wished to maintain between God and the world. Christian theologians referred to creation's relationship with God by using the philosophical notion of "analogy of being" *(analogia entis)*. The doctrine of analogy was a way to speak philosophically about the sacramental relationship between Creator and creation. Thus did Christian theologians explain that the being of creation (as well as its truth, goodness, and beauty) was similar or analogous — and thus not identical — to the being (and the truth, goodness, and beauty)

---

4. See chap. 1, under subheading "Christianity and the Platonic Heritage."

of the Creator. Analogy (or sacramentality) implies that, while creatures may be similar to the Creator, they are in no way identical to him. To be sure, *analogia entis* does imply that there is a link between God and the created order, hence the similarity between creation's being and the being of the Creator. (Just as one might say of a painting that it bears the imprint of the painter, so one could also say of creatures that one sees the Creator in them.)

Indeed, this is one side of the coin of analogy: there is a kind of similarity between God and the world. But the coin has another side as well: the doctrine of analogy does not just argue for similarity but also insists on the infinite *difference* between Creator and creature. In fact, *dis*similarity is the main point of the doctrine of analogy. Although there is a certain similarity between the way God is good and the way creation is good, nonetheless, an infinite difference remains — and never decreases, not even slightly — between the goodness of God and the goodness of creation. Therefore, the Fourth Lateran Council (1215) insisted that "between the Creator and the creature so great a likeness cannot be noted without the necessity of noting a greater dissimilarity between them."[5] The doctrine of analogy basically claimed that the connection between creation and Creator is *merely* sacramental in character. Yes, creation truly participates in its eternal christological anchor; but this participation is strictly a gift of grace and in no way erases the Creator-creature distinction. In fact, sacramental participation *limits* the significance of the created order: its truth, goodness, and beauty are not its own, but are merely derived from the being of God. Idolatrous self-assertion is out of the question. The infinite dissimilarity of the doctrine of *analogia entis* (or, we might say, of the sacramentality of creation) thus serves to sound the Christian negative to Neo-Platonist pantheism: God and creation should not be confused.

It is crucial to observe that the sacramental participation of our being in the being of God upholds the infinite difference between God and creation. The doctrine of analogy allows one to say, along with Augustine, "What then, brethren, shall we say of God? For if thou hast been able to comprehend what thou wouldest say, it is not God; if thou hast been able to comprehend it, thou hast comprehended some-

---

5. Henry Denzinger, *The Sources of Catholic Dogma,* trans. Roy J. Deferrari (Fitzwilliam, NH: Loreto, 2002), 171 (no. 432).

thing else instead of God."[6] The Bishop of Hippo had a deep awareness of the mystery of God. The doctrine of analogy also harked back to Athanasius's insistence that "there is similarity of names between things human and things divine, revealing nevertheless underneath this sameness a wide difference in meanings."[7]

Athanasius, along with most church fathers and medieval theologians, recognized a fundamental tension in Christian theology. On the one hand, the connection between God and this world has to be safeguarded: God truly reveals himself in this world and in human language, so that this world really does have being, and human words really do attain to the mystery of God. On the other hand, over against the Platonic tradition, the otherness of God needs to be preserved as well: God's transcendence implies that it surely would be erroneous to equate our being with the being of God or to assert that human language could adequately comprehend God. The resulting doctrine of *analogia entis* was the Great Tradition's way of avoiding a mingling of the divine and the human. The relationship between creation and Creator is merely a sacramental or analogous relationship. The sacramentality of the relationship implies that, although God is present in his creation, and though creation participates in the eternal Word of God, the sacramental reality *(res)* of the Word infinitely transcends terrestrial objects. The infinite difference between Creator and creature implies the rejection of the pantheism that lurks in straightforward Neo-Platonism.

This doctrine of analogy came to classical expression in the theology of Thomas Aquinas. In important respects, the thirteenth-century theologian took his place within the longstanding Platonist-Christian tradition. This was certainly the case with his understanding of analogy. Thomas argues that God is so much greater than we are that we cannot adequately comprehend God and talk about him in straightforward language. So, if we were to ask, What is God like? What is his essence? we could only answer that his essence is existence or being itself.

6. Augustine, *Sermons on Selected Lessons of the New Testament,* in *Nicene and Post-Nicene Fathers,* 1st ser., vol. 6, trans. R. G. MacMullen, ed. Philip Schaff (1888; reprint, Peabody, MA: Hendrickson, 1994), II.16.

7. Athanasius, *Contra Eunomium,* in *Nicene and Post-Nicene Fathers,* 2nd ser., vol. 5, ed. Archibald Robertson (1893; reprint, Peabody, MA: Hendrickson, 1994), I.39; see also Frances M. Young, *Biblical Exegesis and the Formation of Christian Culture* (Peabody, MA: Hendrickson, 2002), 142.

God, argues Thomas, is being, not becoming. Unlike the world that he made, God himself does not change; thus there is no potentiality in God: he is pure act. All of this is different among created beings. In created beings, there *is* a real distinction between essence and existence. After all, created being is simply of the borrowed kind; created being is being only because by grace it participates in the existence of God. Only of God can we say that there is no distinction between essence and existence and that the two completely overlap.[8]

Of course, if God is so transcendent that we cannot grasp his essence and cannot use straightforward language to describe who he is in his innermost being, this raises the question of how we can talk about God at all. Thomas answers this question by recourse to *analogia entis;* following the Great Tradition, he tries to walk the same fine line. On the one hand, because there is a participatory link between our existence and God's, it is possible for us to talk about God in human language. On the other hand, Thomas is also convinced that when we talk about God, we always have to remember the infinite difference that remains. Hence, in stating that God is wise, we do not imply, according to Thomas, that God is wise in the same way that human beings are wise. In characteristically Scholastic fashion, the angelic doctor argues his case as follows:

> [W]hen any term expressing perfection is applied to a creature, it signifies that perfection distinct in idea from other perfections; as, for instance, by this term *wise* applied to a man, we signify some perfection distinct from a man's essence, and distinct from his power and existence, and from all similar things; whereas when we apply it to God, we do not mean to signify anything distinct from His essence, or power, or existence. Thus also this term *wise* applied to man in some degree circumscribes and comprehends the thing signified; whereas this is not the case when it is applied to God; but it leaves the thing signified as incomprehended, and as exceeding the signification of the name. Hence it is evident that this term *wise* is not applied in the same way to God and to man.[9]

8. See Leo J. Elders, *The Metaphysics of Being of St. Thomas Aquinas in a Historical Perspective,* Studien und Texte zur Geistesgeschichte des Mittelalters, no. 34 (Leiden: Brill, 1993), 170-89.

9. Thomas Aquinas, *Summa Theologica (ST),* trans. Fathers of the English Dominican Province (1948; reprint, Westminster, MD: Christian Classics, 1981), I, q.13, a.5.

Thomas's insistence that human discourse cannot comprehend God shows his faithfulness to the Great Tradition's insistence on the mystery of God. Human beings are unable to comprehend God. The word "wise" cannot possibly apply to God and humans in the same way: the language we use for God does not apply to him in a straightforward fashion. Since the created order *merely* participates in God's being sacramentally, human discourse about God, too, is *merely* analogous language. Thus does Thomas make it quite clear that the doctrine of analogy is meant to offer protection against the excesses of the way the Neo-Platonic tradition understands participation. The form of human beings, Thomas declares, only very distantly resembles God's own form, "not, that is, so as to participate in the likeness of the agent's [i.e., God's] form according to the same specific or generic formality, but only according to some sort of analogy."[10] Such an analogous or sacramental approach is the very best we can do with respect to a God who, on the one hand, is our Creator and who, on the other hand, infinitely transcends us.

In the fourteenth century, however, Duns Scotus argued that the idea of analogous being simply does not make sense.[11] Something either does have being or it does not. To say God exists and to say created objects exist is to say one and the same thing. All being is being in the same sense. Put philosophically, all being is univocal in character. While analogy of being had served to uphold the infinite difference between Creator and creature, Scotus's univocity of being countered that being is an objective, neutral category and that God's being and created being are identical in kind. As James K. A. Smith puts it, for Scotus, "both the Creator and the creature exist in the same way or in the same sense. Being, now, becomes a category that is unhooked from participation in God and is a more neutral or abstract qualifier that is applied *to* God and creatures in the same way."[12] In other words, univocity of being served as one of the blades of modernity's scissors that cut the real, sacramental presence of God in the natural world. Historians of doctrine debate to what extent this representation of Scotus is a fair one.[13] But what does

10. *ST* I, q.5, a.3.

11. See Louis Dupré, *Passage to Modernity: An Essay in the Hermeneutics of Nature and Culture* (New Haven: Yale University Press, 1993), 167-89; see also Smith, *Introducing Radical Orthodoxy*, 95-103.

12. Smith, *Introducing Radical Orthodoxy*, 97.

13. See Robert Sweetman, "Univocity, Analogy, and the Mystery of Being according to

seem clear is that with Scotus there appears an initial flattening of the infinite horizons of the sacramental ontology of the Great Tradition. Theologians in the Radical Orthodoxy movement have rightly drawn attention to this development: in the late Middle Ages, it became possible to "understand being in an unambiguous, sheerly 'existential' sense, as the object of a proposition, without reference to God, who is later claimed 'to be' in the same univocal manner."[14]

The novel assertion of univocity of being has had huge implications for the way people view their relationship with God. For the Platonist-Christian synthesis, a sacramental link between the created order and the eternal Word exists: there is a sacramental connection — a participation — that links the creation to its Creator. Human beings and the created order participate in the divine life. This sacramental ontology becomes problematic with Scotus's univocity of being. If it is true that we can apply "being" to God and creatures *in the same way,* then "being" forms an overarching category in which God and creatures both share. With Scotus, we might say, it became possible to deny the sacramentality of the relationship between earthly objects and the Logos as their eternal archetype. No longer did earthly objects (as *sacramentum*) receive the reality *(res)* of their being from God's own being. Rather, earthly objects possessed their own being. No longer was there a mysterious reality hiding within what could be observed by the senses. The full reality of created objects could be seen, heard, touched, smelled, and tasted. The loss of analogy meant the loss of sacramentality.

Smith points out that a "double idolatry" is involved in this move from analogy to univocity.[15] Although such language may seem rather strong at first blush, there is little doubt that the shift toward univocity implies the substitution of idols for sacraments. First, univocity means a reduction of God: God is subordinated to a higher concept, namely, that of being. For Scotus, God is simply one of many beings — all understood in the same, univocal sense of "being." Thomas's Platonic proclivities had ensured that, for him, God does not simply belong to a *different* category (or genus) of being than creatures

John Duns Scotus," in *Radical Orthodoxy and the Reformed Tradition: Creation, Covenant, and Participation,* ed. James K. A. Smith and James H. Olthuis (Grand Rapids: Baker Academic, 2005), 73-87.

14. John Milbank, "Only Theology Overcomes Metaphysics," *New Blackfriars* 76 (1995): 334.

15. Smith, *Introducing Radical Orthodoxy,* 98.

do, but rather that he far transcends *every* category of being.[16] The new understanding, by contrast, turns God into one of many categories. Second — and this point is particularly important in connection with the origin of an autonomous, desacramentalized realm of nature — univocity in effect renders the created order independent from God. We can now say of the created order that it exists just as much as we can say of God that he exists. No longer does created existence have being by participation *only*. Instead, the created order claims radical independence; it turns into a "discrete, secular order."[17] The Platonist-Christian emphasis on the created order sacramentally participating in God's being, and thus depending for its existence entirely on God's own life, makes way for a separation between the created order and the fullness of God's being. No longer are truth, goodness, and beauty given with the reality of the divine Word. Instead, these universals claim independence from what had once been their christological anchor in the heavenly places. Slowly but surely, the infinite mystery of God will recede from the horizon before this concrete, comprehensible, and malleable concept of being.

The Absolute Power of God

If created being no longer had a real, participatory connection with God, the relationship between Creator and creature — as two distinct beings — would have to be configured differently. The real presence of a sacramental relationship would have to make room for a different kind of relationship. As a result, the participatory or real bond gave way to an external or nominal link. The newly conceived external connection was guaranteed by the will *(voluntas)* of God. For Aquinas, we might say, divine decisions had always been in line with eternal truth. For example, when God condemned theft or adultery, this was not an arbitrary divine decision, but it was in line with the truth of divine rationality. Or, to use another example, when God rewarded almsgiving, this was not because he arbitrarily decided that almsgiving was a commendable practice, but because it was in line with the very truth of God's character.

16. *ST* I, q.5, a.3, reply obj. 2.
17. Smith, *Introducing Radical Orthodoxy,* 99.

Duns Scotus proffered a radical disjunction between will and reason, between goodness and truth. The new voluntarist approach departed from the Platonist-Christian synthesis by arguing that God's will determines the moral status of a particular act and that his intellect simply follows along. The consequences were close at hand: if something is good strictly because God *wills* it to be good, then couldn't God declare anything, even the most horrible act, to be good? Now, it seems, there is nothing in almsgiving itself that makes it an inherently good act; God simply wills and declares it to be so. It is hard to avoid the implication that God has become an arbitrary God who declares the moral status of human actions simply at whim.

The divine arbitrariness resulting from univocity and voluntarism is clear from the way late medieval theologians worked with the distinction between God's absolute power *(potentia absoluta)* and his ordained power *(potentia ordinata)*.[18] The distinction itself had been common among medieval scholastic theologians. They used it to safeguard God's omnipotence. Aquinas, for example, had used the distinction to say that God had ordained to use his power — which, of course, was in itself absolute or unlimited (except for the law of noncontradiction) — in a particular way, in order to bring about some things rather than others. But Duns Scotus — and after him especially the Oxford scholar William of Ockham (c. 1288-c. 1348) — gave far greater rein to God's *potentia absoluta*.[19] These fourteenth-century Franciscans shifted the traditional balance between God's ordained and absolute power by implying that perhaps God might actually *use* his absolute power to do things that were outside the scope of his ordained will. For instance, Ockham points to John 3:5: "Unless someone is born of water and the

18. For this paragraph, I have drawn especially on G. van den Brink, "De absolute en geordineerde macht van God: Opmerkingen bij de ontwikkeling van een onderscheid," *Nederlandisch theologisch tijdschrift* 45 (1991): 205-22.

19. See the comment of Servaes Pinckaers about Ockham: "For him, the divine will was totally free; it governed moral law itself and all the laws of creation. What God willed was necessarily just and good precisely because he willed it. Law, and all moral value or qualification, flowed from this will. Determined in the establishment of good and evil by nothing other than itself, the divine will could at any instant change what we considered to be permitted or forbidden according to the commandments, notably the Decalogue. God could even change the first commandment and, for example, pushing it to the limit, command a person to hate him, in such a way that this act of hatred would become good" (*The Sources of Christian Ethics,* trans. Mary Thomas Noble [Edinburgh: T. & T. Clark, 1995], 246-47).

Spirit, he cannot enter the Kingdom of God." Cannot? Ockham asks. But what about God's *potentia absoluta?* Might it not be possible, by virtue of God's *potentia absoluta,* that people might enter the kingdom of God without water and the Spirit? Ockham answers in the affirmative.

Similarly, when we look at Jacob and Esau, we observe no major moral differences between the two, and so we would expect that God's ordained power would treat them equally. In actual fact, however, we know from Scripture that God elected Jacob while rejecting Esau. Thus, argues Ockham, this divine choice must have followed God's *potentia absoluta.* This implies, of course, that voluntarism had begun to separate God's absolute power from his ordained power and had made allowance for the former to override the latter. Whereas Aquinas had simply used the distinction to look at God's power from two different viewpoints, late medieval theology began to separate the two: God could actually use his absolute power to do things he would not do according to his ordained power.

In the fifteenth century, this voluntarism of Duns Scotus and Ockham found climactic expression in the thought of Gabriel Biel (c. 1425-1495), who, later in life, became a professor at the University of Tübingen.[20] Biel insisted that, by his *potentia absoluta,* God could destroy someone he loved, could lie to human beings, could destroy the grace that he had once given, and could even take on human nature and subsequently abandon it, so that humanity could once more fall into sin. The result of this radical use of God's *potentia absoluta* was a thorough-going skepticism. After all, if God prophesied something in the Bible, did such prophecy actually bind his power, so that he now *must* do what he had promised he would do? It is easy to see how the *potentia absoluta* began to cast its shadow over all divine activity. The absolute freedom of God appeared to undermine the stability of his promises. Thus did Scotus's univocity of being give rise in the fourteenth and fifteenth centuries to a voluntarism that ended up exalting the absolute freedom of the divine will at the expense of the truthfulness of divine judgment. The world's real, sacramental participation in God gave way to an external relationship in which God ruled from afar, by means of the absolute freedom of the divine will: God was in heaven; human beings were on earth. Sacramental participation yielded to the extrinsicism of voluntarism.

---

20. For Biel, see Heiko A. Oberman, *The Harvest of Medieval Theology: Gabriel Biel and Late Medieval Nominalism* (1983; reprint, Grand Rapids: Baker Academic, 2000).

The voluntarism of the Scotist school had a deep impact on both late medieval theology and the direction of Western culture. Louis Dupré succinctly summarizes the impact:

> If creation depends on the inscrutable decision of a God who totally surpasses the law of human reason, nature loses its intrinsic intelligibility. Grace also becomes a blind result of a divine decree, randomly dispensed to an unprepared human nature. The emphasis upon a divine omnipotence unrestricted by rationality results in a "supernatural order" separated from nature's immanent rationality.[21]

In these few sentences Dupré points to a number of serious consequences that resulted from univocity and voluntarism. First, nature, now separate from reason, became fundamentally unintelligible. Over time, skepticism would be the inevitable result. Second, the late medieval emphasis on the "divine decree" appeared to cut the link between divine will and divine knowledge, between God's goodness and his truth. The upshot would be an emphasis on predestination in which God appeared to take arbitrary decisions about the eternal salvation and damnation of human beings.[22] Third, since grace was the "blind result" of this divine decree, theologians could only conceive of grace as an arbitrarily and externally imposed gift. Thomas's notion that God's gift of grace somehow connected to a natural desire *(desiderium naturale)* present in all human beings became unsustainable. Finally, all this implied a distinct, supernatural order, one that was assumed to be strictly separate from the natural order. As we saw in the preceding chapter, it was this separation that *nouvelle théologie* lamented as the foundation underlying secular modernity.

Ockham and the Rise of Nominalism

If univocity (along with the resulting voluntarism) constituted the first blade of modernity's scissors, the other blade was nominalism. One of

---

21. Louis Dupré, *Religion and the Rise of Modern Culture* (Notre Dame, IN: University of Notre Dame Press, 2008), 22.

22. See my critique esp. of later Calvinist views on predestination in *Violence, Hospitality, and the Cross: Reappropriating the Atonement Tradition* (Grand Rapids: Baker Academic, 2004), 53-73.

the important elements that the Great Tradition borrowed from Platonism was the notion that the Forms or Ideas had real existence. The Platonic Forms were attractive to Christian theology because they could easily be reconfigured in christological terms, thus providing a philosophical underpinning for various theological truths. For Christians with a Platonic bent, it was the eternal Logos in which all created being lay anchored. This christological anchor made it possible to assert, for example, that human beings participated in a common humanity, that cats participated in a common "felineness," that dogs participated in a common "canineness," and so on. One could trace back these universals (humanity, felineness, canineness) to the eternal Word of God. Philosophers speak of this notion — that the various members of one species share a common essence — as "realism." It is called realism simply because, according to this understanding, universals (humanity, felineness, and canineness) are real. They're not just figments of the imagination. Because of its link with Platonism, the Christian tradition prior to the late Middle Ages had, by and large, insisted that universals were real.

The fourteenth-century philosopher William of Ockham, however, felt that he could easily dispense with real universals.[23] He maintained that the existence of some kind of extraterrestrial realm of universals (the Platonic Forms) sounded like superfluous philosophical baggage. Sure, human beings do look alike, and so do cats and dogs; but there is an easier way to explain this similarity than by way of the odd assumption that universals have real existence. The principle of "Ockham's razor" is that one should explain observations by making as few assumptions as possible; one should use one's razor to shave off all unnecessary assumptions. And by putting his razor to work, Ockham pretty nearly shaved the universals right off. The tradition that followed Ockham insisted that universals were simply names *(nomina)* that we apply to individual objects that happen to look alike. Hence the term "nominalism" for the philosophical position that universals do not have real existence in the mind of God but are simply names that we assign to particular objects.[24] Summarizing Ockham's thought, Frederick Copleston says this:

23. See the helpful account in Richard E. Rubenstein, *Aristotle's Children: How Christians, Muslims, and Jews Rediscovered Ancient Wisdom and Illuminated the Dark Ages* (Orlando, FL: Harcourt, 2003), 251-57.

24. To be sure, Ockham did acknowledge the existence of universals as concepts in our minds; thus his approach is really, strictly speaking, "conceptualism" rather than "nominalism."

[Ockham's] main point was always that there is no need to postulate any factors other than the mind and individual things in order to explain the universal. The universal concept arises simply because there are varying degrees of similarity between individual things. Socrates and Plato are more similar to one another than either is to an ass; and this fact of experience is reflected in the formation of the specific concept of man. But we have to be careful of our way of speaking. We ought not to say that "Plato and Socrates agree (share) in something or in some things, but that they agree (are alike) by some things, that is, by themselves and that Socrates agrees with *(convenit cum)* Plato, not in something, but by something, namely himself." In other words, there is no nature common to Socrates and Plato, in which they come together or share or agree; but the nature which is Socrates and the nature which is Plato are alike.[25]

The likeness between Socrates and Plato had nothing to do with heavenly participation. In no way was their likeness based on a sacramental connection with the eternal Word.[26]

So, if the similarity between Socrates and Plato is not the result of a shared universal — if there is no real common humanity — then why do they look so incredibly similar? The reason is simple: the will of God.[27] At this point, Ockham has recourse to his voluntarism. God's will is the cause of every individual thing looking the way it does. Ockham's razor has no need for universals: for him, the will of God is sufficient to explain everything he sees around him. In short, the two blades of modernity's scissors, univocity and nominalism, both give rise to an inordinate emphasis on divine freedom and thus to voluntarism. The scissors of modernity — leading from analogy to univocity and from realism to nominalism — cut the sacramental tapestry in two and thus caused the decline and ultimately the near-collapse of the Platonist-Christian synthesis in the modern Western world.

25. Frederick Copleston, *A History of Philosophy*, 3 vols. (New York: Image/Doubleday, 1963), III:69.

26. See the much more robust understanding of humanity expressed by Craig M. Gay: "[I]f our words enable us to build up a common *world*, if they enable us to say 'we,' if it is given to them to bear any fruit at all in this world, this simply reflects the fact that we are graciously allowed to participate in the creative potency of the divine *Word*" (*Dialogue, Catalogue and Monologue: Personal, Impersonal and Depersonalizing Ways to Use Words* [Vancouver: Regent College Publishing, 2008], 18).

27. Gay, *Dialogue, Catalogue and Monologue*, 70.

Heavenly Participation and Human Culture

The outcome was the desacralized culture of modernity, in which the natural order had been cut from its sacramental participation in the life of God. Louis Dupré expresses it as follows:

> The idea of an independent order of secondary causes gradually led to a conception of nature as fully equipped to act without special divine assistance. But if the actual order of nature functioned as an independent entity directed only by its own teleology, the elevation to grace had to be regarded as a divine addition to the realm of nature. Logic required that theology treat this additional order separately from that of nature.[28]

The basic problem of modernity, as Dupré sees it, is that the separation of two distinct orders (the natural and the supernatural) implied that nature could pursue its own ends without considering any natural desire for the supernatural goal of the beatific vision. It now became impossible to discern the sacramental character of the created order. Heavenly participation gave way to a celebration of the natural ends of earthly realities.

The effects would not remain limited to the world of ideas. James K. A. Smith points out that Radical Orthodoxy

> discerns something of a paradigm shift in Western culture that gave birth to remarkably new, quite unparalleled accounts of the world and social relationships. These philosophical and theological shifts gave birth to new social arrangements, new political ideals, new economic models, and new accounts of human nature, all of which were slowly globalized through the exportation of liberal democracy and capitalist economics.[29]

It will be clear that the Radical Orthodoxy perspective does not evaluate the emergence of "new political ideals, new economic models" and of "liberal democracy and capitalist economics" as positive developments. Indeed, univocity and nominalism, by cutting the sacramental

---

28. Louis Dupré, *Passage to Modernity: An Essay in the Hermeneutics of Nature and Culture* (New Haven: Yale University Press, 1993), 177.

29. Smith, *Introducing Radical Orthodoxy*, 91.

connection between creation *(sacramentum)* and the eternal Logos *(res)*, have given birth to social configurations that, as a matter of principle, do not take into account the teleological purpose of creation's return to the divine source of its life in God. This modern perspective has led to the enjoyment of its being (as well as truth, goodness, and beauty) *for its own sake* — an obvious offense against the Augustinian dictum that only God is to be enjoyed for his own sake.

Ironically, modernity's very insistence that creation must be valued and enjoyed for its own sake results in the loss of any and all value and enjoyment. If there is no sacramental participation of creation in God's being, created objects have no inherent relationship to each other or to God.[30] The result is a nihilist constructivism in which value and enjoyment are the result of external or nominal connections rather than of a participatory or real bond with the eternal Word of God.

By drawing us away from heavenly contemplation, modern secularism has placed on us the burden of constructing our own truth, goodness, and beauty. If the experience of postmodern vacuity teaches us anything, it is that such a burden is too much to carry. The task of constructing our own reality has led to numerous political, economic, and moral dilemmas, dilemmas that cannot be resolved without a return to the stability of heavenly participation. Therefore, one of the most important cultural tasks of contemporary theology may well be the *ressourcement* of the Platonist-Christian synthesis of the Great Tradition.

30. See Louis Bouyer's observation: "What, in fact, is the essential characteristic of Occam's thought, and of nominalism in general, but a radical empiricism, reducing all being to what is perceived, which empties out, with the idea of substance, all possibility of real relations between beings, as well as the stable subsistence of any of them, and ends by denying to the real any intelligibility, conceiving God himself only as a Protean figure impossible to comprehend?" (*The Spirit and Forms of Protestantism*, trans. A. V. Littledale [Princeton, NJ: Scepter, 2001], 184-85).

CHAPTER 5

Attempting to Reweave:
The Reformation for Younger Evangelicals

Martin Luther's burning of the papal bull, *Exsurge Domine* ("Arise, O Lord"), on December 10, 1520, irreversibly settled the religious divide between Catholics and Protestants. Despite serious attempts at reunion throughout much of the sixteenth century, the two sides of the divide were unable to mend the rift once it had been demonstrated so dramatically. And with Protestants soon divided among themselves — followers of Luther, of Calvin, of Zwingli, and of Simons all opposing one another on the Continent alone on a variety of doctrinal issues — the restoration of the religious unity of the Holy Roman Empire more and more appeared like a far-off ideal. The garment of Christ's body, which everyone confessed to be seamless (John 19:23-24), was pulled apart and torn by arguments over faith and works, Scripture and tradition, baptism and Eucharist.

Political intrigue of rising nation-states; fear and frustration on the part of nobility, urban merchants, and subsistence farmers; ecclesiastical and academic pride; and, especially, deep convictions about the gospel truth — all these drew the sixteenth century ever further into the spiral of fragmentation. In hindsight, the Reformation emerges as a major juncture between the unity of the Great Tradition and the fragmentation of the modern period. This is not simply to blame the Reformation for the problems of secular modernity. The previous two chapters have made clear that late medieval developments were responsible for separating nature from the supernatural and thus for tearing the sacramental tapestry of the Great Tradition. Nonetheless, if ecumenical dialogue is to proceed with integrity, we cannot avoid the connection between these medieval developments and the break that occurred in the Reformation. The tearing of the garment of Christ's body in the Reformation is related, it seems to me, to the unraveling and cutting of the sacramental tapestry.

I have referred above to chapters 3 and 4 of this book as the most disheartening ones: after all, the cause of the desacramentalizing of Western culture goes back to the developments I described in the preceding two chapters. But in fairness, the current chapter is probably the most challenging one for evangelicals. First, I argue in this chapter that the Reformation, while it attempted to mend the rift between nature and the supernatural, did not succeed in reweaving the tapestry, and as a result some of the problematic late-medieval presuppositions continued in the Reformation tradition as well as in contemporary evangelicalism. Certainly, one can appreciate the need the Reformers saw for a break with the anthropocentrism and the corruptions of the late medieval church. Nonetheless, part of this chapter's argument is the insistence that we, as evangelicals, only do justice to our past if we regard the Reformation not as something to be celebrated but as something to be lamented. Second, while I am sympathetic to the renewed appreciation of mystery among younger evangelicals, in this chapter I will take aim at their linking of mystery with postmodernity. I am convinced that postmodern skepticism is something quite different from premodern sacramental mystery. Sorting out the difference is essential for the future of evangelicalism.

Tearing Tapestry and Garment

The insistence that the sixteenth-century Reformation was a tragedy to be lamented and that it is historically connected to the secularism of the modern age yields an admittedly one-sided picture of our past. The objections to such an approach could be numerous: Wasn't the medieval church in dire need of reform? Are there not gains as well as losses in the Reformation? And are not some of the gains considerable? The typical Protestant emphases such as the centrality of the Word that is witnessed in strong expositional preaching from the Bible and in the study of Scripture both on a personal level and in small groups; catechetical instruction of the youth; the wonderful flourishing of hymnody; the flowering of evangelical missions in the eighteenth and nineteenth centuries; and the general sense of personal engagement and individual commitment — are these all not tremendous gains of the Reformation?

To be sure, some of us may sense that personal commitment too easily gives way to individualism, and we may regret the fragmentation or atomizing that often characterizes our religious commitments. We may also worry that some of the Reformation gains no longer seem quite as secure today as they once were. Some of the younger evangelicals may even question the balance of Reformation theology and may sense that the centrality of the Word and of Christian doctrine has unnecessarily downgraded the Eucharist and led to an unfortunate devaluation of liturgical imagination, as expressed in sacred art and colored vestments, in the smells of incense and the flickering of candles. Perhaps, if we have a sense of history, even the loss of the long and venerable Great Tradition may be disconcerting: Irenaeus and Tertullian, Anselm and Bernard, Thomas and Francis may seem to belong to a borrowed story, one that really belongs to Catholics rather than to evangelicals. But when weighing the balance, gains versus losses, evangelicals do tend to come out in favor of the Reformation. Despite the losses, we gained a great deal through the Reformation. Who would want to return to the corruptions of the medieval Roman Catholic Church?

I freely admit that the reading of this chapter is one-sided. But it presents a side that I believe needs to be heard, because without a careful hearing we not only do selective justice to our past, but we also cannot move forward as we face the cultural and ecumenical challenges of the future. By highlighting a side of the Reformation that does not often get attention among evangelicals, I want to move beyond the balancing act inevitably involved in a search for gains and losses of the Reformation. I quite agree that the Reformation brought both gains and losses, and I appreciate the fact that different people arrive at differing scores. But differing scores are simply the tally of empirical observation. While there is some value to such a mental exercise, it doesn't go deep enough. The sacramental tapestry of the Great Tradition had functioned mostly on a subconscious level: the stories, symbols, and practices of the church had conveyed the unity of nature and the supernatural in a harmoniously woven tapestry.[1] The Reformation undoubtedly brought

---

1. N. T. Wright focuses on the role of stories, symbols, and practices as conveying a culture's worldview, which tends to function mostly at the subconscious level (*Christian*

gains. But what the positive effects of the Reformation failed to do was repair the tapestry that the late Middle Ages had unraveled and cut. In other words, the Reformation, while focusing on doctrinal issues and abusive practices that certainly needed to be addressed, failed to address appropriately the underlying problems that had given rise to the need for reform.

Clearly, then, the reason I lament rather than celebrate the Reformation is not because I feel the need to point an accusing finger at Martin Luther or John Calvin. To do so would be to commit a palpable historical mistake. The abuses of the late Middle Ages were too obvious, and the contributing factors to the Reformation too complex, to place all (or perhaps even most) of the blame on the Reformers. Neither can we say that the Reformation was tragic with the argument that the Reformation churches have been lacking in Spirit-led renewal and growth. I have already pointed to expositional preaching, Bible study, hymnody, and evangelical missions — all of which I believe God has used for the growth of his kingdom. The reason the Reformation was a tragedy is that it split the unity of the church while it failed to address the problematic decline of the Platonist-Christian synthesis. In other words, the Reformation not only continued the disintegration of the sacramental tapestry, but it also rent the supposedly seamless garment of the body of Christ.

These two — the tearing of the tapestry and of the garment — were by no means unrelated. Several of the developments outlined in the preceding chapters directly affected the unity of the church. First, de Lubac's observation that the High Middle Ages made it more difficult to retain the sacramental unity between Eucharist and church is relevant here. The close link between Eucharist and church had implied a strong focus on the unity of the church. Once the Eucharist was no longer seen as constituting the mystery of the church's unity, it became possible to oppose unity and truth to one another. When, for instance, Cardinal James Sadolet charged Calvin with forsaking the church's unity, the Reformer referred to the need to balance love for unity with concern for truth. "My conscience told me," Calvin attested in self-defense to God, "how strong the zeal was with which I burned for the unity of thy Church, provided thy truth were made the bond of con-

---

Origins and the Question of God, vol. I, *The New Testament and the People of God* [Minneapolis: Fortress, 1992], 215-43).

cord."[2] While the unity of the church continued to be dear to Calvin's heart, it is difficult to imagine such a balancing of unity and truth in a theological approach where unity had been the deep sacramental reality resulting from the eucharistic celebration.

Second, a direct connection between the tearing of the sacramental tapestry and the possibility of schism may be observed in Congar's observation about the separation between the authority of Scripture and that of the church in the late Middle Ages. The Reformation went along with the growing disjunction between the two. While the Counter Reformation may well have overemphasized the formal authority of the church, it is equally true that, in self-defense, the Reformation sometimes expressed its *sola Scriptura* principle in a seriously problematic fashion, as if the living tradition did not mediate the continuing relevance of Scripture and as if the church did not have the duty to set appropriate parameters surrounding the interpretation of Scripture. Not satisfied simply with the material sufficiency of Scripture (the idea that in some way Scripture contains all Christian doctrine), many heirs of the Reformation, particularly the Radical Reformers, took for granted its formal sufficiency (the notion that one only needs Scripture itself in order to interpret it rightly). In other words, the Reformation tradition often went beyond simply stating that all Christian doctrine was contained in Scripture by arguing that Scripture was the *one and only* authority in the church. Whereas the earlier, sacramental view had insisted on the Spirit's living presence both in Scripture and in the church, in the late Middle Ages people became increasingly enamored of formal sources of authority, whose dependability (or accuracy) was measurable and manageable. The break of the Reformation would scarcely have been possible without this newly developed, strict focus on the formal authority of Holy Scripture.

Third, and most important, it was late medieval nominalism that allowed for the fragmentation of the church by way of the Reformation. Although nominalism continued to allow Christians to believe in the triune God, who was both Creator and Redeemer, it no longer allowed for the radical christological unity of the medieval tapestry. Nominalism deeply affected human beings' vertical and horizontal relation-

---

2. John Calvin, "Reply by John Calvin to Letter by Cardinal Sadolet to the Senate and People of Geneva," in *Tracts Relating to the Reformation,* vol. 1, trans. Henry Beveridge (Edinburgh: Calvin Translation Society, 1844), 60.

ships. The christological anchor of the Great Tradition had ensured the vertical link between God and humanity: human beings received their being by participation in the eternal Logos. This vertical link with the Word of God meant that, in turn, all human beings were horizontally related to one another: they all participated in a common humanity. The realism of the Platonist-Christian ontology meant that what united human beings was much more important than what divided them. Their common participation in the Logos provided unity and prevented fragmentation.

Within the church, this sacramental unity was sensed particularly strongly. After all, the church's Word and Eucharist bonded people to Christ in a real unity that greatly exceeded the natural unity given with their common humanity. Nominalism subverted this medieval sense of unity, since the new philosophical approach was predicated on the notion that each person was, as it were, a self-subsistent entity, whose being was, in principle, unrelated to the being of other persons. In other words, nominalism was the seedbed for modern individualism. It is easy to see that it is much more difficult for a nominalist than for a realist to concern herself with ecclesiastical unity: fragmentation lies at the heart of a nominalist ontology. Therefore, the Reformation split was also made possible by late medieval developments. The tearing of the unity of the church as the garment of Christ is directly linked to the tearing of the sacramental tapestry of the Platonist-Christian synthesis.

Luther, Calvin, and Late-Medieval Nominalism

We do need to be careful about the way we link the Reformation to late-medieval developments. The question of continuity and discontinuity between the Reformation and the Middle Ages is a much-discussed topic among historians of doctrine, one that touches each of the branches of the Reformation and affects each of the disputed doctrines at the time of the Reformation.[3] The direct connection that Luther and Calvin may or may not have had with nominalist teachers is not en-

---

3. See, e.g., Heiko Oberman, *Forerunners of the Reformation: The Shape of Late Medieval Thought Illustrated by Key Documents,* 2nd ed. (Philadelphia: Fortress, 1981); see also Alister E. McGrath, "Forerunners of the Reformation? Critical Examination of the Evidence for the Precursors of the Reformation Doctrines of Justification," *Harvard Theological Review* 75 (1982): 219-42.

tirely clear, though Luther's early indebtedness to nominalist professors is much more evident than Calvin's.[4] Furthermore, familiarity and links with late medieval nominalism does not necessarily mean that the Reformers uncritically adopted its teaching. Quite the contrary, in Luther's case we have clear evidence that his teaching on justification by faith alone *(sola fide)* was the direct result of the rejection of some of the nominalist teachings that he had received at Erfurt.[5] And Calvin's writings are replete with references to the "sophists," which was shorthand for the Scholastic theologians at the Sorbonne.

It is also important to note that the Reformers did attempt to reconfigure the relationship between nature and the supernatural. Luther was troubled by what he regarded as the inordinate role that medieval theologians were willing to grant to nature and to the corresponding claims of human reason. We would not go wrong by interpreting his protest as at least in part an attempt to counter the naturalism that had been creeping into Western culture ever since the twelfth-century discovery of nature. Aristotle, after all, had allowed Thomas to give the natural realm, along with human reason, a place of relative independence and autonomy. Luther was particularly disturbed by the encroachments of Aristotelian philosophy on the area of theology itself. He disparaged the influence of Aristotelian philosophical concepts and thought patterns on Christian theology. Commenting on the impact of the pagan philosopher, the Wittenberg Reformer explained: "The whole of Aristotle is to theology as shadow is to light."[6] Luther's program of reform was an attempt to purify theology of the negative impact that he believed philosophy — and particularly Aristotelian naturalism — had had on theology. Thus, Luther attempted to correct some of the problems connected with the rise of the autonomy of nature in the High Middle Ages.

---

4. Cf. Alister E. McGrath, "John Calvin and Late Mediaeval Thought," *Archiv für Reformationsgeschichte* 77 (1986): 58-78; McGrath, *Luther's Theology of the Cross: Martin Luther's Theological Breakthrough* (Oxford: Blackwell, 1985), 27-92; Thomas M. Osborne, "Faith, Philosophy, and the Nominalist Background to Luther's Defense of the Real Presence," *Journal of the History of Ideas* 63 (2002): 63-82.

5. McGrath, *Luther's Theology of the Cross,* 128-36.

6. As quoted in Heiko A. Oberman, *Luther: Man Between God and the Devil,* trans. Eileen Walliser-Schwartzbart (1990; reprint, New York: Image/Doubleday, 1992), 160. For a detailed discussion of Luther's critique of Aristotle, see McGrath, *Luther's Theology of the Cross,* 136-41.

This does not mean, however, that Luther tried to restore the sacramental tapestry of the Great Tradition. He was much more concerned about the alien impact of philosophy on theology than he was about the growing rift between philosophy and theology, or between reason and faith. If anything, the nominalist influence on his thinking seems to have inclined him to keep reason and faith as distinct as possible. Heiko Oberman captures the nominalist impact on Luther when he summarizes his position as follows: "Questions of faith must be resolved through the Word of God or not at all. The temptation — or compulsion — to sanctify the words of man and believe in them is satanic. When God is silent, man should not speak; and what God has put asunder, namely Heaven and earth, man should not join together."[7] Luther's position faced the difficulty that the nominalist separation between heaven and earth ran counter to the sacramental integration of the two that had characterized the earlier Platonist-Christian synthesis. His suspicion of philosophy was the result of a separation between faith and reason, between nature and the supernatural, and between heaven and earth. In nominalist fashion, Luther wanted a faith unalloyed by the dross of natural philosophical excess. Unfortunately, he was unaware that the nominalist separation of nature and the supernatural would ultimately lead to modernity's secularism.

Calvin seemed to break down the nominalist division of nature and the supernatural much more effectively. Louis Dupré rightly observes that the influence of humanism on Calvin led him to extol with highest praise both the realm of nature as a mirror of God and the accomplishments of non-Christians. Dupré observes that Calvin "leaves no doubt that the *ordo naturae* continues to manifest God's presence and guidance. In his glorification of the natural qualities of the human mind and of the beauty of the cosmos, the true intent of Calvin's theology appears most clearly. Grace enables nature to overcome its existential insufficiency and to attain its final destiny, but nature continues to form the basis of redemption."[8] Calvin's view of grace overcoming the insufficiency of nature and of nature still forming the basis of redemption would not have been out of place in the integrated cosmos of the Great Tradition.

---

7. Oberman, *Luther*, 160.

8. Dupré, *Passage to Modernity: An Essay in the Hermeneutics of Nature and Culture* (New Haven: Yale University Press, 1993), 209-11.

Still, this positive view of God's presence in and guidance of nature did not fit well with other elements of Calvin's thought.[9] His emphasis on the pervasiveness of human sin, on the radical dependency of the human will on divine grace, and, especially, on the doctrine of double predestination meant that Calvin did not share with the Great Tradition the view that human beings had a natural desire for the beatific vision. The Fall, according to Calvin, had rendered the human will radically incompetent.[10] The resulting opposition between human inability and divine grace caused Calvin — despite his best humanist intentions — to pitch grace over against nature. Calvin's theology was unable to avoid the desacramentalizing of nature that late-medieval nominalist philosophy had introduced. Dupré says: "By a sad irony . . . in downgrading nature as *totaliter corrupta* reformed theology actually weakened the powers to resist the triumphant march that an unfettered naturalism had already begun through modern Europe."[11] Dupré's assessment may well be a difficult pill for many evangelicals to swallow. Still, the modern and postmodern dilemmas resulting from a radical opposition between heaven and earth, and between nature and the supernatural, require that we make a renewed effort at reevaluating some of the key tenets of the Calvinist Reformation.

The nominalist impact on Lutheranism and Calvinism came to the fore particularly in the tendency to interpret the divine-human relationship in external or nominal — rather than in participatory or real — terms. The Reformation teaching of justification by faith alone *(sola fide)* exemplified a great deal of continuity with the nominalist tradition. This continuity centered on the imputation of Christ's righteousness. The imputation — according to the Reformers, a forensic declaration — was external or nominal in nature. Luther's notion that the

9. In an interesting essay, Dennis E. Tamburello argues that Calvin's theology contains fairly pronounced elements of sacramentality ("Calvin and Sacramentality: A Catholic Perspective," in *John Calvin and Roman Catholicism: Critique and Engagement, Then and Now,* ed. Randall C. Zachman [Grand Rapids: Baker Academic, 2008], 193-215). Ultimately, the argument is not quite convincing since it does not distinguish between Calvin's comments on the *manifestation* of God in creation and those on God's *presence* in creation. Of the former (which doesn't require participation or sacramentality) there are many, of the latter but few.

10. See John Calvin, *Institutes of the Christian Religion,* ed. John T. McNeill, trans. Ford Lewis Battles, The Library of Christian Classics, vol. 20 (Philadelphia: Westminster, 1960), II.iii.

11. Dupré, *Passage to Modernity,* 215.

believer was at the same time righteous and sinner *(simul iustus et peccator)* gave strong evidence of the nominal character of salvation.[12] While believers were righteous in Christ, they remained sinners in themselves. One can well understand why Luther's detractors asked this question: But doesn't the grace of God change believers internally? When Luther likened the imputation of Christ's righteousness to Boaz's cloak covering Ruth and to a mother hen's wings covering her chicks, these external metaphors did little to lessen the anxieties of his Catholic opponents.[13] To be sure, Luther did know about the need for good works, and, especially later, he clearly confronted the reckless antinomianism of fellow Lutherans such as Johann Agricola.[14] Nonetheless, it is fair to ask whether Luther's own articulations of justification perhaps gave occasion for some of his followers to express their aberrant views.

Calvin, much like Luther, was intent on keeping justification separate from human works. In order to do this, he, too, maintained that justification was a nominal or external judicial declaration rather than an internal transformation worked by the Holy Spirit.[15] The underlying pattern of the Reformation doctrine, with its strong focus on imputation, would not have been possible without the nominalist developments of the late Middle Ages.

This is not to deny that the Reformers, most notably Calvin, had a strong sense of the sanctifying grace of the Holy Spirit. Certainly, Calvin not only knew of imputation but also of impartation of righteousness.[16] Calvin highlighted the so-called third use of the Law *(tertium usus legis)*, according to which the Law served as a moral guide for one's Christian life. To Calvin, this "third use" was crucial.[17] While he did hold to salvation by faith alone *(sola fide)*, he simultaneously emphasized strongly that justification (the nominal element) and sanctification (the real element) were inseparable: it was impossible to have the

---

12. See Matthew Myer Boulton, *God against Religion: Rethinking Christian Theology through Worship* (Grand Rapids: Eerdmans, 2008), 138-44.

13. Boulton, *God against Religion*, 139-40.

14. See Timothy J. Wengert, *Law and Gospel: Philip Melanchthon's Debate with John Agricola of Eisleben over* Poenitentia (Grand Rapids: Baker, 1997).

15. Calvin, *Institutes*, III.xi.13-23.

16. Calvin even went so far as to speak of an evangelical "works righteousness" that followed upon justification by faith (*Institutes*, III.xvii.9-10; cf. III.iii.20; III.xiv.21).

17. *Institutes*, II.vii.12.

former without the latter.[18] Accordingly, believers genuinely participated in divine grace. In fact, salvation was so "real" for Calvin (especially via his emphasis on the believer's union with Christ) that several
contemporary scholars have recently begun to speak of deification in
Calvin's theology.[19] While I must confess that I am less than fully persuaded by this Eastern spin on Calvin, I do agree that Calvin's participatory language did a great deal to blunt the Catholic criticism that
Calvin's forensic justification undermined a participatory ontology as
well as the urgency of good works.

When we look back in hindsight on the developments of the Reformation, I believe we end up with an ambivalent result. On the one
hand, the Reformers were keenly aware that the Scholasticism and
nominalism of the Middle Ages required adjustment. The theological
reconfigurations of the Reformation also involved an attempt to reconnect, at least in some way, the threads of the earlier cosmic tapestry. On
the other hand, the Reformers continued to build on some of the
wrongheaded developments of the High and late Middle Ages. In particular, they were unable to break with the desacramentalizing that was
initiated by the nominalist turn of the previous two centuries. In order
to reweave the tapestry successfully, the Reformers would have had to
move beyond Luther's ill-directed criticism of pagan philosophy and
also beyond Calvin's opposing of nature and grace. Most fundamentally, they would have had to reassert the sacramental or participatory
ontology that had characterized Western theology until at least a few
centuries prior to the Reformation itself. As it is, the inability of the
Reformers to reweave the tapestry led to the understandable but tragic
divide that still continues to haunt Christians in the West. A successful
reconnection of the threads might also lead to a genuine reconnection
among divided Christians.

Raschke and the Next Reformation

The nominalist atomizing and fragmentation resulting from a desacramentalized worldview needs to be named for what it is: a serious prob-

18. *Institutes,* III.xi.6; III.xvi.1.

19. Carl Mosser, "The Greatest Possible Blessing: Calvin and Deification," *Scottish Journal of Theology* 55 (2002): 36-57; see also J. Todd Billings, *Calvin, Participation, and the Gift: The Activity of Believers in Union with Christ* (Oxford: Oxford University Press, 2007).

lem. The problem needs to be identified especially because some of the so-called younger evangelicals appear to accept and even to take some degree of pleasure in fragmentation — at times with an appeal to the Reformation itself. Just as was the case with the Reformation, so the younger evangelicals' fragmentation is, in itself, understandable enough. Wary of the intellectualism of an earlier generation of evangelicals, many relish a new turn to mystery. Therefore, the "modest" truth claims of postmodernity get celebrated as an approach that may help overcome the propositionalism of earlier (modern) evangelicals. I want to briefly highlight one (admittedly extreme) instance of such fragmentation, one that is, interestingly, defended by way of an appeal to Martin Luther. I am thinking of the book *The Next Reformation: Why Evangelicals Must Embrace Postmodernity* (2004) by Carl Raschke, professor of religious studies at the University of Denver. Here Raschke makes a plea for three of the central Reformation tenets: faith alone, Scripture alone, and the priesthood of all believers.[20] Indeed, Luther in some ways emerges as the hero of Raschke's book.

Luther's *sola fide* implies two things for Raschke. First, it means an unequivocal rejection of the claims of human reason. Radicalizing Luther's rejection of pagan philosophy, Raschke insists that what the apostles proclaimed was "intrinsically ridiculous" (p. 169). "Postmodernism gives me a calling to see how God loves the bizarre. The incarnation is bizarre. The Lord's table is freaking bizarre" (p. 169). Christianity was based not on human reason but on the "absurdity" of the Incarnation (p. 19).[21] Because of his postmodern "Lutheran" nominalist fideism, Raschke demonstrates a remarkable distrust of theology. Hooking into postmodern philosopher Jacques Derrida's view of theology as an idolatrous "naming" of God, Raschke insists that "the One whose name is above all names must be honored not with sound and consistent theology, but with a contrite and humble heart" (p. 114).[22] The vague echo that may remind us of the humility of Gregory of Nyssa, Augustine, and Anselm cannot hide the fact that what we have in Raschke is a rather different approach, one that eliminates the link between theology and spirituality.

20. Carl A. Raschke, *The Next Reformation: Why Evangelicals Must Embrace Postmodernity* (Grand Rapids: Baker Academic, 2004), 26. Hereafter, page references to this work appear in parentheses in the text.

21. The second hero of Raschke's book is Tertullian because of his opposing of Jerusalem to Athens (pp. 19, 129, 152, 169).

22. Similarly, Raschke makes an appeal for "the end of theology" (p. 211).

The sad thing about theological education, says Raschke, is that it "seeks to prevent fragmentation. . . . Athens and Jerusalem are inextricably entangled with each other, and fatefully confused" (p. 169). For Raschke, *sola fide* means a rejection of the claims of human reason and a deliberate collapse into postmodern fragmentation.

Second, *sola fide* also means a deep distrust of morality and holy living. Mary Magdalene "expected nothing and did nothing with her 'religion,'" Raschke claims. "She merely had faith in the man who died for her and rose from the grave" (p. 162; cf. pp. 109-10). Fearful of all moralism and legalism, Raschke's Next Reformation "is all about grace. It is a *revolution of grace*. Luther is reported to have exhorted his followers to 'sin boldly.' That attribution is generally taken out of context. But it emphasizes a discovery that Luther — who until his 'revelation' of 'grace' was completely obsessed like Paul with his inability to live the proper Christian life — tacitly made" (p. 178).[23] I suspect that if Luther and Calvin would have had the slightest inkling of how Raschke would one day appropriate their *sola fide*, they would have gained a new sense of appreciation for the concerns expressed by the Catholic Counter Reformation. Raschke lapses into irrationalism and antinomianism, rejecting reason as well as holiness, truth as well as goodness, both of which the entire tradition — including the Reformation — had considered as the sine qua non of the Christian faith.

When it comes to Luther's principle of the priesthood of all believers, it soon becomes apparent that Raschke has a strong aversion to all forms of authority and hierarchy. Appealing to Luther's "freedom of a Christian," Raschke makes the radical (and unwarranted) comment that the priesthood of all believers "signified the flattening of all ecclesiastical hierarchies in the administration of God's grace. In the grand summation the believer must stand before God and come to a reckoning with him, and him alone" (p. 26). However, Raschke's egalitarianism has less to do with Luther's "priesthood of all believers" than it does with a postmodern flattening of horizons — the ultimate outcome of the nominalist desacramentalizing of the cosmos. Appealing to the "horizontal [flat, immanent] sovereignty" of postmodern theorist Michel Foucault (p. 149), Raschke strongly opposes vertical authority structures in favor of a multiplicity of relationships "in and through society as the 'imma-

---

23. To be sure, Raschke does caution against "cheap grace" (p. 167); but the general scope of his argument is to extol grace and warn against moralism and legalism.

nence' of culture" (p. 151). The Reformation, despite its decentralizing of clerical authority, did not go far enough, claims Raschke, because it did not "bring about a return to the primitive or first-century church, which the Reformers had set about to achieve" (pp. 155-56). It seems hard to imagine a bolder rejection of the authority of church and tradition than what Raschke presents in *The Next Reformation.*

I mention Raschke because his approach echoes a broader — though usually much more gently expressed — tendency among younger evangelicals. It is a tendency that, rather than attempting to reweave the tapestry, threatens to shred the last little bits that may still remain. Although younger evangelicals generally consider themselves quite ecumenical — often regarding denominational divisions as noxious obstacles from the past that we should ignore as much as possible — the reality is rather different. While they in no way intend to add to the existing ecclesiastical fragmentation, the new generation of younger evangelicals nonetheless courts exactly that danger. Radical appeals to *sola fide, sola Scriptura,* and the priesthood of all believers do nothing to heal the tragic wounds of the Reformation divide; instead, they deepen them. Raschke's deliberate postmodern fragmentation runs directly counter to the sacramental reintegration of the cosmos. Each of the three elements I have highlighted in Raschke — the distrust of human reason, the opposition to Christian morality, and the flattening or immanentizing of human structures — makes a potentially fruitful conversation between evangelicals and Catholics a great deal more difficult. We may, as evangelicals, have the impression that the old divisions between Protestantism and Catholicism are slowly but surely being mended. Some of the evangelical students I meet come to the subject of the Reformation with the preconception that the sixteenth-century debates about justification and grace are in large part an example of the ignorance of past generations, something that our post-denominational, emerging churches are finally able to put behind us. For these students, the "Evangelical and Catholics Together" (ECT) dialogue was simply a steppingstone toward the recognition of the obsolete character of our old divisions. As a result, they are quite ready to answer in the affirmative the question that Mark Noll and Carolyn Nystrom raise in the title of their recent book: *Is the Reformation Over?*[24]

---

24. Mark A. Noll and Carolyn Nystrom, *Is the Reformation Over? An Evangelical Assessment of Contemporary Roman Catholicism* (Grand Rapids: Baker Academic, 2005).

I am becoming more and more convinced that such optimism is misplaced. To be sure, Noll and Nystrom paint an upbeat (and truthful) picture of a warming Catholic-evangelical relationship, one that could not possibly have been painted even three or four decades ago. The various ECT statements show that, despite the differences that remain, genuine convergence has become possible on several important issues, most notably that of justification by faith, which for Calvin had been the "hinge on which religion turns."[25] Despite all the positive signs that Noll and Nystrom are able to assemble, however, I am not yet convinced that the Reformation is really over. One of the things I appreciate about ECT is that it is not, to borrow a phrase I recently heard, "sloppy agape."[26] ECT is intent on finding convergence where possible, but it also wants to name the differences where those continue to exist. While the first few ECT documents were able to present a remarkably common front between evangelicals and Catholics, the 2002 statement that dealt with *sola Scriptura* was rather different in character. Gone were the encouraging subheadings — "We Hope Together," "We Search Together," "We Contend Together," "We Witness Together" — that characterized the initial 1994 statement. In the 2002 document on Scripture and tradition, the discussion partners had difficulty speaking with a common voice. Instead, they preferred to summarize the positions of their respective communities. The recently published statement on Mariology suffers from a similar lack of agreement.[27]

The reason ECT appears to be losing its momentum is not just that some of its elder "statesmen" have passed the baton to a new generation. Instead, I suspect that ECT has discovered genuine points of disagreement on difficult theological points of doctrine. The issue underlying the difficulties, I suspect, is an inability to reweave the sacramental tapestry. Postmodern evangelicals like Raschke make it a great deal more difficult to reconnect the threads. In fact, they hinder ecumenical progress much more than did the evangelical propositionalism of previous generations. I am convinced that postmodernism is simply the natural outcome of modernity, both of them predicated on a desacramentalized universe; and I believe that the solutions to our

25. Calvin, *Institutes,* III.xi.1.

26. A comment by Deacon Keith Fournier in a lecture on "The Catholic Social Vision and Ecumenical Dialogue" at Trinity Western University in Langley, B.C., Jan. 16, 2009.

27. "Do Whatever He Tells You: The Blessed Virgin Mary in Christian Faith and Life," *First Things* 197 (Nov. 2009): 49-58.

problems hardly lie in evangelical accommodation to contemporary cultural trends. Instead, as Protestants, we need to relearn to see the world with sacramental eyes.

Richard Mouw, in dealing with Andrew Greeley's book *The Catholic Imagination* (as I mentioned in the introduction), refers to Colossians 1: "He is before all things, and in him all things hold together." Mouw then observes: "Given the increasingly fragmented character of contemporary life, the challenge to explore the meaning of this 'holding-together' dimension of the person and work of Jesus Christ is both urgent and engaging."[28] Mouw is quite right, it seems to me. We need to put an end to our nominalist, (post-)modern fragmentation and instead work toward reintegration and unity. This is not to suggest that ecumenism is a human project that we ourselves can manage; rather, it is a project of prayer and of conversion. As Pope John Paul II once put it, "[T]he commitment to ecumenism must be based upon the conversion of hearts and upon prayer, which will also lead to the *necessary purification of past memories*."[29] I believe that part of this conversion process is acknowledging that the Reformation, as a tearing of the garment of Christ, was ultimately unable to reweave the tapestry. The Reformation simply could not stem the tide of the fragmentation of the Platonist-Christian synthesis. What we need is evangelicals and Catholics who discern the primary demand of our time: a celebration of our heavenly participation in the eternal Word of God. Only a heavenly minded Christian faith will do us any earthly good.

28. Richard J. Mouw, "Restless Hearts in Search of Meaning," unpublished paper, 2008.

29. John Paul II, "*Ut unum sint:* On Commitment to Ecumenism," no. 2, May 25, 1995 (www.vatican.va).

Reditus: Reconnecting the Threads

A theology of heavenly participation requires that we reconnect the threads of the medieval Platonist-Christian synthesis. In part 2, I argue that a retrieval of the sacramental ontology of the patristic fathers and the Middle Ages requires a focus on Christology in every area of theology. Through the Eucharist, the church becomes a sacrament of the fullness of Christ (chapter 6). Tradition is the unfolding of the Word of God, who has become incarnate in Jesus Christ (chapter 7). Scripture needs to be interpreted sacramentally in the light of the mystery of the Incarnation (chapter 8). Truth claims turn out to be a sacramental sharing in the eternal Word of God (chapter 9). And the discipline of theology is an initiation into a divinizing participation in the Son of God (chapter 10). Each of these chapters turns to the mid-twentieth-century Catholic renewal movement of *nouvelle théologie* in order to retrieve a sacramental approach for evangelical theology.

CHAPTER 6

Eucharist as Sacramental Meal

Attempts at recovering the Platonist-Christian synthesis of the Great Tradition have often been piecemeal; they have not been successful in redirecting societal trends in Western culture. The twentieth-century French renewal movement called *nouvelle théologie* was an attempt at exactly such a cultural redirection through a *ressourcement* of the sacramental tapestry woven by the fathers and the Middle Ages. Although it may still be too early to tell to what extent *nouvelle théologie* will influence contemporary culture, it is clear that the movement has had a tremendous impact on the Second Vatican Council and on contemporary Catholic thought in general. In part 2 of this book, then, I will mine some of the writings of the *nouvelle* theologians that I believe to be particularly promising in terms of reconnecting the threads of the tapestry.

Before discussing their actual work, however, allow me to make a caveat. My foray into *nouvelle théologie* does not suggest that we can recapture the sacramental ontology of the Great Tradition only by reading these French theologians. One may also legitimately turn to seventeenth-century Caroline divines such as Lancelot Andrewes (1555-1626), William Laud (1573-1645), Jeremy Taylor (1613-1667), and Herbert Thorndike (1598-1672) to find a flourishing of the sacramental outlook marginalized by modernity. Well-known literary figures such as Coleridge (1772-1834) and T. S. Eliot (1888-1965), too, were keenly interested in recovering a sacramental ontology. It almost goes without saying that the Oxford Movement and John Henry Newman (1801-1890) also reappropriated the sacramental outlook that had characterized the Great Tradition. And the tradition of Eastern Christianity as a whole — very much of interest to *nouvelle* theologians — has never really abandoned the sacramental worldview of the church fathers. Hence, *ressourcement* of a sacramental ontology is not the sole prerogative of the *nouvelle* theologians.

In its recovery of a sacramental ontology, the Catholic *ressourcement* movement made quite a few enemies. Many in the Catholic Church had taken the separation of two distinct realms — the natural and the supernatural — for granted, not realizing how much their Neo-Thomist approach to theology actually furthered the cause of a secular, desacralized culture. *Nouvelle théologie* pointed back to the premodern period, in which the supernatural had referred not to a separate order of reality but to the sacramental means of grace that allowed nature to reach its divinely appointed end: eternal participation in the divine life itself (deification).[1] This attempt at *ressourcement* implied a sharp critique of the five steps away from the Platonist-Christian synthesis (chap. 3 above) and, by implication, of the inroads that univocity and nominalism had made in Catholic theology (chap. 4).

Although *nouvelle théologie's* critique of Scholastic developments in the Middle Ages was aimed at Neo-Thomist Catholicism, we saw in the previous chapter that the French theologians' project also implies a challenge for contemporary evangelicals. After all, the Reformation did not escape the general trend toward a nominalist view of the cosmos. By depicting the Reformation as a tragic (no matter how understandable) outcome of the disintegration of the Platonist-Christian mindset, I am obviously calling for a reevaluation of the Reformation and of the way in which evangelicalism should proceed theologically. The second part of this book goes beyond a critique of the disintegration of the sacramental ontology of the premodern period. In what follows, I want to engage positively the task that lies ahead for evangelicals, if we take the Platonist-Christian synthesis as our point of entry. It will not come as a surprise that I will argue that *nouvelle théologie* offers a number of significant signposts that point evangelical theology in the right direction.

A *ressourcement* of the Great Tradition must begin with a reappraisal

---

1. For discussions of the theology of deification, see Norman Russell, *The Doctrine of Deification in the Greek Patristic Tradition* (Oxford: Oxford University Press, 2004); Daniel A. Keating, *Deification and Grace* (Naples, FL: Sapientia Press of Ave Maria University, 2007).

of ecclesiology. The doctrine of the church has suffered chronically from the Protestant emphasis on the invisible church and particularly from the anti-institutional fear of hierarchical structures that appears common among evangelicals. To be sure, there are signs of change. Some evangelicals recognize the troublesome nature of the relative neglect of Eucharist and church within Protestantism.[2] Still, the overall attitude among evangelicals continues to regard Eucharist and church as belonging to the well-being *(bene esse)* rather than to the very being *(esse)* of the Christian life. The reason for this position seems fairly obvious in the light of my analysis thus far. If our connection with God is primarily an external or nominal one, rather than one that is real or participatory, there is little room for what traditional theology used to call sacraments or means of grace. According to such an understanding, one may still celebrate communion because it is an "ordinance" of God that regulates our common life together; but the Eucharist will hardly be regarded as a sacrament that participates in the life of Christ and thus as something that mediates to us the life of the triune God.

Furthermore, even evangelicals who *are* attracted to the Platonist-Christian synthesis and the sacramental ontology that it implies may take umbrage at the fact that the second part of this book starts off with a chapter on the church. Should an evangelical approach to sacramentality not begin with Scripture rather than with the church? I appreciate that objection, and I am deeply sympathetic with the high regard for Scripture that the question implies. But the careful reader of part 1 of this book will not be surprised by my choice. As we have seen, one of the problems that Yves Congar observed about the late Middle Ages was the separation between Scripture and church.[3] Whether the option was for Scripture (evangelicals) or for the church (Catholics) — for Congar the resolution was wrong in either case. Moreover, I hope to make clear in chapter 7 that it has been *within the church* that the authority of the canon has been recognized historically. Therefore, it is inconceivable to regard Scripture as somehow separate from the church, with the interpretation of the Bible left to individual believers or scholars. The Bible is, first and foremost, the church's book. Consequently, Scripture itself, throughout its pages, points us to the church as the liv-

---

2. I am thinking, for example, of Barry Harvey, *Can These Bones Live? A Catholic Baptist Engagement with Ecclesiology, Hermeneutics, and Social Theory* (Grand Rapids: Brazos, 2008).

3. See chap. 3 above, under subheading "Scripture, Church, and Tradition."

ing embodiment of the truth. The church, not Scripture, is "the pillar and foundation of the truth" (1 Tim. 3:15). Of course, we should in no way neglect the centrality of Scripture, or its ability to sit in judgment on errors in the church. Scripture, after all, is "God breathed and is useful for teaching, rebuking, correcting and training in righteousness" (2 Tim. 3:16). We should in no way try to set up the one Epistle to Timothy against the other. Nonetheless, Scripture serves as the sacramental means to build the church; the church is not the sacramental means to build Scripture. Thus, an authentically evangelical view should begin with the church as the primary object of evangelical *ressourcement.*

Among the *nouvelle* theologians, Henri de Lubac holds a place of prominence for me: I know few theologians who are as careful as de Lubac was with his sources; I know few theologians who, like de Lubac, were able to maintain their love for the very church that silenced them; I know few theologians who were as consistent as de Lubac was in maintaining a sacramental approach throughout their careers;[4] and I know few people who have done as much as de Lubac has for the recovery of an authentically sacramental interpretation of Scripture.[5] Therefore, it has been my personal delight to observe the flurry of studies over the past few years on the theology of the great Jesuit patristic scholar. John Milbank, David Grumett, Rudolf Voderholzer, and Bryan Hollon have all contributed to the retrieval of de Lubac's theology.[6] With only slight exaggeration, we might say that a genuine de Lubac revival appears to have broken out. The recovery of de Lubac is of particular importance because, in his own time and as a Catholic, he did battle with the same problematic heritage of Enlightenment thought that younger evangelicals are opposing today. However, de Lubac points to a way beyond the flat cultural horizons of modernity — and, we might add, postmodernity — by steering us to the intuitions of the premodern sacramental outlook of the medieval tra-

---

4. I have argued this point in "Sacramental Ontology: Nature and the Supernatural in the Ecclesiology of Henri de Lubac," *New Blackfriars* 88 (2007): 242-73.

5. See chap. 8 below.

6. John Milbank, *The Suspended Middle: Henri de Lubac and the Debate concerning the Supernatural* (Grand Rapids: Eerdmans, 2005); David Grumett, *Henri de Lubac: A Guide for the Perplexed* (London: T. & T. Clark/Continuum, 2007); Rudolf Voderholzer, *Meet Henri de Lubac* (San Francisco: Ignatius, 2008); Bryan C. Hollon, *Everything Is Sacred: Spiritual Exegesis in the Political Theology of Henri de Lubac* (Eugene, OR: Cascade/Wipf and Stock, 2008).

dition. Perhaps he did so nowhere more pointedly than in his recovery of what many today call a "communion ecclesiology."[7]

De Lubac's Two Opponents

To illustrate what de Lubac was after, I will turn to his *Corpus Mysticum: The Eucharist and the Church in the Middle Ages* (1944), which has been recently translated — yet another indicator of the flourishing publishing industry surrounding de Lubac. In the conclusion of his study of the development of eucharistic theology in the Middle Ages, de Lubac situates himself against two opponents, both of which he considers extremes. The one opponent is Protestantism: he laments the Protestant weakening of the doctrines of the Eucharist and the church, mentioning Calvin by name and charging him with "watering down" both the reality of Christ's presence in the Eucharist and the traditional idea of the church as the body of Christ. The two necessarily go hand in hand, de Lubac maintains. With only a "virtual presence" of Christ in the sacrament, one would end up with only a "virtual presence" of Christ in the church, too.[8] (As an aside, those of us who have read Calvin will realize that, compared to many evangelicals today, he actually had quite a *high* view both of the Eucharist and of the church. But we'll leave that aside. Perhaps it is true that, compared to de Lubac's "real presence" of Christ, Calvin only had a "virtual presence" of Christ in both the Eucharist and the church.)

The Protestant opponent, however, is not the main antagonist in de Lubac's *Corpus Mysticum*. He devotes a great deal more time and attention to the other opponent, the one on the other extreme of the theological spectrum: Neo-Thomism, or Neo-Scholasticism, to which I have already referred several times. Two characteristics of Neo-Thomist theology are particularly important for our understanding of de Lubac's approach to the Eucharist and the church. First, Neo-Scholasticism was based on the strict separation between nature and the supernatural that the late Middle Ages had introduced. This sepa-

7. See Dennis M. Doyle, *Communion Ecclesiology* (Maryknoll, NY: Orbis, 2000).

8. Henri de Lubac, *Corpus Mysticum: The Eucharist and the Church in the Middle Ages: Historical Survey,* trans. Gemma Simmonds with Richard Price and Christopher Stephens, ed. Laurence Paul Hemming and Susan Frank Parsons (London: SCM, 2006), 252.

ration coincided with the separation between philosophy and theology. Philosophy served to establish truths that human reason could access simply by looking at the natural world. Theology, the teachings of the church, did not enter into the picture until afterwards, once the philosophical foundation of natural truth had been laid. Supernatural, divine grace was something that was "superadded" to the realm of nature. Grace was not able to build on something already present in nature itself; rather, the supernatural world of grace was entirely extrinsic or foreign to the world of nature. Even when grace was superadded to nature, it remained extrinsic to the realm of nature. This extrinsicist view of reality was the cornerstone of Neo-Thomist Scholasticism and dominated the Catholic Church especially in the years during which de Lubac started his theological career.

The second characteristic of Neo-Thomism built on the first. It was the rationalist apologetic approach both to the Bible and to the history of Christian thought. Put somewhat negatively (and perhaps unfairly), one goes to Scripture and the tradition in order to find the truths of the Catholic faith confirmed there. Just in case the reader thinks I am unduly harsh on Catholic thought, let me emphasize that I do not think that this rationalist apologetic approach was limited to Catholic thought. In the period following the Reformers, Protestant Scholastic theology did much the same thing. Rationalist apologetics has also had a fairly strong influence on evangelical theology.[9] This is precisely one of the aspects of the evangelical heritage against which many of the younger evangelicals are reacting. One of the most serious problems with this apologetic use of Scripture and tradition — for de Lubac and others — was the temptation to squeeze the historical data to make them say what one already believed. To give but one example: if a person believed in transubstantiation (the teaching that in the Eucharist the substance of bread and wine change into the substance of Christ's body and blood), Neo-Thomist rational apologetics would scour Scripture and tradition in order to find such a "real presence" affirmed in the positive or historical sources of Scripture and tradition.

---

9. The classic example is perhaps Josh McDowell, *Evidence That Demands a Verdict: Historical Evidences for the Christian Faith* (San Bernardino, CA: Campus Crusade for Christ, 1972).

Augustine's "Allegorized" Texts

In the conclusion of *Corpus Mysticum,* de Lubac tackles his Neo-Thomist opponents and their seventeenth-century Scholastic ancestors, all of whom he believes hardened the theology of Thomas Aquinas into a rationalist system. De Lubac takes particular exception to two prominent cardinals of the Counter Reformation: Robert Bellarmine (1542-1621) and Jacques du Perron (1556-1618). Ever the patristic scholar and always concerned with recovering the Great Tradition, de Lubac accuses both these theologians of misinterpreting Saint Augustine. They were unable to locate the doctrine of transubstantiation in Augustine's writings; they simply could not find in the fifth-century North African bishop the "real presence" that had developed in the church over time and had come to be official church doctrine. And this difficulty, according to de Lubac, led them to engage in mental gymnastics in their interpretation of Augustine.

In one particularly well-known sermon (Sermon 227), Augustine repeatedly speaks about the "unity" of the body of Christ, the "unity" of the church, which he believes resulted from the celebration of the Eucharist. In one fascinating passage he says:

> In this loaf of bread you are given clearly to understand how much you should love unity. I mean, was that loaf made from one grain? Weren't there many grains of wheat? But before they came into the loaf they were all separate; they were joined together by means of water after a certain amount of pounding and crushing. Unless wheat is ground, after all, and moistened with water, it can't possibly get into this shape which is called bread. In the same way you too were being ground and pounded, as it were, by the humiliation of fasting and the sacrament of exorcism. Then came baptism, and you were, in a manner of speaking, moistened with water in order to be shaped into bread. But it's not yet bread without fire to bake it. So what does fire represent? That's the chrism, the anointing. Oil, the fire-feeder, you see, is the sacrament of the Holy Spirit.[10]

---

10. Augustine, "Sermon 227," in *Sermons (184-229Z) on the Liturgical Seasons,* vol. III/6 of *The Works of Saint Augustine,* trans. Edmund Hill, ed. John E. Rotelle (New Rochelle, NY: New City, 1993), 254.

What is a Catholic supposed to do with a passage like this? It contains no talk of real presence, let alone transubstantiation. The focus seems to be on the unity of the believers, on their fellowship or communion, which results from the many grains being joined together in a loaf of bread. It seems as though Augustine draws an arbitrary allegorical comparison between grains joining together into a loaf of bread and believers getting together into the body of the church. How could sixteenth-century Scholastic theologians such as Bellarmine and du Perron appropriate a church father who used such airy-fairy allegorizing in talking about the unity of the body?

De Lubac chastises the inability of the Scholastic Catholic theologians of the Counter Reformation (Bellarmine, du Perron, and others) to deal with these kinds of allegorical passages in Augustine. In fact, the French Jesuit scholar goes further and insists that Scholastic theology was in danger of losing Augustine altogether: "They cheerfully divide up the ancient texts [from St. Augustine and others] relating to the Eucharist into two groups: the first group is made up of 'realist' texts, while all the 'allegorized' texts are lumped into a second group, which is abandoned." We need to pause here for a moment to analyze what de Lubac is saying. It will be clear that the passage from Augustine's Sermon 227 does not refer to "real presence" and that it is not, in de Lubac's terminology, a "realist" text. Rather, Augustine's Sermon 227 presents an "allegorized" text. The unity of the bread functions as an allegory depicting the unity of the church.

According to de Lubac, the Scholastic tradition following the Counter Reformation had been at a loss about what to do with such "allegorized" texts; as a result, they simply ignored and abandoned them. The loss, however, was not restricted to the "allegorized" texts. De Lubac explains that the problem extends to the so-called "realist" texts: "But the so-called 'realist' texts are not always as realist as these historians would have us believe." In other words, de Lubac maintains that people might not find later Catholic teaching on the Eucharist explicitly in Augustine at all. The Scholastic approach to the past is laden with irony, according to de Lubac, for "by abandoning these 'allegorized texts', they sometimes deprive us of the most effective testimony to authentic realism."[11] Translated, this simply means that de Lubac believed that the Neo-Thomists missed out on Augustine al-

---

11. De Lubac, *Corpus Mysticum*, 255.

together: they could not find any "realist" texts, and they ignored the "allegorized" texts.

This brings us to the sacramental outlook that de Lubac was so keen on recovering, especially with regard to Eucharist and church. According to de Lubac, it was "fear of symbolism" that lay behind the Neo-Thomist approach and behind its vain search for "realist" texts, as well as its abandonment of "allegorized" texts. It was the Neo-Thomist fear of the Protestant nemesis of symbolism that rendered them incapable of properly appreciating Augustine and other premodern theologians. Of course, de Lubac agreed with his Neo-Scholastic opponents that Protestant views of the Eucharist were problematic. They were insufficiently sacramental: Calvin's "virtual presence" did not appear to recognize the real presence of Christ in the Eucharist and thus reduced it (at least in de Lubac's understanding) to a mere symbol. So de Lubac was certainly willing to join the Neo-Thomists in their opposition to a merely symbolic view of the Eucharist. However, he was not convinced that fear of Protestant symbolism was sufficient reason to buy into the Neo-Thomist reading of Augustine.

De Lubac vehemently rejects the two presuppositions driving the Neo-Thomist approach: (1) the separation between nature and the supernatural, between philosophy and theology; and (2) the rationalist apologetic that served as the theological *modus operandi*. By contrast, de Lubac's sacramental approach to reality does not regard the world of nature as separate from the supernatural but as the gracious gift of the Creator. For de Lubac, the world of nature is never without God's presence. A sacramental approach to reality *begins* with theology: it begins with the assumption that what we see around us is the gift of the Creator-Redeemer God. Such a starting point in theology clashed with the Neo-Thomist extrinsicism that regarded the supernatural as an arbitrary imposition on a self-sufficient natural world.

De Lubac's sacramental ontology clashed not just with the Neo-Scholastic separation of nature and the supernatural, but also with its rationalist apologetic. Saint Augustine — and along with him much of the Middle Ages — had regarded the created world as a world full of symbols. They were not just symbols, in which symbol X related to some completely different, distant reality called Y. Symbol and reality were not two strictly separate entities. Instead, these symbols functioned as sacraments. And, as we have already seen, a sacrament *(sacramentum)* shares or participates in the reality *(res)* to which it points. According to this understanding, symbols point to and share in a reality that is much greater than the symbols themselves. For the Platonist-Christian synthesis, the symbols give only a small inkling of the great sacramental reality that upholds them. The problem de Lubac saw in the Neo-Thomist rationalist theology was that its "realism" completely or univocally identified symbol and reality. Symbol and reality had being in the same straightforward manner. To Neo-Scholastic rationalists, therefore, "real presence" precluded the use of allegories, as they appeared to represent a flight into an airy-fairy mysticism. Real presence and allegory were antithetically opposed to each other. In other words, the Scholastic Catholic approach insisted that once people grasped the symbol, they also fully comprehended the body of Christ itself. There was no value-added mystery hidden within the symbol; there was no sacramental reality that reached beyond the human symbol.

The Threefold Body

One of the reasons why talk of a participatory link between sacrament and reality is difficult for evangelicals is that this language goes back to the eucharistic controversies at the time of the Reformation. I suspect that evangelicals might be open to a sacramental ontology were it not for the fact that there are significant implications for the way one understands the Eucharist and the church. Worry about those implications was, for quite some time, one of the hesitations that I personally had about a participatory ontology. A book that has been of great help to me in this regard is J.-M.-R. Tillard's *Flesh of the Church, Flesh of Christ.*[12] One of the things Tillard does in this book is trace the patristic exegesis of 1 Corinthians 10:16-17. Tillard shows beyond doubt that the common view of the Great Tradition would read these verses in a participatory or sacramental fashion. Looking at the Pauline passage again, after reading Tillard, I was surprised that I had not seen the sacramental connection earlier. Recently, I came across a book by George Hunsinger, the Reformed Barth scholar, in which he relates a similar experience.

---

12. J.-M.-R. Tillard, *Flesh of the Church, Flesh of Christ: At the Source of the Ecclesiology of Communion,* trans. Madeleine Beaumont (Collegeville, MN: Liturgical, 2000).

Looking back, it seems that the turning point came in 1995 during a Lenten Bible study in my local congregation. Feeling that my New Testament Greek, never very good, was getting ever more rusty by the day, I took an interlinear volume with me to one of the sessions. To my surprise the word *koinonia* [fellowship, participation] showed up in 1 Cor. 10:16. Could it be, I wondered, that the relationship between the bread and Christ's body might be one of mutual indwelling? Over time my hunch was reinforced by Luther, confirmed by Vermigli, and validated by Käsemann.[13]

Hunsinger's discovery of a Pauline passage that had been crucial in the history of biblical interpretation allowed him to accept a more robust participatory or sacramental view of the Eucharist.

So, what did the Great Tradition believe was going on in 1 Corinthians 10? Perhaps the best way to clarify this is by introducing the "three bodies" that de Lubac mentions in *Corpus Mysticum*. The three bodies of Christ are the historical body (the body born of the Virgin), the eucharistic body (signified by bread and wine), and the ecclesial body (the body of the church). De Lubac's book is, in essence, an overview of how the relationship between these three bodies developed in the Middle Ages. It seems obvious that one has to make some kind of distinction between these three bodies. The very fact that we can talk about a historical body, a eucharistic body, and an ecclesial body means that we can distinguish the three. But the question remains — and this is the question whose history de Lubac traces in his book — *how much* should we distinguish them? Maybe a better way of framing the question would be: What is the *nature* of the relationship of the three bodies?

To get hold of de Lubac's reading of the Middle Ages, we need to remember that he attempts to sail between, on the one hand, the Scylla of Protestant symbolism, which regarded the eucharistic bread simply as an arbitrary symbol X referring to a distant reality Y, and, on the other hand, the Charybdis of a strict Neo-Scholastic focus on real presence, which so identified symbol X with reality Y that the spiritual reality in no way exceeded the symbol. How did Augustine situate himself among these various approaches to symbolism? One of the most interesting lines in Sermon 227 says the following about consuming Christ's

---

13. George Hunsinger, *The Eucharist and Ecumenism: Let Us Keep the Feast* (Cambridge: Cambridge University Press, 2008), viii-ix.

body and blood: "If you receive them well, you are yourselves what you receive. You see, the apostle says, *We, being many, are one loaf, one body* (1 Cor. 10:17)."[14] The comment sounds innocuous enough, but it contains two fascinating elements. First, when we talk about transubstantiation, we think of the teaching that the bread becomes the body of Christ. Augustine says something rather different: *You* become the body of Christ; *you* become what you eat. We could perhaps say — somewhat anachronistically — that, for Augustine, transubstantiation meant that the Spirit changed *our* substance into the body of Christ.

This would seem like a peculiar understanding of the Eucharist. What did Augustine mean when he said, "You are what you have received"? To find an answer to this question, we need to turn to the second fascinating element in Augustine's comment. In the second part of his statement, the Bishop of Hippo quotes the apostle Paul: "The bread is one; we, though many, are one body." This is a quotation from 1 Corinthians 10:17. The NIV translation renders verses 16b and 17 as follows: "And is not the bread that we break a participation in the body of Christ? Because there is one loaf, we, who are many, are one body, for we all partake of the one loaf." The word "body" occurs twice in this passage. The first time, it refers to the eucharistic body. ("[I]s not the bread that we break a participation in the body of Christ?") The second time, it refers to the ecclesial body. ("Because there is one loaf, we, who are many, are one body.") Of the three bodies frequently referred to in the Great Tradition (the historical, the eucharistic, and the ecclesial), Paul takes the last two and places them right beside each other. Actually, he does more than place them beside each other; he links them together. He maintains that when, by faith, we share in the one eucharistic body, the Spirit makes us one ecclesial body. As Augustine would put it, we become what we have received. Or, as de Lubac famously phrases it, the Eucharist makes the church.

Here we arrive at de Lubac's objection to the Neo-Thomists with their robust focus on transubstantiation and real presence. De Lubac, in effect, objects by saying: You focus so much on what makes a legitimate Eucharist, and you zero in so unilaterally on the eucharistic body, that you forget that the *sacramental* purpose of the eucharistic body is to create the ecclesial body. The *telos* is communion. (This explains the now common reference to "communion ecclesiology" in contemporary

14. Augustine, "Sermon 227," 254.

Catholicism.) We could also say that, for de Lubac, the sacramental reality to which the eucharistic body points and in which it participates is the ecclesial unity of the church. Thus, there really were not three bodies, but only one body — one threefold body *(corpus triforme)* — the various aspects of which were sacramentally related to one another. For Augustine and the Middle Ages, the one body of Christ was historical, eucharistic, and ecclesial in character; and in their different manifestations, these three were sacramentally linked together.

De Lubac begins *Corpus Mysticum* by reiterating something we have already observed: that for Augustine, and for much of the Middle Ages, Eucharist and church were closely connected: "[T]he Eucharist corresponds to the Church as cause to effect, as means to end, as sign to reality."[15] The goal of the celebration of the sacrament was the unity or communion of the church. In the last part of the Apostles' Creed, we confess our faith in the "communion of saints." At least, that is how we often put it. But the Latin is ambiguous: *sanctorum communio* could be translated either as "communion of saints" or as "communion of holy things." For the medieval tradition, it was not an either/or option. Communion of holy things — meaning, communion with the body and blood of Christ — was related to the communion of saints. The one caused the other and was related to it in a sacramental manner. De Lubac puts it this way: "[I]n the same way that sacramental communion *(communion in the body and the blood)* is always at the same time an ecclesial communion *(communion within the Church, of the Church, for the Church . . .)* so also ecclesial communion always includes, in its fulfilment, sacramental communion. Being in communion with someone means to receive the body of the Lord with them" (p. 21; italics in original). In his own flowery way, de Lubac simply reiterates the central point that the Eucharist makes the church. The theologians of the Middle Ages had consistently emphasized the unity of the one body of Christ. This unity had been the focus even when they distinguished the three aspects (historical, sacramental, and ecclesial) of the threefold body. Sacrament and church were regarded as one and the same.

In the ninth century, de Lubac explains, *corpus mysticum* had served as a technical term for the eucharistic body, distinguishing it from both the "body born of the Virgin" and the "body of the Church,"

---

15. De Lubac, *Corpus Mysticum*, 13. Hereafter, page references to this work appear in parentheses in the text.

while at the same time keeping the three closely connected. Medieval theologians talked about the "mystical body" of the Eucharist and about the "mystery" of the Eucharist, both to indicate that the Eucharist was a sign of something else and to refer to the obscure depths hidden in the Eucharist. The ecclesial body was the sacramental reality to which the Eucharist pointed and in which it participated. Therefore, there was a Spirit-guided movement from the sacrament to its mysterious reality, from the eucharistic body to the ecclesial body. The sacrament was something dynamic, not static. Or, as de Lubac puts it, "[A] mystery, in the old sense of the word, is more of an action than a thing" (p. 49). For de Lubac, this active connotation of the term "mystery" in the Middle Ages stood in opposition to the view, common in his own day, that regarded the Eucharist as an arbitrary, supernatural intervention from above, unconnected to the life of the church. The purpose of de Lubac's meticulous historical study is thus to overcome the extrinsicism of the Neo-Thomists, which treated the Eucharist as unconnected or extrinsic to the fellowship of the church. De Lubac wanted to make people see that, throughout much of the Great Tradition, the Eucharist had been regarded as the activity that created the unity of the church.

The Shifting *Corpus*

According to de Lubac, some — especially Protestants — focused strictly on the sacramental purpose of the body, the church's fellowship or unity as the intended reality of the sacrament (its *res*), while forgetting that this reality was tied to its origin in the eucharistic body; others — especially Catholics — focused strictly on the sacramental presence of Christ in the elements (the *sacramentum*), while forgetting that this real presence was tied, by way of participation, to its purpose in the ecclesial body. De Lubac's point is important with respect to the overall argument of this book. De Lubac recognizes that it would simply not do to lay all the blame for the loss of the Platonist-Christian synthesis at the feet of the Protestants (or the evangelicals). If de Lubac's analysis is correct — and I have no reason to doubt that it is — *both* Protestants and Catholics suffer the loss of a sacramental ontology.

In chapter 3, I briefly mentioned the developments surrounding the Berengarian controversy of the eleventh century as one of the five steps that unraveled the medieval sacramental tapestry.[16] At this point, we need to go into a little more detail and investigate what happened to the participatory relationship among the three bodies. De Lubac points to some significant linguistic shifts (depicted in Diagram 2). Over time, in the High Middle Ages, the word "true" *(verum)* moved from the ecclesial body to the eucharistic body: Christ's body in the Eucharist came to be seen as "the true body." At the same time, the word "mystical" *(mysticum)* moved from the eucharistic body to the ecclesial body: the church as the body of Christ came to be seen as "the mystical body."[17] To be sure, de Lubac does not take issue with the use of the term "mystical body" to describe the church, but he does believe that the *overall* shift in terminology — with the word "true" being used for the eucharistic body and the term "mystical" being reserved for the ecclesial body — is problematic. For de Lubac, these linguistic shifts reflected (1) an increasing focus on the real presence in the Eucharist (the "true" body of Christ); and (2) a loss of the sacramental connection between the eucharistic and the ecclesial body of Christ.

Diagram 2. The Shifting *Corpus*

	Early Middle Ages	High Middle Ages
Eucharistic Body	Mystical $\Longrightarrow$	True
Ecclesial Body	True $\Longrightarrow$	Mystical

As I have mentioned, de Lubac saw the main cause of the changes occurring in the eleventh and twelfth centuries. The eleventh century witnessed a sharp controversy over the Eucharist, which involved Berengar of Tours. To simplify matters somewhat, we might say that Berengar

16. See chap. 3 above, under subheading "Discovery of Nature."

17. For a detailed analysis of these linguistic shifts, see de Lubac, *Corpus Mysticum*, 75-119, 143-67; see also Susan K. Wood, *Spiritual Exegesis and the Church in the Theology of Henri de Lubac* (Grand Rapids: Eerdmans, 1998), 63-68.

was like an eleventh-century Calvinist. He contrasted spiritual eating to bodily eating, insisting that one did not eat the actual body of Christ, but that, instead, the eating of Christ in the Eucharist was a spiritual eating. This contrast between spiritual and bodily eating caused great consternation. Alger of Liège (1055-1131) and others reacted strongly by insisting on a bodily consumption of Christ. And, de Lubac adds, "[f]rom the affirmation of bodily reception, we are led by implication to the affirmation of a bodily presence" (p. 155). The result was that "'spiritualist' vocabulary gradually became, if not suppressed, at least rare," while all the emphasis came to be placed on the real presence in the eucharistic body of Christ (pp. 161-62). The theory of the threefold body quickly turned into a theory of a twofold body: "the historico-sacramental body and the ecclesial body" (p. 162).

The new emphasis on bodily feeding and on real presence in the Eucharist meant that the ecclesial body was no longer regarded as "true body" *(corpus verum).* Prior to the Berengarian controversy, it had seemed fitting to identify the ecclesial body as "true body." The sacramental aim of the eucharistic celebration had been the church as the "fullness of Christ" (Augustine's *totus Christus*), and hence this ecclesial aim used to be described quite suitably as the "truth" *(veritas)* of the Eucharist. But the twelfth-century shift in emphasis from the ecclesial body to the eucharistic body made it difficult to sustain this identification of the unity of the church as the "true body." Instead, the eucharistic elements began to take the place of the unity of the church as *corpus verum.* Consequently, around the twelfth century, the Eucharist turned into the "true body" of Christ.

At about the same time, the church herself became the "mystical body" *(corpus mysticum).* De Lubac points to Peter Lombard (c. 1095- c. 1164), the well-known twelfth-century theologian whose work many later medieval interpreters used as the starting point for their own theological reflections. With Lombard, the Eucharist became the "proper flesh" *(caro propria),* while the church became the "mystical flesh" *(caro mystica),* or the "spiritual flesh" *(caro spiritualis)* (p. 102). Lombard, as well as the great Scholastic theologians of the High Middle Ages, sharply distinguished the eucharistic body from the ecclesial body. And this was only a first step. Now that the expression "mystical *flesh*" was used for the church, theologians would soon also use the expression "mystical *body*" to refer to the church rather than to the Eucharist.

One of the most attractive elements of de Lubac's *ressourcement* of the Middle Ages is the fact that his sacramental approach points to the existence of a middle path between a complete *separation* of sign and reality, on the one hand (the evangelical temptation), and a strict *identification* of sign and reality, on the other hand (the Catholic temptation). The middle path had first been charted by Augustine and medieval theology, and it was predicated on a sacramental link between Eucharist and church, a link that the Great Tradition saw reflected in Saint Paul's own connection between the two in 1 Corinthians 10. Perhaps evangelicals sometimes direct their attention too quickly to the Catholic notion of transubstantiation, in order to reject it as out of line with a proper understanding of Scripture. We do well to keep in mind that de Lubac's moderate view has been tremendously influential in the Catholic Church, as is witnessed by the common acceptance of "communion ecclesiology." The reason for this designation is that communion, or participation *(koinônia)*, for de Lubac, was the means to reach the sacramental reality at which the eucharistic celebration aimed. The Second Vatican Council of the 1960s irreversibly ensconced this communion ecclesiology as the official teaching of the Roman Catholic Church. This common acceptance of the Lubacian view within Catholicism offers new prospects for fruitful dialogue. Just as the Catholic Church has begun to focus more strongly on the fellowship of the church community, so, I would suggest, is it time for evangelicals to celebrate much more unambiguously the real presence of Christ in the Eucharist.

CHAPTER 7

Tradition as Sacramental Time

With the increasingly warm relationships between Catholics and evangelicals over the past few decades, evangelicals inevitably face this question: Can we consider Catholics — at least some Catholics — to be evangelicals? In other words, is there a species called "the Catholic evangelical"?[1] I suspect that one of the main reasons many evangelicals are hesitant to acknowledge that one could legitimately speak of Catholic evangelicals is the belief that Catholics do not share with evangelicals their focus on Scripture as the one ultimate source of authority for the church. Catholics hold to two sources of authority: Scripture *and* tradition (Catholics tend to capitalize "Tradition," while most evangelicals are reluctant to do so). And since tradition is strictly human interpretation and outworking of divinely given Scripture, Catholics would not seem to share evangelicals' concern for the centrality of the Bible. Thus, even evangelicals who are quite ready to acknowledge Catholics as brothers and sisters in Christ may still feel that to acknowledge them as "evangelicals" would render that term meaningless.

I believe that the argument is flawed. There *are* Catholic evangeli-

1. The question is not just an academic one. Evangelical colleges and universities, if they are serious about maintaining their identity, cannot avoid the issue. Individual Catholic scholars are sometimes quite prepared to sign the statements of faith that evangelical institutions have devised, and they may be equally willing to refer to themselves as evangelicals. John L. Allen makes the argument that "evangelical Catholicism" is currently one of the defining currents within the Catholic fold (*The Future Church: How Ten Trends Are Revolutionizing the Catholic Church* [New York: Doubleday, 2009]). See also Bill Portier, "Here Come the Evangelical Catholics," *Communio* 31 (2004): 35-66.

cals. Nonetheless, those who are convinced that the notion of a "Catholic evangelical" is an oxymoron do work with an underlying assumption that I warmly applaud: that evangelicals should guard their identity. Therefore, my argument is not that evangelicalism should just relax a little and allow some folks from different traditions to join their ranks. My argument is just the opposite: it seems to me that contemporary evangelicalism is not nearly as strong in its identity as evangelicals sometimes imagine themselves to be. I am largely convinced by David Wells's argument that "radical, postmodern relativism not only pervades American society but it has also become the majority perception in the evangelical Church."[2] To the extent, therefore, that evangelicals are opening themselves up to Catholics because they can no longer properly articulate their identity, the ecumenical endeavor is bound to fail. My argument is that, as evangelicals, we need Catholic voices precisely in order to maintain and reinforce our evangelical identity.

But, someone may retort, that's exactly the point of debate: Does a Catholicism of the genuinely evangelical kind really exist? Should those overly irenic evangelicals who think that the Second Vatican Council brought reformation to Catholicism perhaps read the Council's statement on divine revelation, *Dei Verbum*? Doesn't one of its articles explicitly point to "Scripture and Tradition" as the two sources of revelation, each to be received with equal devotion and reverence?

> Sacred Tradition and sacred Scripture, then, are bound closely together, and communicate one with the other. For both of them, flowing out from the same divine well-spring, come together in some fashion to form one thing, and move towards the same goal. Sacred Scripture is the speech of God as it is put down in writing under the breath of the Holy Spirit. And Tradition transmits in its entirety the Word of God which has been entrusted to the apostles by Christ the Lord and the Holy Spirit. It transmits it to the successors of the apostles so that, enlightened by the Spirit of truth, they may faithfully preserve, expound and spread it abroad by their preaching. Thus it comes about that the Church does not draw her certainty about all revealed truths from the holy Scriptures alone.

2. David F. Wells, *Above All Earthly Pow'rs: Christ in a Postmodern World* (Grand Rapids: Eerdmans, 2005), 169.

Hence, both Scripture and Tradition must be accepted and honored *with equal feelings of devotion and reverence.*[3]

The statement would seem to indicate that the notion of a Catholic evangelical is based on wishful thinking. In fact, the italicized phrase constitutes a direct quote from the Council of Trent (1545-1563), and the statement seems to explicitly reject the notion of *sola Scriptura.*

Yet, even though the cards may seem to be seriously stacked against me, I will make the argument that the notion of a "Catholic evangelical" is not a contradiction in terms. In fact, at the risk of making my case seem indefensible from the outset, I will push my argument to the limit. Not only should we consider many Catholics to be evangelical, but also vice versa: we should urge many evangelicals to become catholic (lowercase *c,* to be sure) in order to be true to their claim of being evangelical. And, in case the reader may be wondering at this point, let me state clearly that I am not trying to make a clever ploy. The point I am making is that many Catholics hold to an evangelical understanding of the Scripture-tradition relationship, while many evangelicals need to recover the role of tradition if they want to be really evangelical. By turning to Yves Congar and Henri de Lubac, I will argue that the way forward is by anchoring tradition in the eternal Word of God. Participation in the eternal christological anchor provides the warrant for any and all human interpretations of Scripture.

Congar and Augustine on Sacramental Time

To make the point, let me begin with the traditional Catholic argument against evangelical objections. The Catholic argument is that, without a teaching authority (magisterium), the authority of Scripture becomes a nose of wax. If everyone can simply interpret the Bible according to individual insight, it seems that it would become difficult, perhaps impossible, to retain any kind of doctrinal cohesion. And, of course, Catholics are quick to point to the relentless splintering of Protestant and evangelical denominations. The argument is one that

---

3. "Dogmatic Constitution on Divine Revelation" *(Dei Verbum),* in *Vatican Council II,* vol. I, *The Conciliar and Postconciliar Documents,* rev. ed., ed. Austin Flannery (Northport, NY: Costello, 1975), 755 (no. 9) (italics added).

traces its origins all the way back to the second century. Irenaeus, when faced with Gnostic interpretations of Scripture, alluded to the process by which people arranged myriad mosaic pieces into one artwork. The many pieces of the mosaic, each shade and color counted out according to the required quantity, would be transported to the building that would house the mosaic, and there the numerous pieces would be skillfully put together according to the pattern of the image that had been provided along with the pieces. Referring to the interpretive practices of the Valentinian Gnostics, Irenaeus observes:

> Their manner of acting is just as if one, when a beautiful image of a king has been constructed by some skilful artist out of precious jewels, should then take this likeness of the man all to pieces, should rearrange the gems, and so fit them together as to make them into the form of a dog or of a fox, and even that but poorly executed; and should then maintain and declare that *this* was the beautiful image of the king which the skilful artist constructed, pointing to the jewels which had been admirably fitted together by the first artist to form the image of the king, but have been with bad effect transferred by the latter one to the shape of a dog, and by thus exhibiting the jewels, should deceive the ignorant who had no conception what a king's form was like, and persuade them that that miserable likeness of the fox was, in fact, the beautiful image of the king.[4]

The possibility that the image of the king might be rearranged into the shape of a dog or a fox resulted, according to Irenaeus, from the refusal to follow the church's core confession — the so-called "rule of faith" — as the lens through which to look in order to interpret Scripture properly. Realizing that Scripture formed the church's book, Irenaeus refused to surrender the interpretation of Scripture to individual believers or scholars. One needed the tradition of the church in order to make sense of the meaning of the text.

Irenaeus's analogy, compelling though it is, does not settle all discussion. Numerous questions about the Scripture/tradition relationship remain. The *nouvelle* theologians of the mid-twentieth century have taught me that — also with regard to questions about Scripture and tradition — a sacramental approach may offer a way forward that is not

---

4. Irenaeus, *Against Heresies*, in *Ante-Nicene Fathers*, vol. 1, ed. Alexander Roberts and James Donaldson (1885; reprint, Peabody, MA: Hendrickson, 1994), VIII.1.

only ecumenically promising but also dogmatically faithful. It is fascinating to me that Congar explicitly speaks of time as being sacramental in character, while de Lubac deliberately anchors tradition (and thus the development of doctrine) in Christ, referring to it as "cashing in Jesus." It seems to me that if we take these sacramental and christological starting points seriously, we have at least the proper framework within which we can then discuss the Scripture/tradition relationship.

As he discusses the functioning of history and development, Congar makes a comment about what he calls "sacramental ontology" *(ontologie sacramentelle),* which he bases on the words of Saint Paul that God will be "all in all" (1 Cor. 15:28).[5] Congar observes that, for Aquinas, the sacraments had a threefold reference: they referred to Christ's own redemptive acts, which were active in the sacraments (past reference); to eternal life as the sacraments' aim (future reference); and to the effect that the sacraments have in our lives (present reference). Congar then makes it clear that he believes that, according to the Christian understanding, time itself is sacramental in character:

> Thus the sacraments have a peculiar temporal duration, in which past, present and future are not mutually exclusive, as in chronological time. Sacramental time, the time of the Church, allows the sharing by men who follow each other through the centuries in an event which is historically unique and which took place at a distant time; this sharing is achieved not merely on the intellectual level, as I could commune with Plato's thought, or with the death of Socrates, but in the presence and action of the mystery of salvation. (p. 260)

For Congar, "sacramental time" or "the time of the Church" means that past, present, and future can coincide.[6] As a result, people from different historical eras can participate or share in the same event. Congar maintains that it was the Holy Spirit who effected this transcending of ordinary temporal limits: "It is the characteristic work of the Holy Spirit to effect a communication between realities despite

5. Yves M.-J. Congar, *Tradition and Traditions: The Biblical, Historical, and Theological Evidence for Catholic Teaching on Tradition,* trans. Michael Naseby and Thomas Rainborough (San Diego: Basilica, 1966), 259. Hereafter, page references to this work appear in parentheses in the text.

6. For references to the "time of the Church," see also Yves M.-J. Congar, *La Foi et la théologie* (Tournai: Desclée, 1962), 43, 99, 105-06.

their limits and the distances separating them ..." (p. 261). When chronological time thus opens up, as it were, eschatological realities themselves are able to enter into it. According to Congar,

> [w]hen the living God himself is the agent of historical events — not just by his general providence, but acting to constitute another element in salvation history, a "mystery" — he communicates to acts which take place in time certain possibilities and a density which surpass the conditions of earthly time. They are inserted into another sphere of existence, the eschatological order, which has for its principle the Holy Spirit. (p. 261)

By saying that God acted to constitute a "mystery" in salvation history, Congar was using traditional sacramental language. As we have seen, for the Great Tradition, a "mystery" was the reality *(res)* to which sacraments pointed and in which they participated. Therefore, Congar argued, God could insert the dimension of "mystery" into earthly events; as a result, these events were taken up into the eschaton. Earthly events became sacraments of eschatological mysteries. Their sacramental dimension allowed earthly events to participate in other events, both past and future.[7]

Perhaps the most important reason modernity has made it difficult for us to acknowledge any kind of authoritative role for tradition is the fact that we look at history rather differently from the way people interpreted it throughout the millennium of the Platonist-Christian synthesis. In nominalist fashion, we tend to look at time as a simple succession of distinct moments, unrelated to one another; we regard event *X,* which took place ten years ago, as no longer present, and thus in principle as unconnected to event *Y,* which is taking place today. This is not to say that we deny historical cause and effect. We realize quite well that, through a number of traceable historical causes, event *X* gives rise to event *Y.* The point, however, is that we regard the two events as separate. Going back to our discussion about analogy and univocity, we could say that we view the two events as univocal moments in time: they have the same kind of reality or being, and are not intertwined in

---

7. It is not difficult to see that Congar's participatory notion of "sacramental time" could serve to support a "real presence" in the Eucharist. "Every eucharistic consecration," Congar explains, "brings into play the power not only of the presence of Christ and of the Spirit, but also that of the first, unique and historical consecration at the Last Supper" (p. 260n.2).

any real sense.[8] As Charles Taylor puts it: "We have constructed an environment in which we live a uniform, univocal secular time, which we try to measure and control in order to get things done."[9] Univocal time gives us the control that we desire in the secularity of modernity.

Congar's reflections on "sacramental time" undermine this univocal view of time as simply a succession of historically distinct moments. In doing so, he places himself in the long Platonist-Christian tradition, whose view of time was profoundly expressed by Augustine in Book XI of his *Confessions.* Augustine there recognizes that past, present, and future are not simply successive moments of secular or univocal time. His sacramental mindset opened him to the realization that "it is inexact language to speak of three times — past, present, and future."[10] The reason is that for Augustine, these three coexist in the human mind and, even more importantly, are identical in the eternity of God himself. This is not to say that the Bishop of Hippo adopted a strictly Platonic position in which the world of time was simply an imperfect reflection of the eternity of the realm of ideas. Augustine's concept of time was sacramental: time *participates* in the eternity of God's life, and it is this participation that is able to gather past, present, and future together into one.[11]

Taylor illustrates it well by referring to the two events of the sacrifice of Isaac and the Crucifixion of Christ: "These two events were linked through their immediate contiguous places in the divine plan. They are drawn close to identity in eternity, even though they are centuries (that is, 'aeons' or 'saecula') apart. In God's time there is a sort of simultaneity of sacrifice and Crucifixion."[12] The "sacramental time" of Augustine and Congar allows for the sacramental participation of one historical event in another. The sacrifice of Isaac and the Crucifixion of Christ are not simply two univocal and separate events; rather, the sacrifice of Isaac participates sacramentally in the Crucifixion of Christ.

The example of the sacrifice of Isaac and the Crucifixion of Christ is

---

8. See chap. 4 above, under subheading "Scotus and Univocity of Being."

9. Charles Taylor, *A Secular Age* (Cambridge, MA: Belknap/Harvard University Press, 2007), 59.

10. Augustine, *Confessions,* trans. Henry Chadwick (Oxford: Oxford University Press, 1991), 235 (XI.20).

11. I am drawing on Taylor's distinction between "Plato eternity" and "God's eternity" (*Secular Age,* 57).

12. Taylor, *Secular Age,* 55.

not just a random one. It refers to the fact that, for the Great Tradition, it was in Christ that ordinary or successive time participated most fully and gloriously in the eternal time of God. Christ himself, we could say, is *the* great sacrament, the mystery par excellence. In him, the eternal Word enters into the temporal succession of events, thus allowing time to participate sacramentally in eternity. Every other temporal event that takes place in the ordinary time of human history thus derives its being and significance from the great Christ event itself. Temporal events have meaning because of their sacramental connection — their "simultaneity," as Taylor calls it — to the incarnate Logos, Jesus Christ himself.

De Lubac on Development of Doctrine

Henri de Lubac, deeply influenced by this sacramental perspective on time, recognized the implications for the way Christian doctrine developed throughout the tradition. He recognized that Christ is the great sacrament of God.[13] If Christ is the fullness of the revelation of God, then future developments of Christian doctrine can never leave behind that one great sacrament. They always have to remain connected to Christ; they can never add to him, and they can only be an unfolding of his fullness. "The Whole of Dogma" *(le Tout du Dogme)*, de Lubac insists, is present in the redemptive action of Christ himself.[14] Nothing can be added to Christ. Every doctrinal development that follows Christ can only be a "cashing in" of the fullness of Christ's treasury *(monnayer Jésus)*. According to this Platonist-Christian understanding, all of history leading up to Christ was a sacramental anticipation of the Incarnation, while the subsequent tradition of the church is a sacramental memorial of the Christ event. There is a real participation of past and future in the person of Jesus Christ.

The view that tradition is the "cashing in" of Jesus Christ as the supreme sacrament is not limited to Catholics like de Lubac. Karl Barth, in his *Church Dogmatics,* expresses himself in a similar way.[15] For Barth,

---

13. Henri de Lubac, *The Splendor of the Church,* trans. Michael Mason (1956; reprint, San Francisco: Ignatius, 1999), 202.

14. Henri de Lubac, "The Problem of the Development of Dogma," in *Theology in History,* trans. Anne Englund Nash (San Francisco: Ignatius, 1996), 274.

15. I am grateful to my assistant, Alex Abecina, for alerting me to this section of Barth's *Church Dogmatics.*

revelation means sacrament: thus, God's revelation in Christ is "the basic reality and substance of the sacramental reality of His revelation." Barth describes the humanity of Christ as "the first sacrament"; and the Swiss theologian recognizes that this has implications for one's understanding of history and of tradition. He suggests that, while the Incarnation was obviously a unique occurrence, "its attestation through the existence of the man Jesus is a beginning of which there are continuations; a sacramental continuity stretches backwards into the existence of the people of Israel, whose Messiah He is, and forwards into the existence of the apostolate and the church founded on the apostolate."[16] For Barth, the sacramental presence of Christ stretches backward and forward, so that it ties together past, present, and future. To be sure, Barth does not say that he understands this sacramental character of revelation as participatory in nature. In other words, he does not explicitly declare that in past and future events Christ himself is really present. And that additional move is, I believe, crucial to the Platonist-Christian synthesis of the Great Tradition. All the same, Barth correctly recognizes that the Christ event is the great sacrament that gives meaning to everything that precedes and follows it.

The combination of a sacramental and christological approach to time and history holds ecumenical promise. It is true that a return to the Platonist-Christian view of time does present challenges. Congar and de Lubac realized the challenge that their perspective posed to Neo-Thomist theologians, who mostly held to a rational, propositional view of revelation. According to these Scholastics, the church's job is to figure out what the propositions of Scripture really mean. They were convinced that all of the church's contemporary beliefs must have been present in the church from the very beginning — or at least that we should be able to prove current doctrine by way of rational, syllogistic demonstration from the earliest revelation. The difficulty with this view is that it regards any kind of doctrinal development over time as suspect. How can one conclusively prove from Scripture any of the later doctrines of the church, ranging from fourth-century Trinitarian doctrine to nineteenth-century Marian teaching? Despite these difficulties, the Neo-Scholastics held on to their intellectualist view of revelation and of doctrinal development, and they expressed serious objections to

---

16. Karl Barth, *Church Dogmatics,* vol. II/1, *The Doctrine of God,* trans. T. H. L. Parker et al., ed. G. W. Bromiley and T. F. Torrance (London: T. & T. Clark/Continuum, 2004), 53.

the sacramental and christological challenges posed by *nouvelle* theologians such as Congar and de Lubac.[17]

Evangelicals will likewise experience the Platonist-Christian perspective of *nouvelle théologie* as a serious challenge. To be sure, evangelicals should be encouraged by the explicitly christological focus that de Lubac advocates. Viewing tradition as the "cashing in" of Jesus has a distinctly evangelical ring to it. Nonetheless, the Platonist-Christian perspective on time — with past, present, and future somehow co-inhering in one another — is not only a rejection of the modern perspective on history, but also asks evangelicals to give up their ready allegiance to this modern approach. Evangelicals have largely abandoned a sacramental view of time (as have many Catholics), and this desacramentalizing has impacted the way we have decided on doctrinal issues. Because we tend to regard the time period of the biblical author and our own small moment under the sun as two distinct or separate moments, (univocally) identical in kind, we believe that it is our job simply to find out what exactly the biblical author meant in any given biblical text in order then to proclaim it as authoritative. Thus we simply move back from our contemporary time Y to the biblical time X in order to establish the theological or doctrinal teaching of the church today. And where we find discrepancies between our own cultural context and that of biblical times, we try to negotiate the degree to which we should adapt or accommodate to our current situation.

The sacramental understanding of the Platonist-Christian synthesis shakes up this modern evangelical model. If the various historical moments of the church's tradition sacramentally participate in each other in and through the Christ event, theological or doctrinal convictions of the Christian past are much more than interesting ways Christians throughout history have dealt with the biblical text. If the church today shares, by means of a real participation, in the church's earlier tradition, that earlier tradition genuinely lives on in us and we have a sacred responsibility to it. Earlier periods of the Christian tradition and our present time are connected via a common sacramental participation in the eternal Word of God.

A desacramentalized view of time tends to place the entire burden of

---

17. For a helpful general exposition, see Aidan Nichols, *From Newman to Congar: The Idea of Doctrinal Development from the Victorians to the Second Vatican Council* (Edinburgh: T. & T. Clark, 1990).

doctrinal decision on the present moment: I, in the small moment of time allotted to me, am responsible to make the right theological (and moral) choice before God. The imposition of such a burden is so huge as to be pastorally disastrous. Furthermore, to the extent that as Christians we are captive to our secular Western culture, it is likely that this secular culture will get to set the church's agenda. If we do not see ourselves sacramentally connected to the tradition (and thus to Christ), we sense no accountability to the tradition, and we are likely to accommodate whatever demands our culture places on us and capitulate to them. By contrast, when we are faced with a theological and moral conundrum, a participatory approach to tradition will always ask how the catholic, or universal, church throughout time and place has dealt with the issue. The widespread assumption that Christian beliefs and morals are to a significant degree malleable has its roots in a modern, desacralized view of time.

Congar and Vanhoozer on Scripture and Tradition

Evangelicals will be able to overcome their uneasiness with a sacramental understanding of time when they grasp the fact that, for the Great Tradition, this sacramental focus was simply another way of saying that tradition lay anchored in Christ. And, really, what could be more amenable to evangelicals than an approach to doctrinal development that remains centered on Christ? Indeed, if we were to ask de Lubac and Congar what exactly it might mean to "cash in" Jesus, we would find a great deal of commonality. Accordingly, for the remainder of this chapter I want to ask what it means for tradition (or doctrinal development) to "cash in" Jesus. I will do so by briefly comparing Yves Congar's *La Tradition et les traditions* and Kevin Vanhoozer's *The Drama of Doctrine.*[18] The comparison will illustrate that, though differences remain on the relationship between Scripture and tradition, these two scholars — one Catholic and one evangelical — display a remarkable degree of convergence.

Both Kevin Vanhoozer, a leading contemporary evangelical scholar,

---

18. For my lengthier comparative analysis, see Boersma, "On Baking Pumpkin Pie: Kevin Vanhoozer and Yves Congar on Tradition," *Calvin Theological Journal* 42 (2007): 237-55.

and the late *nouvelle* theologian Yves Congar refer to the account of Philip's meeting with the Ethiopian eunuch (Acts 8:26-40) to explain their respective views of the Scripture/tradition relationship. Upon reading Isaiah 53:7-8, the eunuch does not grasp the meaning of the text, and he asks Philip: "Tell me, please, who is the prophet talking about, himself or someone else?" (Acts 8:34).[19] Observing that Philip explains the Old Testament prophecy in the light of "the good news about Jesus" (8:35), Congar comments: "Just as Jesus had done with the apostles, Philip preached to him about Jesus, taking this passage as his theme. To give the meaning of Scripture is to explain it in the light of God's plan, whose focal point is Jesus Christ."[20] Indeed, for Congar, interpretation of Scripture in the light of Christ is primarily what constitutes the tradition. Thus he immediately adds that "the apostles' preaching and tradition did in fact consist in revealing the entire structure of the economy of salvation, in relation to Christ, as to its center, around whom all the rest was arranged, shaped and took its meaning."[21] For Congar, tradition is the interpretation of Scripture in the light of the Christ event.

Vanhoozer likewise takes the narrative of the Ethiopian eunuch as a biblical example of the nature of tradition. "Philip," he comments, "stands for the origin of Christian understanding and hence for the *nature of tradition*." Vanhoozer then explains that there are four ways to gain further insight into Philip's role and thus into the nature of the Christian tradition.[22] First, the passage highlights the role of the Spirit in enjoining Philip to go to the chariot and in whisking him away (Acts 8:29, 39). Second, the passage gives a glimpse into the role of apostolic tradition when we see Philip as a link in that tradition's chain. Third, we may regard Philip as a stand-in for the church when we perceive that

19. For a biblical-theological discussion of the connection between Acts 8 and Isa. 53, see Morna D. Hooker, "Did the Use of Isaiah 53 to Interpret His Mission Begin with Jesus?" in *Jesus and the Suffering Servant: Isaiah 53 and Christian Origins*, ed. William H. Bellinger and William R. Farmer (Harrisburg, PA: Trinity Press International, 1998), 88-103; Mikeal C. Parsons, "Isaiah 53 in Acts 8: A Reply to Professor Morna Hooker," in Bellinger and Farmer, 104-19; Morna D. Hooker, "Response to Mikeal Parsons," in Bellinger and Farmer, 120-24.

20. Yves Congar, *The Meaning of Tradition*, trans. A. N. Woodrow (San Francisco: Ignatius, 2004), 86.

21. Congar, *The Meaning of Tradition*, 86; cf. Congar, *Tradition and Traditions*, 68.

22. Kevin J. Vanhoozer, *The Drama of Doctrine: A Canonical-Linguistic Approach to Christian Theology* (Louisville: Westminster John Knox, 2005), 117-20 (italics in original).

the eunuch comes to read Scripture aright through the "external means" of the church's authority. Finally, there is the indispensable role of the canonical text of Isaiah 53 itself, which can only be understood appropriately if it is read christologically: "Everything is the same, yet different when viewed from the vantage point of the Christ event."[23]

Vanhoozer does not intend his commentary on Acts 8 to be a comprehensive exposition on the nature of the Christian tradition. His initial observations are nonetheless promising. It is clear that Vanhoozer concurs with Congar that the Christian tradition is what happens when, under the guidance of the Spirit and with apostolic authority, the church passes on her interpretation of Scripture in the light of Christ. In other words, both Congar and Vanhoozer agree that the tradition lies anchored in Christ. Furthermore, this starting point has several additional consequences on which Congar and Vanhoozer agree. First, the tradition is essentially interpretation of Scripture in the light of the Christ event. It is not surprising, perhaps, that an evangelical such as Vanhoozer would regard tradition as interpretation of Scripture. But Congar — and, I would submit, most contemporary Catholics — readily agree. For example, Congar says: "The doctrinal content of Tradition, in so far as it is distinct from Scripture, is the meaning of Scripture."[24]

In other words, both Congar and Vanhoozer are convinced that the contents of Scripture are sufficient in order to arrive at Christian doctrine. This is a crucially important point for evangelicals to grasp. Evangelicals often continue to think that Catholics hold to a "two-source" theory of truth, as if the church derived some of her beliefs from Scripture and others from tradition. While it is certainly true that this was once a common view among Catholics, especially in the period following the Council of Trent (1545-1563), this view has been almost universally abandoned.[25] For Catholics like Congar, Scripture and tradition co-inhere, and the former is materially sufficient for Christian doctrine. The Catholic acknowledgment of this point stems from the centrality of the Christ event as the starting point and the continuing anchor for the interpretation of Scripture.

23. Vanhoozer, *Drama of Doctrine,* 119. Vanhoozer makes a plea here for "figural" or "typological" interpretation, something I will pick up on in chap. 8 below.

24. Congar, *Tradition and Traditions,* 32.

25. See Congar, *Tradition and Traditions,* 64, 167, 286, 414; cf. Congar, *Meaning of Tradition,* 37.

Second, if Christ is the anchor of all Christian doctrine, then it is impossible for any one interpretation of Scripture to exhaust its meaning. Tradition, as the interpretation of Scripture over time, takes a certain trajectory in which the church explores imaginatively the infinite implications of the Christ event. Congar explains:

> For the Fathers, the councils and the theologians of the early Middle Ages and scholasticism in general, the progressive understanding of revelation entails the fullest possible disclosure of God; that is, the Church, under the influence of the Holy Spirit, gradually draws out the implications of the deposit of faith. A certain growth thus occurs, in the sense that what was involved in the deposit inherited from the apostles is developed or unfolded.[26]

Congar maintains that doctrine develops over time because the christological deposit — the anchor of Christ — needs to be cashed in throughout the tradition of the church.

Evangelicals may well be nervous about the notion that doctrine develops. Examples of Catholic dogmas such as the Immaculate Conception of Mary and her Assumption immediately come to mind. Isn't that where development of doctrine inevitably leads? However, before we throw out doctrinal development, we might want to listen to what Vanhoozer has to say about it. His understanding is hardly different from Congar's. Although he does not obviously ground development in Christology the way Congar does, I suspect that Vanhoozer would agree with Congar on the christological foundation. Vanhoozer speaks quite freely about the "meaning potential" of biblical texts, and makes this observation: "As the potential of the Old Testament is realized over the 'great time' of the canon, so too the potential of the canon is realized over the 'great time' of church history." Vanhoozer explicitly uses "development of doctrine" language to describe this unfolding of the meaning potential of the biblical text: "The development of doctrine is thus a matter of *improvising with a canonical script.*"[27] In fact, Vanhoozer's language emphasizes development in some ways more strongly than does Congar's. We repeatedly encounter in Vanhoozer the language of "imagination," as well as related terms, such as "improvisation," "spontaneity," and "creative under-

26. Congar, *Tradition and Traditions*, 267.
27. Vanhoozer, *Drama of Doctrine*, 352-53 (italics in original).

standing." For Vanhoozer, development of doctrine is based on the church's creative improvisation on the biblical text.[28]

But what about the *sola Scriptura* of the Reformation? And what about doctrinal developments, especially in Mariology, that to evangelicals seem far removed from the actual biblical text? First, we have already seen how Congar quite agrees that all the church's teaching can and must be traced back to Scripture itself. There is a material sufficiency of the Bible. On that basis, Catholic theologian Thomas Guarino says: "Most Catholic theologians accept the phrase *sola scriptura;* they accept as well the claim that the Bible is the *norma normans non normata* [original norm, not derived norm], the ultimate touchstone for Christian faith."[29]

The influence that *nouvelle théologie* scholars like Congar had on the Second Vatican Council, as well as on the subsequent Catholic tradition, has been such that little or no disagreement remains with regard to the material sufficiency of Scripture. Of course, some evangelicals will be inclined to push *sola Scriptura* further, arguing that we do not need tradition to interpret Scripture and that, accordingly, we should abandon the notion of development of doctrine. But we have already seen that such a view would not appeal to prominent evangelical theologians like Vanhoozer. More important, such a view is based on a modern abandonment of the sacramental view of time, and it limits the interpretation of the Christ event to its historical origins. I believe that it is a great deal safer to go with the sacramental and christological consensus of the Great Tradition.

Second, Congar's approach to the Scripture/tradition relationship should make evangelicals read the statement from Vatican II's *Dei Verbum* carefully (quoted in the introduction to this chapter). Congar himself, along with others who held views similar to his, was quite influential in shaping the documents of Vatican II. Furthermore, Congar and Guarino are clearly in line with the vast majority of Catholics, who

28. To be sure, Vanhoozer does caution against novelty and invention (*Drama of Doctrine,* 162, 424); see also Vanhoozer, "Into the Great 'Beyond': A Theologian's Response to the Marshall Plan," in *Beyond the Bible: Moving from Scripture to Theology,* ed. I. Howard Marshall, Kevin J. Vanhoozer, and Stanley E. Porter (Grand Rapids: Baker Academic, 2004), 81-95.

29. Thomas G. Guarino, "Catholic Reflections on Discerning the Truth of Sacred Scripture," in *Your Word Is Truth: A Project of Evangelicals and Catholics Together,* ed. Charles Colson and Richard John Neuhaus (Grand Rapids: Eerdmans, 2002), 96.

read *Dei Verbum* in a much more evangelical way. And there is plenty of reason for such a reading. The article begins by declaring that tradition and Scripture "are bound closely together, and communicate one with the other," that they flow "from the same divine well-spring," that they "come together" to "form one thing," and that they "move towards the same goal." Each of these quoted phrases functions as a nail in the coffin of a two-source view of revelation. Tradition and Scripture, according to Vatican II, are *not* two separate sources: they belong together. This official acknowledgment should be incredibly encouraging to evangelicals. It's true that the document also says that "the Church does not draw her certainty about all revealed truths from the holy Scriptures alone." And the statement even quotes the Council of Trent by concluding that Scripture and tradition "must be accepted and honored with equal feelings of devotion and reverence." While disagreement over the concluding sentence, in particular, is likely to remain, these comments do not imply a two-source theory. If we put *Dei Verbum* in the best possible light, we could perhaps interpret it as saying that Scripture and tradition both participate sacramentally in Jesus Christ — himself the great revelatory sacrament of God.

Third, my discussion of Scripture and tradition does not represent a claim of complete agreement between evangelicals and Catholics. Although evangelicals and Catholics can find a great deal more commonality on the subject of tradition than we sometimes assume, differences do persist — as they do between Congar and Vanhoozer.[30] Even if we take for granted that the tradition is normative on the basis of a sacramental view of time, and even if we take the Christ event as the central historical moment that absorbs in itself, as it were, every other moment in time, we may still end up differing with each other on what is and what is not a legitimate unfolding of the Christ event. For example, I am not convinced that the Catholic Marian dogmas are legitimate expositions of the christological anchor. But even here we need to be careful how we phrase our disagreement. In discussing Mariology, we need to remember (1) that Catholics accept the evangelical point that all doc-

---

30. In some ways Congar safeguards the Christian deposit better than does Vanhoozer. I am apprehensive of Vanhoozer's strong emphasis on improvisation, a notion that would require a strong doctrine of the church to guide it appropriately. Also, despite Vanhoozer's acceptance of doctrinal development, he fails to mention tradition when he discusses how we can overcome the gap between the text and our own context (*Drama of Doctrine*, 331).

trine is a matter of biblical interpretation, and (2) that evangelicals (at least those like Vanhoozer and me) accept the Catholic point that all doctrine is a matter of development. This means that our disagreements on Marian teaching are disagreements on what constitutes the correct interpretation of Scripture. In other words, for contemporary Catholics, Marian dogmas result from the development of doctrine *as interpretation of Scripture.* The Marian disagreements between Catholics and evangelicals, while they remain a serious obstacle, have, in effect, become *exegetical* disagreements. That recognition in itself means a remarkable step forward in Catholic-evangelical dialogue.

In conclusion, while disagreements remain, the overall Catholic approach to tradition is largely evangelical. On a properly evangelical position, the tradition (the church's developing interpretation of Scripture) is entitled to an authoritative position because of its sacramental participation in the incarnate Word of God. It seems to me, therefore, that evangelicals, if they truly wish to be evangelical, need to follow theologians such as Vanhoozer in taking on board the notion that doctrine develops over time. If they are to remain evangelical in their doctrine, evangelicals cannot do without the tradition. Evangelical identity would be strengthened immeasurably by an acceptance of the Platonist-Christian view of time as sacramental and by the recognition of the tradition as the sacramental unfolding of God's revelation in Christ.

CHAPTER 8

Biblical Interpretation as Sacramental Practice

Evangelicals are known for their high regard for Scripture. While internal squabbles about issues such as inerrancy, verbal inspiration, and the like do flare up on occasion, these differences cannot obscure the fact that one of the main characteristics of evangelicalism is that it is centered on Scripture.[1] To be evangelical is to be biblical. This question should not, of course, keep from view the next very important question: *How* is the Bible central? How does it or how should it *function*? How are we to read it? The preceding chapters give several clues that should help us deal with these questions. If theology is the discipline that facilitates the move from sacrament *(sacramentum)* to reality *(res)*, Holy Scripture itself constitutes the divinely ordained means used by the church to guide people toward the fullness of participation in Christ. This fairly straightforward statement carries important implications for the way we treat the Bible. One such implication is that Scripture belongs to the church. Since Scripture's purpose is a spiritual one that intimately ties in with the sacramental purpose of theology itself, Scripture's home is in the called-out community *(ekklēsia)*, and the Bible must be read with a view to the purpose(s) of that community.[2]

---

1. David Bebbington's fourfold description of evangelicalism is well-known: conversionism, activism, biblicism, and crucicentrism. See David W. Bebbington, *Evangelicalism in Modern Britain: A History from the 1730s to the 1980s* (London: Unwin Hyman, 1989), 1-19; cf. John G. Stackhouse, "Defining 'Evangelical,'" *Church and Faith Trends* 1, no. 1 (Oct. 2007): 1-5.

2. To be sure, as Jaroslav Pelikan rightly observes, since the Bible is the book of *God,* it is, in an ultimate sense, presumptuous for anyone to speak of "possessing" the Bible;

Just as the church has the beatific vision for her ultimate supernatural end, so the Bible serves this purpose.

We saw in the preceding chapter that the Bible itself is a sacrament that participates in the eternal Word of God and makes this Word present to us.[3] This supernatural aim of Scripture is not to deny that we can *study* it; nor is it to deny that we can teach courses in Scripture, or that professors can be rigorous in evaluating their students. A number of years ago, Mark Noll warned the evangelical community that its praiseworthy pious adherence to Scripture should not lead to anti-intellectualism.[4] Piety and intellect are not opposed to one another. Notwithstanding the continuing relevance of this word of caution, in an important sense the Bible's home is the church, not the academy. The church is the place where Scripture was nourished and recognized as canonical; the church is also the place where Scripture, in turn, nourishes the church and where it functions as her canonical guide.

For years, the historical-critical interpretation of the Bible dominated biblical scholarship, so that questions of the supernatural end, or *telos,* of the Bible were bracketed, at best. Of course, such bracketing fit with the ever-increasing rise of naturalism since the late Middle Ages. Historical-critical scholarship was interested in finding the one meaning that the (human) author had in mind: determining the authorial intent and the search for historical meaning set the parameters for biblical study. Today, more and more people question that bracketing of the final end of Scripture. If Scripture's purpose is to serve believers in their pilgrimage to the fullness of Christ, even just a temporary bracketing of that final end would seem out of place. Such bracketing — usually called "methodological naturalism" — may well have gained a certain degree of respectability in some quarters of the academy (which, fortunately, seem to be diminishing rather rapidly); but that bracketing ignores the fact that the eternal Word of God determines the meaning of *all* reality. That is, the very questions we ask of the Bible are established by its supernatural end. Other questions are

---

moreover, our status as "temporary possessors and life-renters" is one that we share with all humanity (*Whose Bible Is It? A History of the Scriptures through the Ages* [New York: Viking, 2005], 247-48).

3. See also Yves M.-J. Congar, *Tradition and Traditions: The Biblical, Historical, and Theological Evidence for Catholic Teaching on Tradition,* trans. Michael Naseby and Thomas Rainborough (San Diego: Basilica, 1966), 404.

4. Mark A. Noll, *The Scandal of the Evangelical Mind* (Grand Rapids: Eerdmans, 1994).

comparatively insignificant, no matter how much "genuine" insight they may yield.

The sacramental or spiritual purpose of Scripture not only has implications for where it is read (in the church), but also for how it is read. In other words, the question of biblical interpretation or hermeneutics is affected by the Bible's purpose of drawing people into the life of the triune God. Younger evangelicals, weary of the dry archaeological attempts at finding the historical meaning of the text, are turning to what they usually call "theological interpretation" — what I will refer to as "spiritual" or "sacramental" interpretation.[5] In this chapter I wish to look more specifically at *how* to interpret Scripture if we take its sacramental purpose seriously. I will particularly argue that a sacramental hermeneutic must, in some way, reappropriate the allegorical exegesis that characterized the church throughout the period of the Platonist-Christian synthesis.

Case Studies: Isaiah 53 and Proverbs 8

At two earlier points in this book, we already briefly encountered the significance of spiritual (as opposed to strictly historical) interpretation, first with regard to Eucharist and church and then in connection with the role of tradition. In chapter 6, I investigated de Lubac's retrieval of the close link that Augustine had posited between Eucharist and church. We saw that, in his Sermon 227, the African bishop connected the grain that is ground and pounded, moistened, and baked with the believers' fasting and exorcism, baptism, and anointing with the Spirit.[6] *Nouvelle théologie*'s Neo-Scholastic opponents, with their "re-

---

5. I am thinking, for example, of Zondervan's "Scripture and Hermeneutics" series (ed. Craig Bartholomew); "Brazos Theological Commentary on the Bible" series (ed. R. R. Reno); Brazos's Foundations of Theological Exegesis and Christian Spirituality series (ed. Hans Boersma and Matthew Levering); as well as of various recent publications on theological interpretation, perhaps most notably Jens Zimmermann, *Recovering Theological Hermeneutics: An Incarnational-Trinitarian Theory of Interpretation* (Grand Rapids: Baker Academic, 2004); and Kevin J. Vanhoozer, ed., *Dictionary for Theological Interpretation of the Bible* (Grand Rapids: Eerdmans, 2005). Although I have no problem with the term "theological interpretation," the language of "spiritual interpretation" does a better job referring to the inner, spiritual dimension of the biblical text.

6. See chap. 6 above, under subheading "Augustine's 'Allegorized' Texts."

alist" focus on the eucharistic elements, were troubled by this Augustinian "allegorizing," and as a result they ignored the many beautiful passages in Augustine where that allegorizing occurs. The interesting thing to observe in the context of this current chapter is that, for Augustine — and, as we shall see, also for de Lubac — one's theology of the Eucharist is intimately tied to one's views of biblical interpretation. Just as a strongly "realist" view of the Eucharist (with a heavy emphasis on "real" presence) might run the danger of forgetting about the greater purpose of the sacrament (namely, the fullness of Christ in the unity of the church), so a strongly "realist" understanding of Scripture (with a heavy emphasis on literal or historical meaning) might end up losing the deeper, spiritual *telos* of the historical event (namely, to illuminate Christ himself).

Therefore, on the one hand, a single-minded focus on the "real presence" in the Eucharist tends to coincide with an approach to the text that restricts itself to the "real" historical meaning; on the other hand, an approach that discerns the link between Eucharist and church will also recognize the sacramental connection between historical and spiritual levels of meaning in the text. In short, a sacramental view that connects the body of the Eucharist to the body of the church implies also a sacramental hermeneutic in which the literal meaning of Scripture sacramentally points to a spiritual meaning. A premodern view of the mystical body does not address *only* eucharistic theology and ecclesiology; it also addresses the interpretation of Scripture. Allegory, it turns out, is a sacramental kind of interpretation that looks for the deeper, hidden meaning beneath the literal, or historical, meaning of the text.

We have also encountered spiritual interpretation in chapter 7 in the discussion of tradition, though there the allegorical approach came to the fore somewhat less conspicuously.[7] We have seen that in Acts 8, Philip explains Isaiah 53 christologically. According to Philip, Christ was the one "led like a lamb to the slaughter" and the one who was silent "as a sheep before her shearers" (Isa. 53:7). A strictly historical method of interpretation would have difficulty reading this passage as referring to Christ. There is a great deal of disagreement about the question of whether or not Isaiah's references to the lamb and the

---

7. See chap. 7 above, under subheading "Congar and Vanhoozer on Scripture and Tradition."

sheep are to be read messianically.[8] For exegetes devoted to a historical method, the questions about whether Isaiah himself was actually thinking of the coming Messiah and whether the original hearers of the prophetic message would have taken the passage messianically are all-important. And the issue seems to take on additional weight from the fact that Philip himself reads the passage in a messianic fashion. Understandably, therefore, readers who take the unity of Scripture seriously tend to be apprehensive about exegetes who argue that Isaiah did not intend his prophetic message in Isaiah 53 messianically. But scholars like Yves Congar and Kevin Vanhoozer have no qualms about following Philip in his christological reading of the prophecy.[9] The reason, I suggest, is that both recognize that the meaning of the text is not restricted to the original intent of the human author. Both Congar and Vanhoozer recognize that a text's meaning is, in part, determined by its reception.

Tradition, as the history of this reception, opens up the text in ways that the original biblical author(s) could not possibly have foreseen. For Congar and Vanhoozer, it is this interplay between text and tradition that allows Christian doctrine to develop over time. Therefore, a hermeneutic that limits itself to the literal or historical meaning of the text tends to coincide with a low view of tradition: the individual reader does not need the church's tradition to find the "objective" meaning of the text.[10] However, a hermeneutic that looks for deeper, spiritual meanings in the text tends to take the authority of tradition more seriously: the church's historical interpretation of the text has entered into its meaning, sometimes in enormously significant ways.

Proverbs 8 is a clear instance of where the church's subsequent interpretation has shaped our reading of the text. Many contemporary exe-

---

8. Cf. John Goldingay and David Payne, *A Critical and Exegetical Commentary on Isaiah 40-55,* vol. 2, The International Critical Commentary (Edinburgh: T. & T. Clark, 2007), 284-88.

9. For a spiritual commentary on Isaiah based on the church fathers, see Robert Louis Wilken, *Isaiah: Interpreted by Early Christian and Medieval Commentators,* The Church's Bible (Grand Rapids: Eerdmans, 2007).

10. See Andrew Louth's comment: "The historical-critical method is, on the analogy of the scientific method, a way of reaching objective truth, that is, truth that inheres in the object, independently of the one who knows this truth" (*Discerning the Mystery: An Essay on the Nature of Theology* [1983; reprint, Oxford: Clarendon/Oxford University Press, 2003], 30).

getes, including evangelical scholars such as Bruce Waltke and Gordon Fee, reject the possibility of interpreting the wisdom of Proverbs 8 as a reference to Christ.[11] Reading that Proverbs chapter christologically, they argue, violates the historical meaning of the text. Furthermore, while one might argue that the New Testament (Acts 8) passage appears to interpret the Isaiah 53 passage christologically, it is much less immediately obvious that the New Testament reads Proverbs 8 as referring to Christ.[12] Accordingly, in this particular instance there may be less need for defensiveness on the part of those who consider the proverbial Lady Wisdom to be a reference to Christ. The unity of Old and New Testaments is not obviously at stake — not, at least, if we can separate the New Testament identification of Christ as wisdom (1 Cor. 1:24, 30; Col. 2:3) from Proverbs 8.

The Platonist-Christian synthesis, however, appears to stand in the way of a purely moral reading of Proverbs 8. In particular, verse 25 — "Before the mountains were founded, before all the hills, he begets me"[13] — played an important role in the theological development of the Great Tradition because the "begetting" language of this verse eventually made it into the church's creed.[14] Indeed, almost the entire tradition of the fathers and the Middle Ages *did* look to Christ as central to the meaning of this chapter. The christological reference was so universally shared that in the fourth century, Arius and Athanasius —

11. Bruce K. Waltke, *The Book of Proverbs: Chapters 15-31,* The New International Commentary on the Old Testament (Grand Rapids: Eerdmans, 2005), 126-33; Gordon D. Fee, *Pauline Christology: An Exegetical-Theological Study* (Peabody, MA: Hendrickson, 2007), 317-25, 595-630.

12. N. T. Wright, while sharing the historical approach of Fee and Waltke, argues that the New Testament *does* read Proverbs 8 christologically (*The Climax of the Covenant: Christ and the Law in Pauline Theology* [Minneapolis: Fortress, 1991], 110-13).

13. This is my rather literal translation of the Septuagint, the Greek translation of this Proverbs passage that Arius and Athanasius both used.

14. For the use of Proverbs 8 in the Arian controversy, see Allan Lee Clayton, "The Orthodox Recovery of a Heretical Proof-Text: Athanasius of Alexandria's Interpretation of Proverbs 8:22-30 in Conflict with the Arians" (PhD diss., Southern Methodist University, 1988); John Behr, *The Nicene Faith,* vol. 2/1, *The Formation of Christian Theology* (Crestwood, NY: St. Vladimir's Seminary Press, 2001), 123-61; Frances M. Young, *Biblical Exegesis and the Formation of Christian Culture* (Peabody, MA: Hendrickson, 2002), 29-45; Wendy Elgersma Helleman, "Gregory's Sophia: 'Christ, the Wisdom of God,'" *Studia Patristica* 41 (2006): 345-50. For further reflection on the relationship between biblical "wisdom" language and Christology, see David F. Ford and Graham Stanton, eds., *Reading Texts, Seeking Wisdom: Scripture and Theology* (Grand Rapids: Eerdmans, 2003).

while in radically opposing camps with regard to the deity of Christ — *both* took for granted that the "wisdom" of Proverbs 8 referred to Christ.[15] While this chapter was central to the disagreement between the Arian and the Nicene parties, both sides of the debate were in full agreement that Christians could not read the passage without thinking of Christ as the wisdom of God. Such widespread agreement about the need for a christological reading should make us pause. Apparently, the historical focus is so strong among contemporary Christians, including many evangelicals, that we are willing to jettison even the little agreement that did at least exist between Arians and Nicene Christians.

Some might wish to argue that the church's dogmatic language should not drive the exegesis of particular texts. Bruce Waltke, for instance, observes: "The notion that Wisdom is eternally being begotten is based on Christian dogma, not on exegesis."[16] However, this separation between dogma and exegesis forgets that the dogma of the eternal "begetting" of the Son from the Father depends, historically at least, on a particular exegesis of Proverbs 8, over which Athanasius did valiant battle with Arius in the fourth century. More broadly, Waltke's comment posits an unsustainable disjunction between exegesis and doctrine. If dogmatic claims do not derive from exegesis, one wonders what their origin might be.

In chapter 7, I was at pains to describe tradition as the historical development of the church's interpretation of Scripture. The church's dogma — including her christological dogma — must remain exegetically based, no matter how much this tradition may develop over time. As evangelicals, we often question Roman Catholic doctrines when they seem to move too far away from the explicit teachings of the biblical text. We should likewise be wary of dogmatic convictions (including those about the eternal generation of the Son) if they are not exegetically based. Indeed, if we really take Waltke's statement at face value, the sound evangelical conviction that dogma must be based on exegesis will render us incapable of retaining the church's teaching about the Son being eternally begotten of the Father. Jason Byassee

---

15. Frances M. Young says: "Everyone, up to and including Arius, took it that the whole passage referred to the creative activity of the pre-existent Logos" (*Biblical Exegesis,* 37).

16. Waltke, *Book of Proverbs,* 409n104.

puts it well when he says, "You cannot have patristic dogma without patristic exegesis; you cannot have the creed without allegory."[17]

De Lubac and Medieval Exegesis

Up to this point, I have argued that we need to go beyond a purely historical or literal reading of the text both when the New Testament demands a christological reading (as is arguably the case with the interpretation of Isaiah 53 in Acts 8) and when the dogmatic confession of the church is at stake (as the history of interpretation of Proverbs 8 suggests). However, it strikes me that a more basic principle underlies the christological approach to both Isaiah 53 and Proverbs 8. That principle is the same sacramental ontology that determined the Great Tradition's approach to the church (chap. 6) and to the tradition (chap. 7). In other words, a move beyond a purely historical reading of the text is demanded by the very sacramental grammar of the Christian faith. Also here, the *nouvelle* theologians were quite aware of the sacramental cast of the Platonist-Christian synthesis. Henri de Lubac, in particular, did a tremendous amount of work in trying to recover the sacramental approach to interpretation that he believed had been at work in the spiritual exegesis of the early church and the Middle Ages. His main books on spiritual interpretation — his book on Origen, *Histoire et esprit* (1950), and his four volumes on medieval interpretation, *Exégèse médiévale* (1959-64) — provide a wealth of material on the Great Tradition's approach to Scripture and a spirited defense of a premodern biblical hermeneutic.[18]

A brief discussion of de Lubac's recently translated *Histoire et esprit*

17. Jason Byassee, *Praise Seeking Understanding: Reading the Psalms with Augustine* (Grand Rapids: Eerdmans, 2007), 16.

18. Henri de Lubac, *History and Spirit: The Understanding of Scripture According to Origen,* trans. Anne Englund Nash with Juvenal Merriell (San Francisco: Ignatius, 2007); de Lubac, *Medieval Exegesis: The Four Senses of Scripture,* 3 vols., trans. Mark Sebanc and E. M. Macierowski (Grand Rapids: Eerdmans, 1998, 2000, 2009). For de Lubac's most accessible material in English, see de Lubac, "Spiritual Understanding," trans. Luke O'Neill, in *The Theological Interpretation of Scripture: Classic and Contemporary Readings,* ed. Stephen E. Fowl (Malden, MA: Blackwell, 1997), 3-25; de Lubac, "Typology and Allegorization," in *Theological Fragments,* trans. Rebecca Howell Balinski (San Francisco: Ignatius, 1989), 129-64; and de Lubac, *Scripture in the Tradition,* trans. Luke O'Neill (1968; reprint, New York: Herder and Herder/Crossroad, 2000).

may serve to illustrate what was at stake in his *ressourcement* of a Platonist-Christian interpretation of Scripture. The title of the book indicates what de Lubac believed lay at the heart of scriptural interpretation found in Origen (c. 185-c. 254) For Origen, there were ultimately two levels of Scripture — the one historical, the other spiritual. There are several reasons why it is interesting to take note of this. For one thing, the Alexandrian father has often been accused of ignoring the historical meaning of the text. His allegorical flights of fancy are commonly thought to be bereft of history, and as a result without foundation. For Origen — many people think — any word of Scripture could take on any kind of allegorical meaning, whatever would strike the interpreter's fancy.[19] The beauty of de Lubac's newly translated book is that he shows here, with example after example, that Origen was, in fact, very concerned with history and with the historical meaning of the text. The examples of where Origen supposedly ignores history are usually taken from his exegesis of Genesis 1 and 2. And de Lubac acknowledges that the "one exception," where Origen indeed believed that Scripture did *not* have a historical level of meaning, was in the "texts concerning our origins and last ends."[20] In a wonderful passage, worth quoting in full, de Lubac notes:

> Origen reacted against those who, in their interpretation of the eschatological texts, let themselves be deceived by the words and images to the point of concocting "inept fables and empty fiction"; to the point, for example, "of going so far as to believe that after the resurrection one would use bodily food and that one would drink wine, not at all from that true Vine destined for eternal existence, but from a material vine." (p. 16)

De Lubac's overall message comes through loud and clear throughout his book on Origen: it is simply impossible to charge the third-century theologian with ignoring or denying the importance of the historical or literal meaning of the text.

To be sure, this still leaves us with the second element of de Lubac's

---

19. This criticism has been classically expressed in R. P. C. Hanson, *Allegory and Event: A Study of the Sources and Significance of Origen's Interpretation of Scripture* (London: SCM, 1959).

20. De Lubac, *History and Spirit,* 116. Hereafter, page references to this work appear in parentheses in the text.

title, *History and Spirit.* De Lubac readily acknowledges that, for Origen, the historical meaning was not everything; in addition, there was a spiritual dimension to the text. Origen often looked for a threefold meaning in the text of Scripture: historical, moral, and mystical (or allegorical). Having determined, as best we can, the literal (or historical) meaning, we have to look for the other two levels of meaning. The basic reason Origen believed that we cannot ignore these deeper levels of meaning is, de Lubac explains, the fact of the Incarnation:

> What makes [Origen] break with the letter of the Jewish law is not a historical illusion or a prejudice for abstract spiritualism: it is faith in Christ and adherence to his Mystery. The Jewish Bible is for him the *old* Testament, and it is as old that he views it: not precisely as what it was — as if we imagined ourselves the contemporaries of Moses or David — but as what it has become since the coming of Christ and because of that coming. (pp. 143-44)

In other words, de Lubac explains that, for Origen, the only way we can make sense of the Old Testament is by reading it in the light of its historical fulfillment in Christ. Allegorizing cannot simply take wings arbitrarily. It is always bound to the historical fact of the Incarnation of the Son of God.

All of this means, according to de Lubac, that the common interpretation of Origen as simply following the allegorizing method of the first-century Jewish interpreter Philo is largely wrong. Harnack's Hellenization thesis, which maintains that things went awry pretty much from the start — as soon as early Christians substituted abstract Greek methods of interpretation (notably the allegorical method) for historically based Hebrew methods — simply does not hold up, according to de Lubac (pp. 39, 177). Harnack was unable to see the great significance that history held both for Origen and for the later tradition, and he also missed the fact that Christian allegory does not take its primary starting point in Philo, but rather in Paul himself (pp. 172-90). It seems to me that evangelicalism, especially where it is wedded to the Radical Reformation, is easily tempted by the Hellenization thesis, and as a result it is often wary of any kind of theological interpretation, let alone any allegorical exegesis. De Lubac's writings remain of value — including to evangelicals — because they demonstrate that Christian interpretation of Scripture did not go off the rails early on in the history of the church.

Christian Mystery and the Plurality of Meaning

This is not to say that either Origen or de Lubac was without fault. De Lubac made clear that he himself already had reservations about some of the moralizing exegesis of Origen, and he lamented the influence that Philo had exercised in that regard. In other words, de Lubac was willing to concede that the christological lens of interpretation was not always as strong in Origen as it should have been. De Lubac also recognized that because of this, Origen's allegorical exegesis did at times suffer from a degree of arbitrariness. For instance, de Lubac acknowledges: "As for the claim of discovering a hidden sense beneath the letter of the evangelical text, it does not always, in its detail, escape the arbitrary" (p. 228). Nor was de Lubac himself, it seems to me, entirely without fault. Both in his book on Origen and in his other writings on spiritual interpretation, it would have been good to read more about what allowed both Origen and the later Christian tradition to allegorize particular details of the biblical text. It is one thing to insist that Old Testament historical events refer, allegorically, to Jesus Christ (and I am in firm agreement with the general approach of the fathers, which interpreted Scripture this way); but perhaps de Lubac was satisfied a little too quickly. What was it, for example, that allowed the church fathers to see the lamb and the sheep mentioned in Isaiah 53:7 as a reference to Christ? What was it that enabled them to see Christ in the wisdom of Proverbs 8?[21] These questions do have some urgency if spiritual interpretation is to avoid the common charge that it renders interpretation arbitrary and subject to the whims of individual interpreters. We might wish that de Lubac had touched on these kinds of questions.

De Lubac likely did not concern himself with these particulars because he believed that the charge of arbitrariness was obviously based on faulty presuppositions. The basic erroneous prejudice of a great deal of historical-critical exegesis was the belief that any given biblical passage could only have one meaning, the one intended by the author. Seeing that, for the Great Tradition, Scripture had been like an "infinite forest of meanings" — an expression from Saint Jerome (c. 347-420), whose implications de Lubac explored in his *Medieval Exegesis* —

21. For a helpful approach to these kinds of exegetical particularities, see John J. O'Keefe and R. R. Reno, *Sanctified Vision: An Introduction to Early Christian Interpretation of the Bible* (Baltimore, Md.: Johns Hopkins University Press, 2005).

the French Jesuit could not get himself to be nitpicky about which allegorical meaning was legitimate and which one was not.[22] He made the
viewpoint of Origen and other church fathers his own: "If in fact the
detail of their explanations, in so many instances, seems so fanciful, it
is because that was not for them the essential thing. They spread out
comfortably 'in the vast field of divine Scriptures.'"[23] De Lubac, along
with the Great Tradition, refused to be squeezed into the confines of
the modern reduction of meaning to the original intent of the human
author.

De Lubac's insistence on plurality of meaning seems to me a crucially important insight. The medieval tradition often distinguished
four different levels of interpretation. A common medieval distich, to
which de Lubac often alludes, runs as follows:

> Littera gesta docet,
> quid credas allegoria,
> moralis quid agas,
> quo tendas anagogia.[24]

In English, one could render the rhyme somewhat freely as follows:

> The letter shows us what God and our fathers did;
> The allegory shows us where our faith is hid;
> The moral meaning gives us the rule of daily life;
> The anagogy shows us where we end our strife.[25]

Convinced that the Holy Spirit was the divine author behind the individual human authors of Scripture, de Lubac believed that the theologians of the Great Tradition had been right to approach the biblical
text not only with historical questions in mind, but also with theological concerns about Christ and the church, about the individual believer
and his or her life of faith, and about eternal life. Multiplicity of meaning was the natural outcome of such an approach to Scripture.

But for de Lubac, plurality of meaning is given not just with the dif-

22. De Lubac, *Medieval Exegesis,* 1:75-89.

23. De Lubac, *History and Spirit,* 374.

24. See Henri de Lubac, "On an Old Distich: The Doctrine of the 'Fourfold Sense' in
Scripture," in *Theological Fragments,* 109-27.

25. Robert M. Grant, with David Tracy, *A Short History of the Interpretation of the Bible,*
2nd ed. (Philadelphia: Fortress, 1984), 85.

ferent spiritual levels of meaning. He recognizes that different readers might well come up with different interpretations *within* the same level. In other words, two exegetes might well present two (or more) different allegorical or christological readings of the same passage. This hardly presents a problem for de Lubac. Convinced that interpretation is a sacramental entry into the infinity of the spiritual realm, he maintains that the sacramental reality *(res)* of the biblical text cannot possibly be captured by one particular allegorical rendering of the text. Therefore, plurality of meaning is not a danger to be avoided and does not constitute an argument against spiritual exegesis; rather, plurality of meaning is something to be *expected,* precisely because exegesis is the Spirit-guided means that enables human participation in heavenly realities.

Not surprisingly, then, de Lubac devotes a section of his *Medieval Exegesis* to the notion of "mystery," where he explains that the word "allegory," as well as the terms "mystery" and "mystical," were common in the medieval tradition.[26] The medieval reader of Scripture was interested in finding the "mystical sense" of the text, "a reality, at first hidden in God, and then revealed to human beings at the same time as realized in Jesus Christ." De Lubac explains that this christological realization of the mystery was, for the Middle Ages, the sacramental reality *(res)* to which the earlier historical event itself pointed and in which it participated. After all, in the Middle Ages the Latin term *mysterium* was sacramental in character: "In Latin *mysterium* serves as the double for *sacramentum.* For Saint Augustine, the Bible is essentially the 'writing of the mysteries,' and its books are the 'books of the divine sacraments.' The two words are often simply synonyms."[27] Further, de Lubac argues, if and when medieval theologians did distinguish between *sacramentum* and *mysterium,* they saw the former as the sacramental sign and the latter as the spiritual reality:

> They are sometimes distinguished as the two terms of a relation or as the two poles of an alternating movement. Then *sacramentum* designates rather the exterior component, the "envelope," as Saint Augustine says: "Christ has been preached by the prophets almost everywhere with a wrapping of sacrament." This is the sign or the letter as

26. De Lubac, *Medieval Exegesis,* 2:19-27.

27. De Lubac, *Medieval Exegesis,* 2:20. Jason Byassee also makes the point that, for Augustine, interpretation was sacramental in character (*Praise Seeking Understanding,* 233-39).

bearer of the sign: "the signs of things are in the sacraments." Whether thing or person, fact or rite, it is the "type," the correlative of the mystery, just as the "figure" or "image" is the correlative of the "truth": "the sacrament comes before the truth of the thing." It is the *sacrum* [sacred thing] rather than the *arcanum* [hidden thing]. The mystery is this *arcanum* itself. It is the interior component, the reality hidden under the letter and signified by the sign, the truth that the figure indicates; in other words, the object of faith itself.[28]

This quotation may be somewhat lengthy and dense, but it captures the heart of de Lubac's approach. The "exterior" of the letter, while indispensable, has a purpose that lies beyond itself. Its purpose is the "interior" of the Spirit. The type or figure of the Old Testament had as its *telos* the hidden reality of Christ, revealed in the New Testament.

None of this is meant to undermine the historical "envelope" of the Old Testament. De Lubac's objection to a historical method that rejects the presence of deeper, sacramental realities in the text is that it cannot do justice to the unity of the Scripture. By reducing the meaning of the text to the historical level, such a method separates Old and New Testaments and thus letter and spirit, sacrament and reality. A purely historical method, de Lubac realized, reduces the story of salvation to a temporal, horizontal narrative, and in the process undermines the unity of the biblical revelation of Old and New Testaments. De Lubac believed that this unity could be maintained only by reasserting the vertical, sacramental link between historical events and the eternal Logos revealed in Christ.

Retrieving Spiritual Interpretation Today

At this point, it should not be difficult to understand why allegorical exegesis declined in the late Middle Ages. The allegorical or sacramental interpretation of the Great Tradition had been the result of a Platonist-Christian synthesis. De Lubac was often at pains to counter accusations that the church fathers depended on Philo or on the Platonic tradition for their interpretation of Scripture.[29] And he was cer-

---

28. De Lubac, *Medieval Exegesis*, 2:21.

29. See esp. Henri de Lubac, "Hellenistic Allegory and Christian Allegory," in *Theological Fragments*, 165-96.

tainly correct that it is the centrality of Christ, not pagan philosophy, that ultimately legitimates the allegorical interpretation of Scripture. Still, it seems undeniable that the practice of allegory in the Hellenic context of the early church did influence the exegetical practices of church fathers such as Origen and Gregory of Nyssa. I am just not sure that such influence is necessarily problematic. In the first few chapters of this book, I have observed that one of the reasons the Platonic tradition captured the imagination of the early church was the fact that it allowed for divine transcendence. More significantly, the Platonic Forms or Ideas were capable of reinterpretation, as Christians insisted that created realities lay anchored in the eternal Logos of God. Sacramental participation of created realities in the eternal Word of God was the Christian theological response to the church's encounter with the Platonic mindset of her surroundings. It is hardly surprising that in this context the church fathers also saw the possibility of a sacramental reworking of the allegorical method that they witnessed in the world around them. As long as (1) allegory centered on Christ and his church and (2) one allowed for the real participation of the historical in the spiritual, one could hardly go wrong with allegory. The sacramental interpretation of allegory fit squarely within the Platonist-Christian ontology that developed through the early church's encounter with a Greek environment. It was the focus on heavenly participation that drove the church's development of allegorical interpretation.

The scissors of modernity — univocal being and the rejection of universals — rendered impossible this sacramental interpretation that had been common throughout the Great Tradition. By rejecting the idea that earthly objects (as *sacramentum*) received the reality *(res)* of their being from God's own being, modernity could no longer see that history was significant precisely because it centered in Christ and issued in the spiritual reality of the beatific vision. Instead, according to the new approach, history had significance in and of itself. Furthermore, by rejecting the reality of universals in the eternal Word of God, nominalism reduced history to flattened horizons in which any talk of purpose (teleology) seemed but an arbitrary and ultimately useless imposition of meaning. By thus reducing time to its horizontal dimension, modernity eradicated its sacramental character. Modernity lodged all of history's significance in its secular, temporal character, thereby rendering impossible the Origenist project of an interpenetration of "history and spirit." For modernity, history had no deeper meaning than the horizontal causes and effects that led from one event to another. It is hardly surprising that neither the Reformation nor later Catholic (and Protestant) Neo-Scholasticism had much use for the medieval fourfold interpretation. The reason is that neither knew what to do with the multiplicity of meaning and the allegorizing that directly flowed from the sacramental tapestry of the Great Tradition.[30]

Perhaps the deepest reason why both Protestants and Catholics need to read the *nouvelle* theologians lies in their *ressourcement* of the spiritual interpretation of Scripture.[31] Again, this should be of great interest to the younger evangelicals who want to move beyond purely historical-critical exegesis. Their renewed interest in theological interpretation — perhaps more accurately referred to as spiritual or sacramental interpretation — does not (at least, should not) imply a complete jettisoning of the genuine insights that the historical-critical method can give. Also on this score, the younger evangelicals would do well to take their cue not from a postmodern skeptical attitude toward all meaning. Instead, by recovering the insights of the Platonist-Christian synthesis, the proponents of genuine spiritual interpretation will take the literal sense seriously, since it is the starting point *(sacramentum)* of a search for the greater, more christological reality *(res)* of the gospel.[32] Augustine expresses the sacramental character of this approach perhaps better than anyone: *"Novum in vetere latet et in novo vetus patet."* ("The New lies in the Old concealed; the Old is in the

---

30. For a contemporary appropriation of premodern exegesis, see Peter J. Leithart, *Deep Exegesis: The Mystery of Reading Scripture* (Waco, TX: Baylor University Press, 2009).

31. In this chapter I have focused on de Lubac. Jean Daniélou and Hans Urs von Balthasar were also keenly interested in spiritual interpretation. For Daniélou, see Hans Boersma, *Nouvelle Théologie and Sacramental Ontology: A Return to Mystery* (Oxford: Oxford University Press, 2009), 168-90. For Balthasar, see W. T. Dickens, *Hans Urs von Balthasar's Theological Aesthetics: A Model for Post-Critical Biblical Interpretation* (Notre Dame, IN: University of Notre Dame Press, 2003). For an excellent approach to a participatory theory of interpretation, see Matthew Levering, *Participatory Biblical Exegesis: A Theology of Biblical Interpretation* (Notre Dame, IN: University of Notre Dame Press, 2008).

32. Even "the literal sense" is hardly a static given; I do not believe in the existence of an objectively given, historical meaning that one can discover and solve just as one does scientific problems. For Thomas Aquinas's appreciation of the plurality of literal meanings, see Mark F. Johnson, "Another Look at the Plurality of the Literal Sense," *Medieval Philosophy and Theology* 2 (1992): 117-41; see also Eugene F. Rogers, "How the Virtues of an Interpreter Presuppose and Perfect Hermeneutics: The Case of Thomas Aquinas," *Journal of Religion* 76 (1996): 64-81.

New revealed.")[33] A sacramental reading of Scripture enables us to see the unity between the two Testaments while we retain the genuine "newness" that comes with the Christ event.

De Lubac's recovery of a premodern sacramental hermeneutic allows for a spiritual interpretation that from the outset is guided by faith in the Christ proclaimed by the church. Although I have discussed the church and the tradition before coming to Scripture itself, it is arguably the retrieval of the spiritual interpretation of Scripture that should form the basis for a recovery of the sacramental ontology of the Great Tradition. If theology is interpretation of Scripture, then a sacramental hermeneutic must be the backbone that gives shape to Christian theology. Evangelicals have nothing to lose and much to gain from such an ecumenical engagement of *nouvelle théologie* and from a reacquaintance with the interpretive approach of the premodern tradition. A sacramental hermeneutic will allow evangelicals to retain the centrality of the Bible while they rediscover its hidden spiritual depths.

33. Augustine, *Quaestiones in Heptateuchum* 2.73; see also de Lubac's reference to the Second Vatican's quotation of Augustine in *Dei Verbum*, no. 16 (*Scripture in the Tradition*, ix).

CHAPTER 9

Truth as Sacramental Reality

Throughout this book we have seen that the sacramental tapestry of the Great Tradition had tremendous regard for mystery. The church fathers and medieval theologians were much less interested in comprehending the truth than in participating in it; and participating in the truth meant to be mastered by it rather than mastering it. The supernatural was not a distinct or separate realm of being that superimposed itself onto an independent and autonomous realm of nature. Instead, the supernatural was simply the divine means to bring created realities of time and space to their appointed end in Christ. Therefore, created realities participated in the heavenly mystery of Christ as their sacramental reality. Access to truth meant sacramental participation in the unfathomable mystery of Christ.

In this chapter I will outline a way of articulating such a sacramental view of truth: I am thinking here particularly of human discourse about *God*, the human "naming" of God. I hope to make clear that *nouvelle théologie*'s return to the earlier Platonist-Christian synthesis also holds great promise for the nature of human truth claims. Hence, I will turn to several of the *nouvelle* theologians in order to draw from them a sacramental view of truth that looks to human language as a suitable means to make present the eternal mystery of the divine Logos, while at the same time recognizing that this mystery will always elude the human grasp.[1]

---

1. For detailed discussions of *nouvelle théologie*'s approach to truth, see Agnès Desmazières, "La 'Nouvelle théologie', prémisse d'une théologie herméneutique? La

Modern Knowledge: Exaltation of Reason

The recovery of truth as sacramental reality seems to me particularly urgent today. Especially since the seventeenth century, the modern approach to truth has started out with mathematical certainty and empirical observation. The former was articulated by René Descartes (1596-1650), who in his *Discours de la méthode* (1637) famously commented that he was resolved "never to accept anything as true that I did not know to be evidently so: that is to say, carefully to avoid precipitancy and prejudice, and to include in my judgements nothing more than what presented itself so clearly and so distinctly to my mind that I might have no occasion to place it in doubt."[2] The latter was the method used by the British philosopher and scientist Francis Bacon (1561-1626), an approach that gave rise to the modern scientific method and thus to the contemporary successes of science and technology. The achievements of mathematics and the scientific method would have been unthinkable without the developments as I have described them in chapters 3 and 4 above.

What I have somewhat audaciously called the "revolt of nature" may be traced all the way to the twelfth century; ironically, this revolt has ultimately yielded many of the comforts of our modern Western world. These successes would also have been unthinkable without the watershed of the seventeenth-century crowning of mathematics and the natural sciences to positions of regal authority. The new methods ensured that truth became something that human beings were able to manipulate by means of proven techniques. As a result, truth was equated with certainty — not the certainty of faith, but the certainty based on a neutral and universally shared human reason.

Despite the accomplishments of the Cartesian and Baconian methods, the past fifty years or so have been marked by an amazing decline of confidence in them, and thus a debilitating sense that truth may be inaccessible after all. The extent to which the skeptical approaches of postmodern philosophers such as Jean-François Lyotard, Jacques

Controverse sur l'analogie de la vérité (1946-1949)," *Revue thomiste* 104 (2004): 241-72; Hans Boersma, "Analogy of Truth: The Sacramental Epistemology of *nouvelle théologie*," in *Ressourcement: A Movement for Renewal in Twentieth-Century Catholic Theology,* ed. Gabriel Flynn and Paul D. Murray (Oxford: Oxford University Press, in press).

2. René Descartes, *Discourse on Method and the Meditations,* trans. F. E. Sutcliffe (1968; reprint, Harmondsworth, UK: Penguin, 1986), 41.

Derrida, and Michel Foucault have influenced the contemporary cultural malaise will likely be a point of discussion for many years to come. Whatever answers that discussion may yield, it seems clear that, particularly since the 1960s, a widespread skeptical relativism has affected Western culture. Many of us are no longer quite as assured of the certainties that modern methods claimed to bring as were preceding generations. While, ironically, we continue to make use of the ever-increasing prowess of technical progress, many of us have become less confident about universal truth claims. Rationality, we have learned from postmodern philosophy, gets shaped by the particularities of time and place, and it is thus very much tradition-dependent; the validity of truth claims is thus limited to particular linguistic communities. In my own evangelical teaching context, I notice a fairly pervasive hesitation of students to claim that their own particular convictions carry weight beyond their personal lives (or, at best, beyond their own cultural or ecclesiastical associations).[3] Trepidation about the imposition of our own viewpoints and fear of the violent enforcement of hegemonic opinions have made us increasingly modest in our truth claims. It is probably not too much to say that modern certainty has given way to postmodern skepticism.[4]

This situation leaves contemporary evangelicals in a dilemma. As I have suggested in chapter 1, younger evangelicals are reacting against the assertive truth claims of earlier generations, which they charge with accepting "modern" notions of truth that were borrowed from mathematical and scientific methods.[5] Younger evangelicals tend to be much more modest in their claims. And they are rightly nervous about treating theology as if it were one of the natural sciences. But this hardly means that a lapse into skepticism or relativism is called for. In fact, the paradoxical argument of this book leads to the conclusion that postmodern skepticism is simply the logical outcome of modern claims of certainty. Such an argument may seem counterintuitive:

3. See David F. Wells, *No Place for Truth; or, Whatever Happened to Evangelical Theology?* (Grand Rapids: Eerdmans, 1993), 168-69.

4. For evangelical discussions on the impact of postmodernism, see Myron B. Penner, ed., *Christianity and the Postmodern Turn: Six Views* (Grand Rapids: Brazos, 2005); James K. A. Smith, *Who's Afraid of Postmodernism? Taking Derrida, Lyotard, and Foucault to Church* (Grand Rapids: Baker Academic, 2006).

5. See Robert E. Webber, *The Younger Evangelicals: Facing the Challenges of the New World* (Grand Rapids: Baker, 2002), 90-92.

skepticism would hardly seem to follow from certainty. Nonetheless, if we start with the observation that the "revolt of nature" isolated the realm of nature from the supernatural, it is easy enough to see the link between modern and postmodern approaches to truth.

Modernity arrived at truth by taking its starting point in "pure nature" (whether that be disembodied mathematical equations or abstract, repeatable experiments). Such a realm of "pure nature" was, in principle, shorn of any connection with the supernatural: the unity of the tapestry had unraveled and finally been cut. Truth, therefore, in the natural realm was forced to stand on its own two feet. The eternal Word of God (the Logos) no longer provided support for human truth claims. As long as the celebration of this independence from God and from the church was in full swing, everything seemed to go along well. In the end, however, a sobering realization set in that a purely natural truth was unable to provide its own support: truth was in need of at least *some* kind of transcendence to uphold its claims. In other words, postmodern relativism unmasked the vacuity of modern claims of certainty: the emperor had no clothes.

The dilemma we now face, while serious, is by no means without resolution. If it is true that the spurious certainty of modernity resulted from the late medieval undoing of the Platonist-Christian synthesis, then we may expect that the Great Tradition offers resources that allow for the recovery of a solid grounding of human truth claims, a grounding that avoids both the Scylla of modern presumption and the Charybdis of postmodern abdication. In order to show how this may be the case, I will turn to three Jesuit scholars from Fourvière. First, I will describe how Henri de Lubac and Jean Daniélou appropriated a premodern sacramental view of truth. Then I will trace the way Henri Bouillard turned to the doctrine of analogy to provide theological support for this participatory account of truth. We will see that each of these *nouvelle* theologians avoided the modern exaltation of human reason without lapsing into the danger of relativism.

Mystical Knowledge: De Lubac, Daniélou, and Gregory of Nyssa

We have already encountered de Lubac's book *Corpus mysticum*, when we examined the relationship between Eucharist and church in chapter 6.

The overall argument of de Lubac's book, I pointed out there, was to recover the unity of the threefold body of Christ.[6] The connection between the historical and sacramental body, on the one hand, and the
ecclesial body, on the other hand, had been severed especially via the
Berengarian controversy of the eleventh century. This disconnect implied that the eucharistic body no longer participated in the greater sacramental reality of the unity of the church. De Lubac's aim was to reconnect Eucharist and church and thereby to restore the "mystery" of the
church to its proper place as the *telos* of the eucharistic celebration.

De Lubac's argument has implications beyond the Eucharist and the
church. If the connection between the two is a sacramental one, it implies
that much more is going on in the Eucharist than the reception of
Christ's body by individual believers. Participation in the sacramental
body of Christ means that the believers themselves are mystically transformed into the ecclesial body of Christ. De Lubac was convinced that
both Berengar's denial of "real presence" and the Catholic reaction that
strongly emphasized transubstantiation suffered from the same problem: both had lost a sense of sacramental mystery, the fact that the "real
presence" in the Eucharist mysteriously makes present the reality of
Christ in his body, the church. An intellectualist hardening had taken
hold of both Berengar and his opponents. The former focused strictly on
the reality *(res)* of the spiritual unity of the church, while the latter paid
attention only to what happened to the elements *(sacramentum)* of the
Eucharist. Both had lost sight, to some degree, of the mysterious nature
of the sacramental unity that existed between Eucharist and church.

De Lubac forcefully presents his charge of intellectualism in the last
chapter of his book, which is entitled "From Symbolism to Dialectic."
There he intimates that the changes in the eleventh and twelfth centuries were part of a much larger shift, a shift in theological methodology
from symbolism to dialectic. Or, we might say, it was a shift from a sacramental entry into the mystery of God to a syllogistic mastering of rational truths. De Lubac argues that the separation between Eucharist
and church was the result of a modern rationalist mindset that had
transformed "symbolic inclusions" into "dialectical antitheses." Both
Berengar and his Catholic opponents had taken for granted the ill-
conceived separation between the eucharistic body and the ecclesial
body. And the cause of this was the way both sides approached the

6. See chap. 6 above, under subheading "The Threefold Body."

nature of theological discourse itself. Berengar, de Lubac maintains, had introduced a dialectical, syllogistic approach to theology. This rationalist approach proved unable to affirm the mystery of the "mutual immanence" between the presence of Christ in the Eucharist and his presence in the unity of the church. According to de Lubac, a new mentality, a new way of thinking, and new categories were emerging and catching people's interests. He points directly to Saint Anselm and Peter Abelard (1079-1142) as the ones responsible for changing the sacramental approach of Augustine. De Lubac obviously laments the resulting Christian rationalism that now began to approach the mysteries of faith mainly by means of intellectual demonstration.[7] Whereas the earlier sacramental symbolism had regarded truth as participation in divine mystery, the new rationalist dialectics maintained that truth meant complete rational comprehension of propositional statements. De Lubac had little doubt that this modern dialectical approach had also infiltrated the Neo-Thomist Scholasticism that was prevalent in early twentieth-century Catholicism. Neo-Thomism, in other words, was able to thrive because, with the tapestry undone, truth had been reduced to the autonomous claims of a universally shared rationality.

Jean Daniélou was quite sympathetic to these criticisms voiced by his former teacher; as a result, he sharply critiqued the separation between theology and life that he observed in Scholastic thought.[8] Daniélou also followed de Lubac in his *ressourcement* of the church fathers and Scripture. He became particularly interested in the mystical theology of Saint Gregory of Nyssa, about whom he published a number of books and articles. One of Daniélou's books on Gregory was an anthology in which he collected some of the most interesting sections of the Cappadocian's well-known writings, such as *The Life of Moses, Commentary on the Song of Songs, On Virginity,* and *Homilies on the Beatitudes.*[9] Daniélou wrote a per-

---

7. Henri de Lubac, *Corpus Mysticum: The Eucharist and the Church in the Middle Ages: Historical Survey,* trans. Gemma Simmonds with Richard Price and Christopher Stephens, ed. Laurence Paul Hemming and Susan Frank Parsons (London: SCM, 2006), 226, 228, 236-38.

8. See esp. Jean Daniélou, "Les Orientations présentes de la pensée religieuses," *Études* 249 (1946): 5-21.

9. Gregory of Nyssa, *From Glory to Glory: Texts from Gregory of Nyssa's Mystical Writings,* intro. by Jean Daniélou, ed. and trans. Herbert Musurillo (1961; reprint, Crestwood, NY: St. Vladimir's Seminary Press, 2001). Hereafter, page references to this work appear in parentheses in the text.

ceptive introduction to this anthology in which he outlines some of the major themes of the fourth-century theologian's mystical writings. Daniélou makes clear in his introduction that, for Gregory, knowledge of God was an important theological theme. At the same time, this knowledge had precious little in common with modern truth claims: (1) Gregory's knowledge was not merely rational in character; (2) it was limited by its inability to grasp the essence of God; and (3) it progressed infinitely. First, Gregory points to the suprarational character of mystical knowledge by insisting that the ascent of Moses proceeded by way of three steps: his vision of God began with light; after that God spoke to him in a cloud; and finally, Moses saw God in darkness (p. 23). The first way, the way of light, was the way of purgation, in which the soul struggled against the passions. The second way, the way of the cloud, allowed the believer to come to knowledge of God by means of the senses. The objects of the created order gave access to God himself. Abraham, for instance, "gained a yearning to gaze upon the archetypal Beauty" by observing the beauty of the world around him (p. 120). Gregory obviously valued the knowledge of God's beauty. In particular, the reflection of God in the purified soul gave a kind of knowledge — albeit obscure in character — of God himself. The soul mirrored the beauty of God:

> So it is that the soul that has been purified by the Word and has put off all sin, receives within itself the circular form of the Sun and shines now with this reflected light. Hence the Word says to her: You have become fair because you have come near to my light, and by this closeness to me you have attracted this participation in beauty. (p. 171)

Gregory's term "participation" is a significant one. It indicates that the soul did not simply have an external or nominal connection with God, but that it was privileged to enjoy a real, heavenly participation in the life of God.

Paradoxically, Gregory describes the most intimate union with God (the third way) as an entry into darkness. The soul, Gregory explains,

> keeps on going deeper until by the operation of the spirit it penetrates the invisible and incomprehensible, and it is there that it sees God. The true vision and the true knowledge of what we seek consists precisely in not seeing, in an awareness that our goal tran-

scends all knowledge and is everywhere cut off from us by the darkness of incomprehensibility. Thus that profound evangelist, John, who penetrated into this luminous darkness, tells us that *no man hath seen God at any time* (John 1.18), teaching us by this negation that no man — indeed, no created intellect — can attain a knowledge of God. (p. 118)

Gregory, who had a predilection for paradoxical expressions, speaks of "luminous darkness" to describe the goal of the mystical life. Clearly, this goal is not just an intellectual knowledge of God. The goal, Gregory suggests, transcends all knowledge because the "darkness of incomprehensibility" means that the goal lies beyond us. No one is able to attain knowledge of God, the Cappadocian father declares boldly.

Second, for Gregory, human knowledge is limited because it is unable to grasp the essence of God. We have already seen that, in a real sense, for Gregory human discourse is unable to grasp the truth of God. Hence, Gregory observes that the injunction of Ecclesiastes that there is "a time to be silent and a time to speak" (Eccles. 3:7) prioritizes silence over speech. This observation provides occasion to reflect on the transcendence of God, which far exceeds the human ability to express in words:

> [I]n the present text I think that silence is mentioned first because human speech finds it impossible to express that reality which transcends all thought and every concept, which the soul that has been torn from evil constantly seeks, and to which it yearns to be united once it has been found. And he who obstinately tries to express it in words, unconsciously offends God. For He Who is believed to transcend the universe must surely transcend speech. (p. 126)

For Gregory, the essence of God is beyond human comprehension, and this is the ultimate reason for human silence. Observation of the created order and of the purified soul may give some degree of knowledge of God. But God himself remains beyond human ken. Gregory thus had a real sense of humility with regard to the human ability to know God. He was, Daniélou explains, ultimately a negative, or "apophatic," theologian, for whom positive speech about God finally had to give way to negation (p. 30). For Gregory, "the man who thinks that God can be known does not really have life; for he has been falsely diverted from true Being to something devised by his own imagination" (p. 146). While Gregory (an ardent defender of Nicene Trinitarian theology) in no way discourages the positive naming of God, he always reminds his readers that such naming must be rooted in the humble acknowledgment of the infinite otherness of the incomprehensible God.

Third, Daniélou gives a special highlight to Gregory's doctrine of *epektasis*, which results from his insistence that human knowledge is participatory in character and that it is inadequate because of the incomprehensibility of God's essence. Gregory takes the notion of *epektasis* from Philippians 3:13, where Paul says that he is "straining" *(epekteinomenos)* toward what lies ahead. To Gregory, this means that the soul's ascent into God will never cease. The infinity of God implies that despite our growth in knowledge, God remains beyond our understanding. Thus, according to Gregory, Philippians 3:13 means that

> in our constant participation in the blessed nature of the Good, the graces that we receive at every point are indeed great, but the path that lies beyond our immediate grasp is infinite. This will constantly happen to those who thus share in the divine Goodness, and they will always enjoy a greater and greater participation in grace throughout all eternity. (pp. 211-12)

The infinity of God implies, according to Gregory, that no matter how much we might progress in virtue and thus in the knowledge of God, God always remains greater. In fact, the journey of heavenly participation in no way lessens the distance that still separates the soul from her goal: "Thou art always to the same degree higher and loftier than the faculties of those who are rising" (p. 212).

Daniélou, clearly attracted to the mystical approach that the doctrine of *epektasis* represents, explains that there are two aspects to the soul's progression, both of which are implied in the Greek expression:

> On the one hand, there is a certain contact with God, a real participation, a divinization (Greek *epi:* "at" or "towards"). The soul is, in a true sense, transformed into the divine; it truly participates in the Spirit, the *pneuma*. But God at the same time remains constantly beyond, and the soul must always go out of itself (Greek *ek:* "out of") — or, rather, it must continually go beyond the stage it has reached to make a further discovery. (p. 59)

Daniélou recognized that Gregory's approach to human truth claims about God implies real heavenly participation, while at the same time it retains infinite divine transcendence.

Gregory's approach is a wonderful example of the Platonist-Christian synthesis I have discussed throughout this book. But the question remains: How can one uphold participation and transcendence at the same time? We have already observed that modernity's truth claims left little room for mystery and transcendence. And the Neo-Thomist theology that de Lubac and Daniélou opposed was hardly positively inclined toward *nouvelle théologie*'s retrieval of Eastern fathers such as Gregory of Nyssa. De Lubac and Daniélou were convinced that the Neo-Thomist suspicion of their *ressourcement* project could be traced to the intellectualism that bedeviled the Scholastic tradition. For Scholastic theology, the eternal dogmatic truths of God had come down to earth, and a proper theology would be able to grasp this dogmatic deposit adequately — as evidenced in the dogmas of the church. These, the Neo-Thomists were convinced, properly corresponded to divine truth itself. But while Scholastic theology was strong on positive truth claims, it was less clear that it had inherited Gregory's apophatic humility. For Scholastic theology, knowledge was less about entering into truth than it was about comprehending truth.

Nouvelle théologie's Neo-Thomist detractors viewed the retrieval of the Platonist-Christian synthesis with suspicion. Truth, according to the leading Neo-Thomist, Réginald Garrigou-Lagrange (1877-1964), was correspondence between object and intellect *(adaequatio rei et intellectus)*.[10] Either a human statement did correspond to reality or it did not. Paradoxical language like "luminous darkness" and statements that seemed to exalt silence over speech did not sit well with the Scholastic Catholic establishment. The Neo-Thomists were convinced that, beneath *nouvelle théologie*'s retrieval of the church fathers, they could discern the subjectivist focus on human experience that the eighteenth-century philosopher Immanuel Kant (1724-1804) had introduced into theology. By focusing on the human experience of faith rather than the propositional character of truth, theologians such as de Lubac and Daniélou surrendered the dogmatic contents of the

---

10. On Garrigou, see Richard Peddicord, *The Sacred Monster of Thomism: An Introduction to the Life and Legacy of Réginald Garrigou-Lagrange* (South Bend, IN: St. Augustine's, 2005).

truth of the gospel. In other words, it was *nouvelle théologie,* not Neo-Scholasticism, that capitulated to modernity.

Henri Bouillard's Analogy of Truth

While the Neo-Thomist accusations against *nouvelle théologie* were understandable, they were largely unfounded. The Neo-Thomist accusation of collusion with modernity failed to recognize the significance of one important element that permeated many of the writings of *nouvelle théologie:* the notion of "analogy of truth" *(analogia veritatis).* This notion is a sacramental principle that serves to underscore two things: on the one hand, it means that, just like a sacrament, human discourse participates in divine truth, so that God's truth is really present in the dogmatic statements of the church; on the other hand, it also means that, just as with a sacrament, the mystery of divine truth infinitely transcends the human words themselves. In other words, *nouvelle théologie*'s "analogy of truth" reflected Gregory's approach: the notion implies real heavenly participation, while at the same time it retains infinite divine transcendence.

So, what exactly did the *nouvelle* theologians mean by "analogy of truth"? In chapter 4, I discussed a more common concept, that of "analogy of being" *(analogia entis).*[11] There we saw that the Great Tradition wanted to make clear that it did have serious reservations about the pantheism of the Platonic tradition. "Analogy of being" means that the being of creation is similar or analogous to the being of God, while at the same time there is an infinite difference between Creator and creature. The connection between Creator and creature is *only* sacramental in character: the infinite difference between God and creature remains. The "analogy of truth" notion maintains that one can speak not only of an analogous or sacramental relationship between the *being* of God and that of the creature, but also of an analogous or sacramental relationship between the *truth* of God and of the creature. Indeed, one could say of each of the three eternal transcendentals — truth, goodness, and beauty — that they are reflected in earthly truth, goodness, and beauty. Put differently, human truth, goodness, and beauty participate sacramentally in heavenly truth, goodness, and beauty.[12]

---

11. See chap. 4, under subheading "Scotus and Univocity of Being."

12. The notion of analogous truth can be found in several of the precursors to *nou-*

Nouvelle théologie's notion of "analogy of truth" is not just an abstract way of explaining the relationship between divine and human truth. The notion had traction with regard to particular theological issues, as became clear from Henri Bouillard's *Conversion et grâce chez S. Thomas d'Aquin* (1944), in which de Lubac's younger colleague at the Jesuit Fourvière scholasticate advances several quite controversial ideas about Thomas Aquinas's theology.[13] In particular, Bouillard's interpretation seems to put question marks behind transubstantiation and the priority of the divine initiative in justifying grace. We don't need to concern ourselves with these particular theological issues here, important though they may be. What is of interest is the way Bouillard defends his theological moves. He was, of course, well aware that Neo-Scholastic theologians would be worried that he was attempting to change established Catholic dogma, which would be unthinkable to them. How could truth — as correspondence between object and intellect — change? In particular, if the church was the recipient of God's own, eternal truth, then what right did a young Jesuit scholar from Fourvière have to change it?

Bouillard did have some sympathy with these concerns. He was not a postmodern relativist for whom truth was entirely dependent on one's historical and cultural context. Such skepticism, Bouillard realized, would cut the link between eternal, divine truth and temporal, human truth claims. Put philosophically, we could say that such a view regards human knowledge of God as purely equivocal: there is no correspondence whatsoever between the language that we use about God and the reality of God himself. Such equivocity, says Bouillard in agreement with the Neo-Thomists, would render dogmatic truth claims impossible. Or, at the very least, dogmatic truth claims would then be entirely limited to our sublunary horizons, and the church would be unable to make any positive, enduring truth claims on which one could rely because they result from divine revelation. To be sure, one might try to defend such equivocity with an appeal to Gregory's apophatic, or negative, statements about God, but Gregory's humility before the incomprehensible God never prevented him from claiming

---

velle théologie (Maurice Blondel, Pierre Rousselot, and Joseph Maréchal), as well as in Louis Charlier, Marie-Dominique Chenu, Henri Bouillard, Jean-Marie Le Blond, and Hans Urs von Balthasar. See Boersma, "Analogy of Truth."

13. Henri Bouillard, *Conversion et grâce chez S. Thomas d'Aquin: Étude historique*, Théologie, no. 1 (Paris: Aubier, 1944).

that we do, in some sense, have access to God — that, in fact, the soul enjoys a heavenly participation in God. Equivocity is quite different from Gregory's apophaticism: it is the postmodern outcome of the cutting of the cosmic tapestry.

But Bouillard was not convinced that the Neo-Thomist alternative to equivocity was itself faithful to the Great Tradition. The intellectualism of the Scholastic tradition seemed to him a little too confident of the human ability to comprehend truth — and particularly, to comprehend *divine* truth. It was one thing to insist that there was a link between God's eternal truth and our temporal truth claims, but Bouillard was nervous that the Neo-Thomists, by emphasizing this link, were losing sight of the infinite difference between the two. After all, any claim that human knowledge was a full and adequate rendering of divine self-knowledge would be the height of superciliousness. Human beings could never claim to comprehend fully the truth of God, even if one accounted for the fact that we were dealing with divine revelation and with the church's officially proclaimed dogmatic statements of truth. The Neo-Thomist confidence regarding the adequacy of human truth claims seemed out of line with a Platonist-Christian perspective like that of Gregory, who had maintained that "true knowledge of what we seek consists precisely in not seeing."

The Neo-Thomists appeared to jump from the one extreme to the other, from equivocity to univocity: they did not seem to acknowledge a differentiation between human knowledge and divine knowledge, but regarded the church's dogmatic statements as true in the same way that God's eternal truth was true. Throughout the era of the Great Tradition, theologians had shied away from such univocal truth claims. Along with his respected colleague, Henri de Lubac, Bouillard realized that such univocal truth claims were the result of the modern eclipse of mystery. Once symbolism had given way to dialectic, the participatory approach to truth was lost to a univocal approach according to which truth was something to be mastered.

The question that Bouillard and other *nouvelle* theologians faced was a difficult one: Was there really a way out of the dilemma between the imperious attitude of univocity and the skeptical abdication of equivocity?[14] To express it differently, how could one articulate theo-

---

14. Thomas G. Guarino deals with this dilemma in a lucid exposition in *Foundations of Systematic Theology* (New York: T. & T. Clark, 2005), 239-53.

logically the earlier Platonist-Christian approach of theologians such as Gregory of Nyssa? Bouillard and others believed that the traditional doctrine of analogy offered a genuine alternative. Jean-Marie Le Blond was one of the theologians who came to Bouillard's defense as the battle over his book was joined.[15] Le Blond maintained that, just as one could speak of analogy of being *(analogia entis),* so one could also speak of analogy of truth *(analogia veritatis)* — and, for that matter, of analogy of goodness and of beauty. This meant concretely that even the masterful system of Thomas Aquinas was not identical to divine truth itself. There was no univocal relationship between human and divine truth. Any human articulation of truth was *only* an analogous participation in divine truth. While divine revelation certainly allowed one to make positive statements about God, such truth claims did not yield true knowledge in the same sense that God's self-knowledge was true knowledge. The doctrine of analogy, while positing a similarity, was meant to uphold the infinite difference between Creator and creature.

Therefore, an infinite difference obtained between truth as it was in God himself and truth as creatures were able to apprehend it. Bouillard succinctly describes his alternative approach as follows: "If one and the same revealed truth is expressed in different systems (Augustinian, Thomist, Suarézian, etc.), the various notions that one uses to translate it are neither 'equivocal' (or else one would no longer speak of the same thing), nor 'univocal' (otherwise all the systems would be identical), but 'analogous', that is to say that they express the same reality in a different way."[16] In other words, Bouillard argues that "analogy of truth" represents a third way, a way that avoids the pitfalls both of equivocity and of univocity.

Bouillard articulates the difference between truth as it is in God and truth as it is found here below by distinguishing between eternal "affirmations" and temporal "representations": "History . . . manifests at the same time the relativity of notions, of schemes in which theology takes shape, and the permanent affirmation that governs them. It is necessary to know the temporal condition of theology and, at the same time, to offer with regard to the faith the absolute affirmation, the divine

15. Jean-Marie Le Blond, "L'Analogie de la vérité: Réflexion d'un philosophe sur une controverse théologique," *Recherches de science religieuse* 34 (1947): 129-41.

16. Henri Bouillard, "Notions conciliaires et analogie de la vérité," *Recherches de science religieuse* 35 (1948): 254.

Word that has become incarnate."[17] Bouillard maintains that it was possible to articulate the same eternal affirmations by means of different representations. This means, he believes, that theology is not always and necessarily bound to particular expressions that the church has used in the past. Twentieth-century French theologians lived in different cultural circumstances than did those of thirteenth-century Paris. As a result, Bouillard believes, today's theologians were called to use different representations to express the same unalterable and eternal affirmations.

Bouillard's approach was surrounded by pitfalls, and it is easy to see why his Neo-Thomist detractors were nervous. Let's assume that the Platonist-Christian tradition had it right and that human truth statements do indeed sacramentally participate in God's truth. This means that there is a "real presence" of divine affirmations in our human representations. Doctrinal language is, as it were, caught up with (even if it doesn't fully grasp) divine truth. Therefore, any change in our human representations will raise the question of what this change does to their relationship with the eternal divine affirmation. For example, while Catholics would not maintain that the philosophical Aristotelian distinction between substance and accidents is Christian dogma, the language of "transubstantiation" is nonetheless closely caught up in the Catholic doctrine of the Eucharist. Changing the representation (the discourse of "transubstantiation") inevitably leads to the question of how this might affect the eternal affirmation of divine truth. Likewise, the creeds use Greek philosophical terms — "nature" *(ousia)* and "person" *(hypostasis)* — to express Trinitarian doctrine. The creeds do not mean to cast the particular philosophical distinction between universals *(ousia)* and particulars *(hypostasis)* in stone; at the same time, however, any change in terminology would affect what Bouillard calls the eternal "affirmation." Sacramental participation of human discourse in God's own truth means that human language is sacred and must be treated with the utmost care that it deserves. The difficulty is that there doesn't appear to be a distinct method that, from the outset, ensures a safe outcome.

Immersed as they were in the mystical theology of the Great Tradition, de Lubac, Daniélou, and Bouillard were unwilling to abandon the sacramental approach to truth that they discovered there. What they

17. Bouillard, *Conversion et grâce,* 220-21.

found in theologians such as Gregory of Nyssa was a remarkable combination of (1) a positive insistence on human truth claims — based on the real participation of human statements of truth in the eternal truth of God; and (2) an acknowledgment that the eternal truth of God infinitely transcends any truth claims we might make, based on the fact that the mystery of the sacramental reality *(res)* far transcends the particularity of human discourse *(sacramentum)*. To be sure, this "third way" of analogous participation in divine truth is not an easy path to chart. Some might be tempted to subvert it into relativism by separating human representations from divine affirmation. Others might be tempted to undermine it by insisting on a static identity between the two. Despite these difficulties, the Platonist-Christian tradition was attractive to *nouvelle théologie* because it appeared to do justice to the sacramental reality of the cosmos.

I believe it is a propitious time for evangelicals to turn to *nouvelle théologie*'s view of truth as a sacramental reality that lies anchored in the truth of the eternal Word of God. The certainty of the Cartesian and Baconian methods may long have held sway in Western culture. More and more, however, evangelicals are realizing that the univocal view of truth implied in these methods is deeply problematic — and most certainly unfitting for theological discourse that aims at the mystery of God. At the same time, it would be a tragic mistake for evangelicals to veer off into the equivocity of postmodern skepticism. A bold retrieval of the Platonist-Christian synthesis offers a genuine way out of the current dilemma evangelicalism faces. Furthermore, such a *ressourcement* would be a most welcome ecumenical opportunity. It goes without saying that, despite their sacramental heritage, contemporary Catholics face many of the same challenges that evangelicals face. At times, the post-Vatican II pluralism in Catholicism seems to stretch the connection between representations and affirmations to the breaking point, and thus are Catholics no strangers to postmodern equivocity. A common search for a renewed articulation of a sacramental view of truth would go a long way toward fostering mutual recognition between Catholics and evangelicals.

CHAPTER 10

Theology as Sacramental Discipline

One of my favorite movies is Gabriel Axel's *Babette's Feast* (1987). It tells the story of a French cook who, by reason of circumstances in the French-German War of 1870-71, ends up in a reclusive and ingrown Lutheran sect on the remote Danish coast of Jutland. Something is clearly awry in the sect. Life is not as it should be. The rugged physical shape of the Danish landscape symbolizes the harsh realities of the community, in which time appears to have torn relationships, and in which ascetic practices, separated from the religious focus of the community's founder, have made people lose their vision of a life that is true, good, and beautiful. The small hamlet should be a paradise of fellowship. Instead, gossip, hatred, sexual infidelity, intolerance, fraud, and theft have incapacitated the community. The members of the tiny village consider earthly love "of scant worth and merely empty illusion," says the film's narrator.[1]

Few places seem more inhospitable or unlikely for a French chef than this small sectarian community; nonetheless, it is the place that Babette gets catapulted into. Martina and Philippa, daughters of the sect's founder (whose names are feminine tributes to Martin Luther and Philip Melanchthon), warmly welcome the bedraggled stranger into their home as their guest — even though her place is to be the maid of the house. While Martina and Philippa are aware that their

---

1. I have discussed the eucharistic implications of *Babette's Feast* in *Violence, Hospitality, and the Cross: Reappropriating the Atonement Tradition* (Grand Rapids: Baker Academic, 2004), 219-20.

guest is able to cook, they do not realize that, in her former life, she was the master chef of Café Anglais, the most prestigious restaurant in Paris. Babette enters the tiny Lutheran village as stranger and guest, but she ends up organizing a lavish French dinner for the villagers. In her own self-denying love, Babette gives every last penny of the money she has won in a lottery to express her gratitude to the group of people who, despite their internal animosity, have accepted her as one of their own. The dinner not only involves a remarkable role reversal — in which the stranger, Babette, paradoxically initiates the community into a life of joyous sacramental participation *(koinōnia)* — but also throws into disarray their engrained asceticism. In the words of one of the dinner guests, Babette demonstrates her ability to "transform a dinner into a kind of love affair that made no distinction between bodily appetite and spiritual appetite."[2] The love and care that Babette offers in this sumptuous feast become the occasion for the villagers to deal with their mutual grievances and to offer each other forgiveness and reconciliation. Much of the film is taken up by the delicate intricacies of the meal itself, through which the twelve disciples of the community undergo their transformation.

Comparing the discipline of theology to the person of Babette is a precarious endeavor. On the one hand, some may wish to point out that Babette arrives in Denmark as a bedraggled refugee, and, making the analogy to theology, they will insist that theology, too, has become a rather worn-out and disheveled figure. Doesn't theology resemble Babette, who has long forgotten her former glory as a master of Parisian cuisine? After all, how long has it been since theology has occupied the place Thomas Aquinas assigned to her by referring to her as "queen of the sciences" *(regina scientiarum)*? Furthermore, doesn't the cultural captivity of evangelicalism pose a serious threat to the movement's future well-being?[3]

2. The comment is made by General Löwenhielm during the dinner that Babette has prepared. Löwenhielm, the twelfth guest, is actually an outsider to the community; indeed, he clearly behaves like a stranger throughout the meal. He has led a sophisticated life and is familiar with the intricacies of Parisian cuisine, so he is the only one who truly appreciates the generous character of the meal. This outsider is needed to complete the community (as a community of twelve) and to assist them in their transformation, even as he himself also comes to see his life in an entirely new perspective.

3. See David F. Wells, *Above All Earthly Pow'rs: Christ in a Postmodern World* (Grand Rapids: Eerdmans, 2005).

On the other hand, there will be those who may wish to focus, instead, on the restoration of Babette's former glory. She has retained a connection with her Parisian past in the form of a lottery ticket, which a friend in Paris has renewed for her from year to year. When she receives a letter in the mail, indicating that she has won the lottery, her position suddenly changes: she now has the financial means to host the elaborate meal, which is worth the entire lottery of 10,000 francs. Considering the numerical quantity as well as the academic quality of much contemporary evangelical theology, would it not almost seem that evangelical theology has, so to speak, won the lottery?[4] Though this latter position does have a good deal of truth to it, it seems to me that we would do well not to ignore the cultural captivity that often ties evangelicals far too closely to the desacramentalized ontology of modernity. For theology really to reassume her former position of glory — with the task of leading the faithful into the sacramental participation of the divine life — she needs to have a clear sense of what it is that she has been given to do.

Theology as Twofold Discipline

Faith does not place its hope in the fate of lotteries, but in the providence of a gracious God. Therefore, regardless of the comparisons we may draw between the state of theology and the figure of Babette, there is reason for hope. This chapter is, more than anything else, an exercise based on hope. I give expression here to my hope for what I passionately desire theology may yet again become: a regal figure like Babette that will initiate the faithful into sacramental participation in the eternal Word of God and thus in the life of the triune God. Since I have no illusions about the task that lies ahead, I want to reflect somewhat carefully on the *discipline* of theology in contemporary society.

The word "discipline" has a variety of meanings. According to the *Oxford English Dictionary,* among the most common definitions are the following: (1) "A branch of instruction or education; a department of learning or knowledge; a science or art in its educational aspect." In

---

4. See Alister E. McGrath, *Evangelicalism and the Future of Christianity* (Downers Grove, IL: InterVarsity, 1995); McGrath, *A Passion for Truth: The Intellectual Coherence of Evangelicalism* (Downers Grove, IL: InterVarsity, 1996).

this sense, we may describe theology as a discipline alongside other academic disciplines, such as jurisprudence, medicine, and philosophy. (2) "Instruction having for its aim to form the pupil to proper conduct and action; the training of scholars or subordinates to proper and orderly action by instructing and exercising them in the same; mental and moral training."[5] According to this understanding, we may describe theology as a discipline that trains believers — just as we say of "spiritual disciplines" such as meditation, prayer, fasting, and the like that they train, instruct, and exercise believers in the Christian life. Theology is initiation into the Christian life. Although I am a professional theologian teaching at an academic institution, I am convinced that the first of these two definitions is the one of lesser importance. Without in any way wanting to denigrate the academic character of theology as a discipline, the purpose of this chapter is to show that it can fulfill its proper role only if it takes with utmost seriousness the second way in which it is a discipline. The theologian has the sacred task of initiating others, along with him- or herself, into the Christian life — that is, into the very life of God. In other words, theology as academic instruction leads to theology as moral practice; truth serves goodness; teaching gives life; knowledge implies initiation. Theology fulfills its task as an academic discipline faithfully only if it leads to initiation and thus to Christian virtue.[6]

I want to take my starting point in the second Oxford definition of theology: theology as the discipline of initiating believers in the Christian life by training, instructing, and exercising them mentally and morally. Such a description of discipline fits closely with the Platonist-Christian tapestry whose warp and weft I have described in part 1 of this book. According to this perspective, the natural order has participation in the eternal life of God as its divinely appointed end. Thus, nothing can be more important than initiating people into the Trinitarian life of God: the supernatural end of the beatific vision determines the task of theology as discipline. Of course, such a Platonist-Christian perspective implies, as Andrew Louth rightly emphasizes,

---

5. The two quotations are from "discipline," *OED Online*, 2nd ed., 2009, http://dictionary.oed.com (accessed May 7, 2009).

6. Stanley Hauerwas's theology displays a commendable emphasis on initiation, discipleship, and virtue, though he may not share the sacramental (Platonist-Christian) slant that I give to this. See Hauerwas, "Discipleship as a Craft, Church as a Disciplined Community," *Christian Century* 108, no. 27 (Oct. 1, 1991): 881-84.

that theology is not primarily about words; it is about realities.[7] Theology doesn't thrive in a context where the relationship with God is explained primarily as external or nominal; theology as discipline requires an environment in which we experience the relationship with God as participatory and real. Theology is a sacramental discipline: it is an initiation in which our ordinary created existence is taken up into the truth, goodness, and beauty of the eternal Word of God and thus participates by grace in the triune life of God.

If theology is a sacramental discipline, that means that all the subjects of the four preceding chapters of part 2 inform our understanding of theology: the way we approach Eucharist, tradition, Scripture, and truth gives direction to the process of initiation. The discipline of theology cannot breathe, as it were, without the harmonious cooperation of these four elements. Marie-Dominique Chenu, the great Aquinas scholar and enthusiastic supporter of the revolutionary Parisian worker-priest movement in the years following World War II, reflected particularly carefully on how theology (as initiation) was supposed to connect with each of these four elements. Beginning with his 1920 dissertation on contemplation in Thomas Aquinas,[8] the Dominican's career was marked by consistent reflection on the nature of theology, on the relationship between the contemplative and the active life, and on questions surrounding faith and reason.[9] His book *La Théologie est-elle une science?* (1957) presents a particularly lucid exposition on the nature of theology. The nuanced way Chenu answers the question of his title makes clear that he believed theology could thrive only in the context of an appreciation of the elements of the four previous chapters. This means that, for Chenu, theology was ultimately a sacramental discipline in both of the ways described by the *Oxford English Dictionary*. As I

---

7. Andrew Louth, *Discerning the Mystery: An Essay on the Nature of Theology* (1983; reprint, Oxford: Clarendon/Oxford University Press, 2003), 89: "[T]he heart of the Christian faith is not something simply conceptual: it is a fact, or even better, an action — the action, the movement, of the Son sent into the world for our sakes to draw us back to the Father." Cf. Louth, *Discerning the Mystery*, 74-75.

8. Carmelo Giuseppe Conticello, "*De contemplatione* (Angelicum, 1920): La Thèse inédite du P. M.-D. Chenu," *Revue des sciences philosophiques et théologiques* 75 (1991): 363-422.

9. For an excellent introduction to Chenu's overall thought, see Christophe F. Potworowski, *Contemplation and Incarnation: The Theology of Marie-Dominique Chenu* (Montreal: McGill-Queen's University Press, 2001).

have indicated, it seems to me that many evangelicals do take seriously the first definition of the word "discipline." Going beyond this, however, I want to make a plea for the restoration of theology as a sacramental discipline, something we cannot do without taking the second definition of the word equally seriously.

Chenu's book does not present a detailed discussion of each of the four elements — Eucharist, tradition, Scripture, and truth. He does focus a great deal on the first element, though he does not discuss the Eucharist-church relationship in the way we have seen de Lubac discuss it. Instead, the Dominican from the Saulchoir studium focused on the broader role that liturgy plays in providing the basis for theology. He was convinced that theology found its proper place within the church, because it was in the church's liturgy that one heard the Word that informed theology: "The Church is the spiritual home of the theologian, who finds in her both his material and his light." Furthermore, Chenu argues that the sensible and material signs of the sacraments — "a bath of water, a meal, etc." — were crucial for theology itself: "If . . . we recall that the liturgy is one of the living sources of theology, one of its 'homes', as it were, we may assess how much the symbolic and sacramental expression of the revelation can nourish from within our appreciation of the faith."[10] Theology, for Chenu, is not about abstract, intellectual apprehension; it is reflection on and engagement with what God has done in Christ and continues to do in the church.

Chenu did not examine in any detail the role that tradition played in the discipline of theology. Indeed, Chenu probably emphasized the malleability of the tradition more than any other *nouvelle* theologian; he certainly had the most strongly developed rebellious inclinations. He was quite willing to shed what he considered unnecessary traditional ballast, and it was important to him that the church take seriously the philosophical and social developments of her contemporary context. Chenu often speaks of the "signs of the times," convinced as he was that the church had the duty to connect with them.[11] Whatever

10. In what follows, I will use the English translation: Marie-Dominique Chenu, *Is Theology a Science?* trans. A. H. N. Green-Armytage (New York: Hawthorn, 1959), 43, 84-85. Hereafter, page references to this work appear in parentheses in the text.

11. Cf. Potworowski, *Contemplation and Incarnation*, 171-80. Chenu's repeated appeals to "signs of the times" rendered him vulnerable to the charge of careless accommodation to modernity. Indeed, Chenu was at bottom quite sympathetic to the desacramentalizing of modernity. See my criticism of Chenu in chap. 3, under subheading "Dis-

the tradition was, Chenu certainly did not consider it simply a collection of dead relics from the past. We could even say that, for Chenu, tradition served as the path by which he arrived at his revolutionary spirit. Chenu was a careful medievalist, and his books mine the twelfth and thirteenth centuries in particular for contemporary implications. His study of Aquinas — a *ressourcement* project that opened up new possibilities throughout his life — reinforced his sense that the church could not afford to live in isolation from her cultural context.

The very fact that Chenu's lifelong commitment was to the work of *ressourcement* is nonetheless also evidence of a desire for continuity with the tradition of the church. Precisely because the church's liturgy is theology's primary home, Chenu was keen to regard the tradition as both alive and in continuity with the past:

> I do not find this Word only in archaic and sacred texts which date from an increasingly distant past. I find it today, in the daily reading of the Gospels. I find it in the Church — for the Church, the community of believers, is a real and visible society linked to Christ by the apostolic succession, the store-house and dispensary of the revelation, and the dwelling-place of the Spirit according to Christ's promise. (p. 43)

For Chenu, the tradition is something received today, by way of the visible church, that is linked to the past through apostolic succession. In this light, it is hardly surprising that Chenu — repeatedly and vehemently — rejects the division between what Catholics often call "positive" and "Scholastic" theology, with the former focusing on the historical sources of Scripture and tradition, and the latter on doctrinal elaboration. Chenu considers this separation a post-Reformation "blunder" (p. 45), and he believes that it led to problems in both fields: "historicism" among positive theologians (naturalism or immanentism, we might also call it) and "theologism" among Scholastic theologians (supernaturalism or extrinsicism, we might say) (p. 118). It is not surprising, then, that Chenu's reflections on the nature of theology are peppered with historical references. Chenu did not believe he could do theology without the tradition of the church.

---

covery of Nature." As we will see below, Chenu nonetheless had a deep sympathy for a Platonist-Christian approach to theology, and his book on the nature of theology presents an excellent way forward.

Chenu's plea for a reintegration of positive and Scholastic theology meant that not only tradition, but also Scripture itself, should be central in the theological discipline. Chenu makes comments about the role of Scripture that should warm the heart of any evangelical Christian. The Scriptures, Chenu observes,

> are not for the theologian a mere preliminary to his real work, preceding it and outside of it, the raw material which he will have to bring to a kind of abstract maturity. The study of Scripture is not, as has sometimes been said, a science auxiliary to theology; rather is it its very soul, alive and always fresh. Indeed, history shows us in the most striking manner that a return to the Gospel has always been rejuvenating and cleansing for theology and the awakenings it has caused were not the result of external pressure but were inner awakenings of theological contemplation itself, as also in the teaching of the faith. (pp. 43-44)

Chenu had a deep-seated passion for Scripture to function as the soul of theology. Hence, he highlights the fact that in medieval universities the "masters" of theology were not just "professors." They were engaged in "a complete energizing of the Word of God," which involved *legere* (the exegesis of Scripture), *disputare* (the working out of the questions one would ask of Scripture), and *predicare* (the preaching of Scripture). In short, theology as sacred teaching *(sacra doctrina)* requires grounding in the sacred word *(sacra pagina)* (p. 98). Chenu goes as far as to say: "Theology was literally biblical. The basic text for a master's degree in theology was the Bible. St Thomas, in his magisterial thesis, commented on the Bible" (p. 94). Chenu does not go into detail about biblical interpretive issues of the kind I looked into in chapter 8. Impressed as he was with the historical method,[12] he often expresses his distaste of what he considered excessive allegorizing, especially in the High Middle Ages.[13] But whatever the interpretive approach, there can be no doubt that theology, for Chenu, was not an abstract Scholastic discipline, separate from the Bible. The entire discipline of theology is based on and takes its contents from sacred Scripture.

---

12. Cf. Potworowski, *Contemplation and Incarnation*, 98-113.

13. At the same time, Chenu also realized the limitations of the historical method: without faith, a "purely critical reading of the text of Scripture . . . would be a mere nibbling at the rind (St Gregory)" (Chenu, *Is Theology a Science?* 24).

Finally, Chenu's understanding of theology relies on an intimate, sacramental link between human and divine truth. Chenu was convinced that one could not have a "pure" theology, stripped of its historical association with Greek philosophy. Listing a number of well-known patristic and medieval theologians, Chenu declares:

> To be sure there are some people who would like to purge away the philosophies of these masters, calling them Platonist or Aristotelian blemishes on the purity of their Christian spirituality. But this is the same old error — of regarding theology as something outside the faith, banished by its intellectualism from the very realm of faith; whereas it is in truth produced within the human mind by the very incarnation of that faith. (pp. 50-51)

For Chenu, philosophy and theology were not antithetically opposed to each other. The historical association of theology with Hellenistic philosophy did not in any way remove theology from the faith of the church.

Theology as Initiation

His constant study of Thomas Aquinas meant that Chenu drank deeply from the Platonist-Christian well, especially with regard to his understanding of truth. Theology, Chenu observes, "is a participation in God's own knowledge of himself" (p. 24).[14] This participatory understanding of human truth means, according to Chenu, that one could never "reduce faith to a mere recitation of verbal and conceptual truths accepted in blind obedience" (p. 29). It is difficult not to interpret this comment as a pejorative barb at the intellectualism of the Neo-Thomists. For Chenu, truth is a participatory entry of the believer into God's very own knowledge of himself and of the world. Truth, in other words, is sacramental in character. This implies that every believer's participation in divine knowledge *(scientia divina)* can be described as theology. Theology is the discipline of initiation. "Theology," Chenu maintains in typically Neo-Platonic fashion, "involves an initiation — or, to use the words of Dionysius, untranslatable in the west, the theo-

---

14. Cf. pp. 29 and 122 for nearly identical expressions.

logian is a mystagogue, an initiator" (p. 38).[15] The theologian was a guide leading people to heavenly participation. This is not to deny that Chenu had reservations about the Platonic tradition. He clearly did.[16] But he also recognized that the Great Tradition was, in an important sense, the product of a Platonist-Christian synthesis. Chenu felt a particularly strong attraction to the sixth-century Syrian Neo-Platonist Denys, whom he encountered in Aquinas's writings.[17] For Chenu, we could say, Babette modeled the role of theology: initiation of the community into the divine life of joyous sacramental participation *(koinônia)*.

It will be clear at this point that Chenu's vision of theology was very much in line with the overall vision that I am attempting to recover in this book. We could almost describe Chenu's *Is Theology a Science?* as a commentary on the previous four chapters. More than anything, my attraction to this book by Chenu stems from the way he integrates and balances faith and reason, mystery and concept. Chenu devotes two of the seven chapters of his book to faith and mystery, respectively. In chapter 2, entitled "Understanding the Faith," Chenu argues that faith is "pregnant" with theology (p. 33). As a result, faith rests in God, not just in concepts about God. Chenu beautifully expresses the aim of theology in the following quotation:

> Consider first the fertility of the object. In a revelation where the light of faith puts me on a level with his transcendence and initiates me into his mystery and incarnate mercy, the living God, the living truth, becomes for me not a mere mental object; he offers himself as a gift from the spirit in an ever more intimate communion, welcomed by love. (pp. 30-31)

For Chenu, the aim of theology's discipline was "intimate communion," which he also expressed rather evangelically as an "inner personal relationship" (p. 31). Thus, in chapter 3 of *Is Theology a Science?*

15. In reliance on Denys, Chenu often spoke of theology as "initiation." See, e.g., Chenu, *Is Theology a Science?* 30, 33n4, 63.

16. This is especially clear from Chenu's emphasis on history and his opposition to the Augustinian body-soul dualism. Cf. Potworowski, *Contemplation and Incarnation,* 85-98.

17. Chenu's positive references to Platonism were fairly limited. His admiration for Denys, however, coruscates from the pages of many of his writings. See Chenu, *Is Theology a Science?* 23, 33, 38-39, 58, 76, 84, 88.

(entitled "Theology and Mystery"), Chenu reiterates that theology depends on the life of faith and is really the expression of one's spirituality: "It is in prayer and adoration, and in the profoundest sense of the word devotion, that theology, the understanding of the Word of God, is born and lives" (p. 41).[18] If faith is the soil in which theology can grow, mystery is its aim. So, even though Chenu speaks of God as the "object" of theology, he is quite aware of the limitations of the term: "The very word 'object' is philosophically awkward and does not fit the Absolute to the letter. He is, in fact, literally super-natural; and therefore even when this communion of love which his grace concedes me is fully realized, God will remain incomprehensible until I meet him face to face" (p. 39). Chenu very much felt at home in the Platonist-Christian world of negative theology, which was embodied by Gregory of Nyssa, Denys, and others.

Still, Chenu's focus on faith and mystery does not imply a disregard for reason and concept; on the contrary, it would not be inappropriate to describe his book as a defense of theology as a science. To be sure, when Chenu uses the word "science," he does not have in mind the contemporary connotation of the "natural sciences," based on a particular method. Primarily he has in mind the Thomist notion of knowledge *(scientia)* of God (p. 31). And, as we have already seen, Chenu regards this human knowledge as a participation in God's own knowledge: science is mystical in character. For Chenu, however, the mystical character of theology does not preclude a significant rational component. The focus on faith and mystery does not come at the cost of reason and concept. While the discipline of theology means that it is initiation, it can also take the form of an academic discipline. The paradoxical combination of these seemingly mutually exclusive elements is possible because of the paradox of the Incarnation:

> The same law which once made us ask for the incarnation of God's Word in human words and on the stage of history now makes us accept in full the whole corpus of knowledge which this incarnation must imply. Theology is at one with the theandric mystery of

18. In 1937, Chenu wrote a book on the nature of theology in which he describes the discipline as a spirituality based on religious experience (*Une école de théologie: Le Saulchoir* [Kain-Lez-Tournai: Le Saulchoir, 1937]). This book caused him a great deal of trouble from the dominant school of Neo-Thomism. See Potworowski, *Contemplation and Incarnation,* 46-55.

the Word of God, the Word made flesh. There alone can it dare to find confidence in the coherence of faith and reason. (p. 50)

Chenu looks to the theandric (divine-human) mystery of the Incarnation, and he observes in it the coming together of the supernatural with the natural world, and thus the confluence of faith and reason.

Faith, therefore, is not simply a supernatural element, strangely out of place in the human. Even though God's gift of faith is a "total gift," it does become "human property." Faith is a human habit *(habitus)*, a "virtue" that becomes "embedded" in human nature. "Faith has its dwelling within reason," Chenu notes, "and it is thus entitled to 'theologize'. . ." (p. 49). As a result, theology naturally strives toward an understanding of the faith. Saint Anselm was right, therefore, to define faith as a quest for understanding *(fides quaerens intellectum)*. Studying theology is the "healthy act of a faith whose appetite, like a physical appetite, is the measure of a healthy constitution" (p. 35).

Chenu even goes so far as to applaud the medieval rise of theological systems, understanding by the word "system" "a logical whole, planned architecturally, wherein the various elements are so disposed as to knit together and buttress the entire structure" (p. 100). While cautioning against the exaltation of particular systems to the level of divine truth, Chenu believes that such excesses do not render theological systems suspect in and of themselves. Instead, he argues that "the truth of reason and the truth of faith are better and more truly served by maintaining theological systems in their full integrity — while recognizing, of course, in all orthodoxy, the relativity of each system in regard to the absolute truth of faith" (p. 104). As long as one recognizes the relativity of the various theological systems — including the Thomist system, though it is second to none (pp. 111-13) — systematization of the faith witnesses to the health of an ardent faith commitment. The discipline of theology as initiation legitimately gives rise to theology as an academic discipline.

The Unity of the Discipline

Chenu's integration of mystery and concept, as well as of faith and reason, is really a plea for a reintegration of academic theology. Chenu is suspicious of any dualism between wisdom *(sapientia)* and science *(scientia)*. He recognizes that a straightforward reduction of theology to science will be problematic: "A science holds no jot of mystery" (p. 119). But Chenu is equally unhappy with Augustine's restriction of theology to wisdom. Augustine's approach, he believes, ignores the fact that "wisdom . . . is not to be attained by turning out of doors all the manifold sciences of this world" (p. 121). The faithful theologian will attempt to reach the aim of *sapientia* precisely by means of *scientia*. The highest aim of theology is no doubt mystical participation in the mystery of God's own self-knowledge. Thus, in no way bypassing the very human mode of academic knowledge, the theologian aims at the unity of wisdom (p. 120).

Chenu's book is a plea for the unity of the discipline of theology. Academic and initiatory discipline, science and wisdom, dogmatic and spiritual theology — they all belong together. Together they have their origin in the church and in the faith of the church; together they are shaped in and by the tradition; together they are nourished by Holy Scripture; and together they participate in the divine knowledge of the truth. Chenu's guiding light in this process is undoubtedly Thomas Aquinas. His theology has served in the glorious position of the master chef of thirteenth-century Parisian cuisine. It is Chenu's hope that, by restoring the unity of faith and reason, mystery and concept, theology will again take up its role of initiating the community of faith into the sacramental participation of the divine life. Chenu's *Is Theology a Science?* recognizes that neither of the two meanings of the word "discipline" can thrive without the other: theology is an academic discipline that serves the discipline of initiation into the mystery of God.

The second Oxford definition of the word "discipline" has an element, however, that I have not yet had an opportunity to discuss. The definition reads: "Instruction having for its aim to form the pupil to proper conduct and action; the training of scholars or subordinates to proper and orderly action by instructing and exercising them in the same; mental and moral training." The focus of this definition appears to be on "conduct," "action," and "moral" training. In this chapter I have focused on contemplation of the mystery of God; and that is certainly the aim of the discipline of theology. But such initiation into the mystery does not bypass the life of the Christian virtues. Contemplation and action go together.

Chenu's book does not say much about the active life, except for a brief lament about the divorce between dogmatic and moral theology

(p. 116). But I would be doing Chenu an injustice if I were to fail to mention his deep desire to keep these two together. I have already mentioned Chenu's involvement in the worker-priest movement. To many people, this involvement in the socioeconomic issues of the day has seemed completely separated from his research as a medievalist. Chenu himself joked that people would sometimes think there were two Chenus, "one old medievalist, who does palaeography, and a kind of scoundrel who runs in the lines of fire of the holy Church."[19] But Chenu himself would argue that such a perception rests on a misunderstanding. He says that, from the very beginning of his career, contemplation and action went hand in hand. Throughout his writings Chenu insists on the unity of the two. In fact, despite his strong Neo-Platonic leanings, the Dominican scholar even expresses some hesitation about the language of "contemplation." He was nervous about the possibility that it might lead to a disdain of the active life:

> There is a sort of snobbery [*aristocratisme*] here, in contemplative life as well. And I, who (when I entered the Order) had experienced so strongly the contemplative life and its absoluteness — I thank God that I did not lose my bearings when I was in the vortex. Nonetheless the contemplation-action duo still seems to me to be insufficient to account for the reality. It is not part of the Gospel vocabulary. One never finds the distinction between contemplation and action in the Gospel. The distinction is applied to the episode of Martha and Mary; but this is a dislocation of the episode. In other words, I give priority to this immersion in the world; without casting oneself into it so as to lose one's identity as a Christian.[20]

For Chenu, "immersion" in the world was the natural outcome of the theandric mystery of the Incarnation. A contemplation that did not give way to action would be a form of "snobbery."

One might wish, perhaps, for Chenu to have highlighted the mutual dependence between contemplation and action, between participation and virtue. Like Chenu, Gregory of Nyssa also often emphasizes the unity between the two. But there is also a difference between the two

---

19. Marie-Dominique Chenu, *Un théologien en liberté: Jacques Duquesne interroge le Père Chenu*, Les interviews (Paris: Centurion, 1975), 61.

20. Marie-Dominique Chenu, *Conférence aux Provinciales à Monteils*, 1978 (Archives OP de France), 15; as quoted in Potworowski, *Contemplation and Incarnation*, 26-27.

theologians. Concerned about "snobbery," Chenu stresses the importance of contemplation giving way to action: the theologian has the duty to get involved! I recognize my evangelical students in Chenu. They, too, want nothing more passionately than for theology to serve the social and economic needs of the community around them. And, to be sure, that is exactly the service that Babette rendered to the small Danish community in which she found herself.

Contemplation must, indeed, give way to action. However, Gregory emphasizes that the obverse is also true: action is also the road to contemplation. The life of virtue renders possible human participation in the divine life. From this perspective, it is contemplation that is the highest aim; but the two approaches do not necessarily exclude each other. Chenu correctly intimates that contemplation necessarily issues in charity, and Gregory is right to see virtue as the very process of initiation. The journey of initiation is a never-ending cycle: from action to contemplation, back to action, and on to contemplation again, until the sacramental journey of the theological discipline will have reached the fullness of the "real presence" of the mystery of the beatific vision.

Christ-Centered Participation

This book has presented an apologia for the Platonist-Christian synthesis of the Great Tradition. I have described this synthesis in a variety of complementary ways, using the language of participation, of analogy, and of sacrament to refer to the way God draws us into the divine life. As should be clear by now, it seems to me that these three expressions — participation, analogy, and sacrament — refer to one and the same reality. Each of them expresses the way God graciously condescends in order to allow the created order to share in the reality of his life. Philosophers commonly make a distinction between "predicamental participation" and "transcendental participation." In predicamental participation, the participating object fully shares in something else. My dog, Trooper, for instance, fully shares in the canine species; there is nothing in the species of "canineness" in which Trooper does not share. In transcendental participation, however, the participating object shares in something else in only some small way. While I am quite impressed with Trooper's intelligence, I am relatively confident that my intelligence outshines hers: she is the dog, and I am the owner. In other words, Trooper shares only dimly in the characteristic of intelligence. Similarly, we could say, there is a transcendental participation of human beings in the attributes or perfections of God. Although human beings may be wise, their wisdom will be in evidence particularly if and when they recognize that their wisdom isn't anything like God's. God's wisdom far outshines human wisdom.[1]

---

1. See Leo J. Elders, *The Metaphysics of Being of St. Thomas Aquinas in a Historical Perspec-*

Epilogue

Transcendental participation and the doctrine of analogy serve the same function. In fact, as Francis Martin indicates, transcendental participation "is the 'ontology of analogy,' allowing God's being to be correctly though inadequately spoken of on the basis of those perfections in creatures which participate, through God's efficient causality, in something of which he is the ineffable exemplar."[2] When Martin says that we can "correctly though inadequately" speak of God's being, he refers to the doctrine of analogy of being *(analogia entis),* which, as we have seen, was the way the Great Tradition explained that, though one can use human language to speak about God, our "naming" of God in no way exhausts the ineffable mystery of God's being.[3] Likewise, the doctrine of (transcendental) participation maintains that while created beings really do share in the perfections of God — particularly in the transcendentals of truth, goodness, and beauty — these perfections are present in God in an infinitely dissimilar fashion. Participation and analogy are like two different angles from which to approach the relationship between heaven and earth.

The sacramental ontology whose history I have traced in part 1 of this book is simply yet another angle from which to view the relationship between heaven and earth. For a sacramental ontology, heaven and earth are not like two essentially unconnected stories in which the bottom half at best vaguely resembles the top half. Such a separation can only end up in a tug-of-war between heaven and earth. As a result, many evangelicals find the temptation of contemporary (perhaps nonreductive) materialism almost irresistible: if the tug-of-war is between heaven and earth, it is easy to see which side will win in a largely secular culture. Thus, when contemporary evangelicals deal with eschatology, they tend to emphasize that it is a physical *body* that will inherit the resurrection kingdom, and they highlight the fact that the new creation is an *earthly* reality.[4]

It should be clear by this point that I do not have a quarrel with ei-

---

tive, Studien und Texte zur Geistesgeschichte des Mittelalters, no. 34 (Leiden: Brill, 1993), 225-30.

2. Francis Martin, "Reading Scripture in the Catholic Tradition," in *Your Word Is Truth: A Project of Evangelicals and Catholics Together,* ed. Charles Colson and Richard John Neuhaus (Grand Rapids: Eerdmans, 2002), 153.

3. Cf. chap. 4 above, under subheading "Scotus and Univocity of Being."

4. See, for instance, N. T. Wright, *Surprised by Hope: Rethinking Heaven, the Resurrection, and the Mission of the Church* (New York: HarperOne, 2008), 100-101, 147-63.

ther the idea that God is faithful to his good created order or with the earthly character of the new creation. What I do question is the antiheaven rhetoric among evangelicals.[5] Not only does such discourse focus unduly on this-worldly realities — as if they, rather than the tri-une God himself, were ultimate — but it is also unable to make sense of the traditional doctrine of the beatific vision. Beatific vision is predicated on the Platonist-Christian integration of heaven and earth. To see God "face to face" (1 Cor. 13:12) is only desirable if the heavenly reality of God is the ultimate "object" of human desire. Heaven and earth are opposed once we buy into a nominalist ontology that foregoes earthly participation in heavenly realities. By contrast, a sacramental ontology completely bypasses the tug-of-war metaphor and regards it as the unfortunate outcome of a late medieval nominalist understanding of reality. With a sacramental ontology, one can be grateful for created reality precisely because, as a sacrament, it really makes present the heavenly reality of God himself.

Thus, like participation and analogy, sacramental language recognizes both the real presence of God in our earthly, time-space realities and the infinite transcendence of the mystery that is the triune God himself. This sacramental participation will reach its perfection in the New Jerusalem, which John describes as a "new heaven and a new earth" (Rev. 21:1). In this eschatological reality, the sacramental intimacy or real presence will be such that heaven and earth will seem nearly indistinguishable. Earthly participation in heavenly realities will be such that God's "dwelling" will be among us (Rev. 21:3) without the existence of a temple in the city (Rev. 21:22). The reason, John explains, is that "the Lord God Almighty and the Lamb are its temple." And he unpacks this statement by commenting that the glory of God's very being — once limited to the Most Holy Place of the temple — will suffuse the entire city: "The city does not need the sun or the moon to shine on it, for the glory of God gives it light, and the Lamb is its lamp" (Rev. 21:23).

The transformation of the created order is staggeringly beyond anything that human language is able to express. If sun and moon will disappear from the new heaven and earth, it should be obvious that any language that Scripture may use to describe the eschaton is merely ana-

---

5. I am thinking, for instance, of the title of Paul Marshall's book, written with Lela Gilbert, *Heaven Is Not My Home: Living in the Now of God's Creation* (Nashville: Word, 1998).

logical in character. If the very glory of God's essence will fill the New Jerusalem, this must mean that anything entering into the city will get thoroughly divinized. This earth will be sacramentally transformed into a heavenly reality. The New Jerusalem means heavenly participation of a kind that far outstrips earthly imagination.

"It's all in Plato, all in Plato, bless me, what *do* they teach them at these schools?" joked Lord Digory near the end of C. S. Lewis's *The Last Battle*.[6] Lewis obviously had a great deal of appreciation for the Platonic tradition. But I doubt that he really meant that it's literally *all* in Plato. Lewis was a Christian, and Christians are not straightforward Platonists. The free and loving will of the Creator ("I am making everything new!" — Rev. 21:5); the goodness of earthly, creaturely activities ("The glory and honor of the nations will be brought into it" — Rev. 21:26); and the personal character of the triune God ("He will wipe every tear from their eyes" — Rev. 21:4) — these all put up stiff barriers to a straightforward appropriation of Platonic thought. Most importantly, for Christians, the Platonic Forms or Ideas are merely a vague indicator of the glorious reality of the eternal Word, the Logos of God. Vivian Boland summarizes Augustine's Christian transposition of Platonic Forms as follows: "Christian faith believes that creation proceeds from God's wisdom and love and that the 'place of the ideas' can only be the Word through whom God made all things [Genesis 1; John 1.3, 4; Colossians 1.16; Psalm 103.24]."[7] For the Platonist-Christian synthesis, the eternal Word provides the anchor that secures both the goodness of the created order and its merely penultimate character. The Word is the sacramental reality that creation participates in and that invests time and space with meaning.

Christology, then, lies at the heart of the Christian transposition of the Platonic tradition. Past, present, and future cohere in Christ, the eternal Word become flesh. The Incarnation becomes the norm and standard that reaches backward and forward, redeeming past and future through God's gracious entry into the created order. It is by taking the Word, incarnate in Christ, as the interpretive key to all reality that we will be able to make theological progress and draw evangelicals and

6. C. S. Lewis, *The Chronicles of Narnia* (New York: HarperCollins, 2001), 760.
7. Vivian Boland, *Ideas in God According to Saint Thomas Aquinas: Sources and Synthesis,* Studies in the History of Christian Traditions, no. 69 (Leiden: Brill, 1996), 79 (brackets in original).

Catholics closer together. This is what I have tried to make clear throughout part 2 of this book. The church is the body of Christ, and thus does the church make Christ present in the world. Through the Eucharist, the unity of the church takes sacramental shape.

It is through the eucharistic celebration, therefore, that the church herself becomes a sacrament of the eschatological reality of the fullness of Christ (chapter 6). In Christ, God's eternal present enters into the world, so that past, present, and future come together sacramentally in the "time of the church." Doctrine can develop over time without breaking up into atomized bits of discontinuous teaching because the development is simply the unfolding of the eternal Word of God, who has become incarnate in Jesus Christ (chapter 7). Old Testament events are not reduced to mere memories of a history long past. In Christ they take on sacramental significance, so that it becomes possible to look for deeper, spiritual levels of meaning. After all, Christ himself is the mystery to which Old Testament events point and in which they participate (chapter 8). Human knowledge itself turns out to be a sacramental sharing in the eternal self-knowledge of God in Christ. Truth is not simply correspondence between object and intellect, as if adequate human mastery were possible. Instead, human knowledge is an exploration of the mystery of realities that have their truth in Christ. Human statements of truth share sacramentally in the truth of God, which is the eternal Word as expressed in Jesus Christ (chapter 9). As a result, theology is the Christ-centered discipline that initiates believers into the reality of communion with the incarnate Son of God and so into divinizing fellowship with the eternal Word of God. Theology has the sacramental task of guiding the community of faith into the participatory enjoyment of the triune life (chapter 10).

There is little doubt that each of these five reconfigurations presents a challenge to evangelical thought. And while sacramental language may be more at home in a Roman Catholic context than in an evangelical one, the sacramental participation that I have advocated in this book also challenges contemporary Catholics. Both evangelicals and Catholics, after all, have been seriously affected by the desacramentalizing of modernity. Regardless of the challenge, I have become convinced that the only faithful way forward — not only theologically but also ecumenically — is by way of a sacramental ontology. The sacramental ontology of the Great Tradition preceded the tragic split of the Reformation. It will be impossible to heal the rift without at the same time addressing the problem of a radically autonomous natural realm. For Catholics and evangelicals to find each other, they need to engage in a common *ressourcement* of the Great Tradition. As I have tried to make clear in this book, I believe that *nouvelle théologie* offers important resources for such a common engagement of the Platonist-Christian synthesis. Catholics will turn evangelical and evangelicals will become Catholic if we deepen our common sacramental participation in the eternal Word of God.

Bibliography

Allen, John L. *The Future Church: How Ten Trends Are Revolutionizing the Catholic Church*. New York: Doubleday, 2009.

Anselm, Saint. "Proslogium." In *St. Anselm: Basic Writings*. Translated by S. N. Deane. 2nd ed. La Salle, IL: Open Court, 1968.

Aquinas, Saint Thomas. *Summa Theologica*. Translated by Fathers of the English Dominican Province. 1948. Reprint, Westminster, MD: Christian Classics, 1981.

Augustine, Saint. *Concerning the City of God against the Pagans*. Translated by Henry Bettenson. London: Penguin, 1984.

————. *Confessions*. Translated by Henry Chadwick. Oxford: Oxford University Press, 1991.

————. *The Enchiridion on Faith, Hope and Love*. Introduction by Thomas S. Hibbs. Edited by Henry Paolucci. 1961. Reprint, Washington, DC: Regnery, 1995.

————. *On Christian Teaching*. Translated and with Introduction by R. P. H. Green. Oxford World's Classics. 1997. Reprint, Oxford: Oxford University Press, 2008.

————. "Sermon 227." In *Sermons (184-229Z) on the Liturgical Seasons*. Vol. III/6 of *The Works of Saint Augustine*. Translated by Edmund Hill. Edited by John E. Rotelle. New Rochelle, NY: New City, 1993.

Ayres, Lewis. *Nicaea and Its Legacy: An Approach to Fourth-Century Trinitarian Theology*. Oxford: Oxford University Press, 2004.

Barth, Karl. *Church Dogmatics*. Vol. II/1, *The Doctrine of God*. Translated by T. H. L. Parker et al. Edited by G. W. Bromiley and T. F. Torrance. London: T. & T. Clark/Continuum, 2004.

Bebbington, David W. *Evangelicalism in Modern Britain: A History from the 1730s to the 1980s*. London: Unwin Hyman, 1989.

Behr, John. *The Nicene Faith*. Vol. 2/1, *The Formation of Christian Theology*. Crestwood, NY: St. Vladimir's Seminary Press, 2001.

Boersma, Hans. "Accommodation to What? Univocity of Being, Pure Nature, and the Anthropology of St. Irenaeus." *International Journal of Systematic Theology* 8 (2006): 266-93.

———. "Analogy of Truth: The Sacramental Epistemology of *nouvelle théologie*." In *Ressourcement: A Movement for Renewal in Twentieth-Century Catholic Theology*, edited by Gabriel Flynn and Paul D. Murray. Oxford: Oxford University Press, in press.

———. "Being Reconciled: Atonement as the Ecclesio-Christological Practice of Forgiveness in John Milbank." In *Radical Orthodoxy and the Reformed Tradition: Creation, Covenant, and Participation*, edited by James K. A. Smith and James H. Olthuis. Grand Rapids: Baker Academic, 2005.

———. "The Eucharist Makes the Church." *CRUX* 44, no. 4 (2008): 2-11. Abbreviated version to be published in *Books and Culture* 16, no. 6 (Nov./Dec. 2010).

———. *Nouvelle Théologie and Sacramental Ontology: A Return to Mystery*. Oxford: Oxford University Press, 2009.

———. "On Baking Pumpkin Pie: Kevin Vanhoozer and Yves Congar on Tradition." *Calvin Theological Journal* 42 (2007): 237-55.

———. "On the Rejection of Boundaries: Radical Orthodoxy's Appropriation of St. Augustine." *Pro Ecclesia* 15 (2006): 418-47.

———. "Redemptive Hospitality in Irenaeus: A Model for Ecumenicity in a Violent World." *Pro Ecclesia* 11 (2002): 207-26.

———. "Sacramental Ontology: Nature and the Supernatural in the Ecclesiology of Henri de Lubac." *New Blackfriars* 88 (2007): 242-73.

———. "Theology as Queen of Hospitality." *Evangelical Quarterly* 79 (2007): 291-310.

———. *Violence, Hospitality, and the Cross: Reappropriating the Atonement Tradition*. Grand Rapids: Baker Academic, 2004.

Boland, Vivian. *Ideas in God According to Saint Thomas Aquinas: Sources and Synthesis*. Studies in the History of Christian Traditions, no. 69. Leiden: Brill, 1996.

Bordeianu, Radu. "Maximus and Ecology: The Relevance of Maximus the Confessor's Theology of Creation for the Present Ecological Crisis." *Downside Review* 127 (2009): 103-26.

Bouillard, Henri. *Conversion et grâce chez S. Thomas d'Aquin: Étude historique*. Théologie, no. 1. Paris: Aubier, 1944.

———. *The Knowledge of God*. Translated by Samuel D. Femiano. New York: Herder and Herder, 1968.

———. "Notions conciliaires et analogie de la vérité." *Recherches de science religieuse* 35 (1948): 251-71.

Boulton, Matthew Myer. *God against Religion: Rethinking Christian Theology through Worship*. Grand Rapids: Eerdmans, 2008.

Bouyer, Louis. *The Spirit and Forms of Protestantism*. Translated by A. V. Littledale. Princeton, NJ: Scepter, 2001.

Bradshaw, David. *Aristotle East and West: Metaphysics and the Division of Christendom*. Cambridge: Cambridge University Press, 2004.

Bibliography

Byassee, Jason. *Praise Seeking Understanding. Reading the Psalms with Augustine.* Grand Rapids: Eerdmans, 2007.

Calvin, John. *Institutes of the Christian Religion.* Edited by John T. McNeill. Translated by Ford Lewis Battles. The Library of Christian Classics, vol. 20. Philadelphia: Westminster, 1960.

———. "Reply by John Calvin to Letter by Cardinal Sadolet to the Senate and People of Geneva." In *Tracts Relating to the Reformation.* Vol. 1. Translated by Henry Beveridge. Edinburgh: Calvin Translation Society, 1844.

Chenu, Marie-Dominique. *Aquinas and His Role in Theology.* Translated by Paul Philibert. Collegeville, MN: Liturgical, 2002.

———. *Une école de théologie: Le Saulchoir.* Kain-Lez-Tournai: Le Saulchoir, 1937.

———. *Faith and Theology.* Translated by Denis Hickey. New York: Macmillan, 1968.

———. *Is Theology a Science?* Translated by A. H. N. Green-Armytage. New York: Hawthorn, 1959.

———. *Nature, Man, and Society in the Twelfth Century: Essays on New Theological Perspectives in the Latin West.* Preface by Étienne Gilson. Translated and edited by Jerome Taylor and Lester Little. Medieval Academy Reprints for Teaching, no. 37. 1968. Reprint, Toronto: University of Toronto Press, 1997.

———. *Un théologien en liberté: Jacques Duquesne interroge le Père Chenu.* Les interviews. Paris: Centurion, 1975.

———. *Toward Understanding Saint Thomas.* Translated by Albert M. Landry and Dominic Hughes. Chicago: Regnery, 1964.

Cherniss, Harold F. *The Platonism of Gregory of Nyssa.* Philosophy Monograph Series, no. 81. 1930. Reprint, New York: Franklin, 1971.

Clayton, Allan Lee. "The Orthodox Recovery of a Heretical Proof-Text: Athanasius of Alexandria's Interpretation of Proverbs 8:22-30 in Conflict with the Arians." PhD diss., Southern Methodist University, 1988.

Congar, Yves M.-J. *L'Église: De saint Augustin à l'époque moderne.* Histoire des dogmes, no. 3. Paris: Cerf, 1970.

———. *La Foi et la théologie.* Tournai: Desclée, 1962.

———. *The Meaning of Tradition.* Translated by A. N. Woodrow. San Francisco: Ignatius, 2004.

———. *Tradition and Traditions: The Biblical, Historical, and Theological Evidence for Catholic Teaching on Tradition.* Translated by Michael Naseby and Thomas Rainborough. San Diego: Basilica, 1966.

Conticello, Carmelo Giuseppe. "*De contemplatione* (Angelicum, 1920): La Thèse inédite du P. M.-D. Chenu." *Revue des sciences philosophiques et théologiques* 75 (1991): 363-422.

Copleston, Frederick. *A History of Philosophy.* Vol. III/1. New York: Image/Doubleday, 1963.

Crockett, William R. *Eucharist: Symbol of Transformation.* Collegeville, MN: Liturgical, 1999.

Bibliography

Daniélou, Jean. *The Advent of Salvation: A Comparative Study of Non-Christian Religions and Christianity.* Translated by Rosemary Sheed. New York: Paulist, 1962.

——. *The Bible and the Liturgy.* Liturgical Studies, no. 3. Notre Dame, IN: University of Notre Dame Press, 1956.

——. *From Shadows to Reality: Studies in the Biblical Typology of the Fathers.* Translated by Wulstan Hibberd. London: Burns and Oates, 1960.

——. *Holy Pagans of the Old Testament.* Translated by Felix Faber. London: Longmans, Green and Co., 1957.

——. *The Lord of History: Reflections on the Inner Meaning of History.* Translated by Nigel Abercrombie. 1958. Reprint, Cleveland: Meridian/World, 1968.

——. "Les Orientations présentes de la pensée religieuse." *Études* 249 (1946): 5-21.

——. *Origen.* Translated by Walter Mitchell. New York: Sheed and Ward, 1955.

De Lubac, Henri. *Augustinianism and Modern Theology.* Translated by Lancelot Sheppard. Introduction by Louis Dupré. New York: Crossroad/Herder and Herder, 2000.

——. *Catholicism: Christ and the Common Destiny of Man.* Translated by Lancelot C. Sheppard and Elizabeth Englund. San Francisco: Ignatius, 1988.

——. *Corpus Mysticum: The Eucharist and the Church in the Middle Ages: Historical Survey.* Translated by Gemma Simmonds with Richard Price and Christopher Stephens. Edited by Laurence Paul Hemming and Susan Frank Parsons. London: SCM, 2006.

——. "Hellenistic Allegory and Christian Allegory." In *Theological Fragments.* Translated by Rebecca Howell Balinski. San Francisco: Ignatius, 1989.

——. *History and Spirit: The Understanding of Scripture According to Origen.* Translated by Anne Englund Nash with Juvenal Merriell. San Francisco: Ignatius, 2007.

——. *Medieval Exegesis: The Four Senses of Scripture.* 3 vols. Translated by Mark Sebanc and E. M. Macierowski. Grand Rapids: Eerdmans, 1998, 2000, 2009.

——. *The Mystery of the Supernatural.* Translated by Rosemary Sheed. New York: Herder and Herder/Crossroad, 1998.

——. "On an Old Distich: The Doctrine of the 'Fourfold Sense' in Scripture." In *Theological Fragments.* Translated by Rebecca Howell Balinski. San Francisco: Ignatius, 1989.

——. "The Problem of the Development of Dogma." In *Theology in History.* Translated by Anne Englund Nash. San Francisco: Ignatius, 1996.

——. *Scripture in the Tradition.* Translated by Luke O'Neill. 1968. Reprint, New York: Herder and Herder/Crossroad, 2000.

——. "Spiritual Understanding." Translated by Luke O'Neill. In *The Theological Interpretation of Scripture: Classic and Contemporary Readings,* edited by Stephen E. Fowl. Malden, MA: Blackwell, 1997.

——. *The Splendor of the Church.* Translated by Michael Mason. 1956. Reprint, San Francisco: Ignatius, 1999.

————. "Typology and Allegorization." In *Theological Fragments*. Translated by Rebecca Howell Balinski. San Francisco: Ignatius, 1989.

Denzinger, Henry. *The Sources of Catholic Dogma*. Translated by Roy J. Deferrari. Fitzwilliam, NH: Loreto, 2002.

Descartes, René. *Discourse on Method and the Meditations*. Translated by F. E. Sutcliffe. 1968. Reprint, Harmondsworth, UK: Penguin, 1986.

Desmazières, Agnès. "La 'Nouvelle théologie', prémisse d'une théologie herméneutique? La Controverse sur l'analogie de la vérité (1946-1949)." *Revue thomiste* 104 (2004): 241-72.

Dickens, W. T. *Hans Urs von Balthasar's Theological Aesthetics: A Model for Post-Critical Biblical Interpretation*. Notre Dame, IN: University of Notre Dame Press, 2003.

Doyle, Dennis M. *Communion Ecclesiology*. Maryknoll, NY: Orbis, 2000.

Dupré, Louis. *Passage to Modernity: An Essay in the Hermeneutics of Nature and Culture*. New Haven: Yale University Press, 1993.

————. *Religion and the Rise of Modern Culture*. Notre Dame, IN: University of Notre Dame Press, 2008.

Elders, Leo J. *The Metaphysics of Being of St. Thomas Aquinas in a Historical Perspective*. Studien und Texte zur Geistesgeschichte des Mittelalters, no. 34. Leiden: Brill, 1993.

Elgersma Helleman, Wendy. "Gregory's Sophia: 'Christ, the Wisdom of God.'" *Studia Patristica* 41 (2006): 345-50.

Fee, Gordon D. *Pauline Christology: An Exegetical-Theological Study*. Peabody, MA: Hendrickson, 2007.

Flannery, Austin, ed. *Vatican Council II*. Vol. 1, *The Conciliar and Postconciliar Documents*. Rev. ed. Northport, NY: Costello, 1975.

Flynn, Gabriel. *Yves Congar's Vision of the Church in a World of Unbelief*. Burlington, VT: Ashgate, 2004.

Ford, David F., and Graham Stanton, eds. *Reading Texts, Seeking Wisdom: Scripture and Theology*. Grand Rapids: Eerdmans, 2003.

Gay, Craig M. *Dialogue, Catalogue and Monologue: Personal, Impersonal and Depersonalizing Ways to Use Words*. Vancouver: Regent College Publishing, 2008.

Goldingay, John, and David Payne. *A Critical and Exegetical Commentary on Isaiah 40-55*. Vol. 2. The International Critical Commentary. Edinburgh: T. & T. Clark, 2007.

Grant, Robert M., with David Tracy. *A Short History of the Interpretation of the Bible*. 2nd ed. Philadelphia: Fortress, 1984.

Greeley, Andrew M. *The Catholic Imagination*. Berkeley: University of California Press, 2000.

Gregory of Nyssa. *From Glory to Glory: Texts from Gregory of Nyssa's Mystical Writings*. Introduction by Jean Daniélou. Edited and translated by Herbert Musurillo. 1961. Reprint, Crestwood, NY: St. Vladimir's Seminary Press, 2001.

————. *On the Soul and the Resurrection*. Translated by Catharine Roth. Crestwood, NY: St. Vladimir's Seminary Press, 1980.

Bibliography

———. On "Not Three Gods": To Ablabius. In Nicene and Post-Nicene Fathers, 2nd ser., vol. 5. Edited by William Moore and Henry Austin Wilson. 1893; reprint, Peabody, MA: Hendrickson, 1994.

Grumett, David. Henri de Lubac: A Guide for the Perplexed. London: T. & T. Clark/Continuum, 2007.

Guarino, Thomas G. "Catholic Reflections on Discerning the Truth of Sacred Scripture." In Your Word Is Truth: A Project of Evangelicals and Catholics Together, edited by Charles Colson and Richard John Neuhaus. Grand Rapids: Eerdmans, 2002.

———. Foundations of Systematic Theology. New York: T. & T. Clark, 2005.

Hanson, R. P. C. Allegory and Event: A Study of the Sources and Significance of Origen's Interpretation of Scripture. London: SCM, 1959.

Harvey, Barry. Can These Bones Live? A Catholic Baptist Engagement with Ecclesiology, Hermeneutics, and Social Theory. Grand Rapids: Brazos, 2008.

Hauerwas, Stanley. "Discipleship as a Craft, Church as a Disciplined Community." Christian Century 108, no. 27 (Oct. 1, 1991): 881-84.

Hindmarsh, D. Bruce. "Retrieval and Renewal: A Model for Evangelical Spiritual Vitality." In J. I. Packer and the Evangelical Future: The Impact of His Life and Thought, edited by Timothy George. Grand Rapids: Baker Academic, 2009.

Hollon, Bryan C. Everything Is Sacred: Spiritual Exegesis in the Political Theology of Henri de Lubac. Eugene, OR: Cascade/Wipf and Stock, 2009.

Hooker, Morna D. "Did the Use of Isaiah 53 to Interpret His Mission Begin with Jesus?" In Jesus and the Suffering Servant: Isaiah 53 and Christian Origins, edited by William H. Bellinger and William R. Farmer. Harrisburg, PA: Trinity Press International, 1998.

———. "Response to Mikeal Parsons." In Jesus and the Suffering Servant: Isaiah 53 and Christian Origins, edited by William H. Bellinger and William R. Farmer. Harrisburg, PA: Trinity Press International, 1998.

Hunsinger, George. The Eucharist and Ecumenism: Let Us Keep the Feast. Cambridge: Cambridge University Press, 2008.

Husbands, Mark. "The Trinity Is Not Our Social Program." In Trinitarian Theology for the Church: Scripture, Community, Worship, edited by Daniel J. Treier and David Lauber. Downers Grove, IL: InterVarsity, 2009.

Irenaeus. Against Heresies. In Ante-Nicene Fathers, vol. 1. Edited by Alexander Roberts and James Donaldson. 1885; reprint, Peabody, MA: Hendrickson, 1994.

John Paul II, Pope. "Ut unum sint: On Commitment to Ecumenism." May 25, 1995. www.vatican.va.

Johnson, Mark F. "Another Look at the Plurality of the Literal Sense." Medieval Philosophy and Theology 2 (1992): 117-41.

Keating, Daniel A. Deification and Grace. Naples, FL: Sapientia Press of Ave Maria University, 2007.

Kerr, Fergus. After Aquinas: Versions of Thomism. Malden, MA: Blackwell, 2002.

Kilby, Karen. "Aquinas, the Trinity and the Limits of Understanding." *International Journal of Systematic Theology* 7 (2005): 414-27.

Le Blond, Jean-Marie. "L'Analogie de la vérité: Réflexion d'un philosophe sur une controverse théologique." *Recherches de science religieuse* 34 (1947): 129-41.

Leithart, Peter. *Deep Exegesis: The Mystery of Reading Scripture.* Waco, TX: Baylor University Press, 2009.

Levering, Matthew. *Participatory Biblical Exegesis: A Theology of Biblical Interpretation.* Notre Dame, IN: University of Notre Dame Press, 2008.

Lewis, C. S. *The Chronicles of Narnia.* New York: HarperCollins, 2001.

_____. *God in the Dock: Essays on Theology and Ethics.* Edited by Walter Hooper. Grand Rapids: Eerdmans, 1970.

_____. *The Great Divorce.* 1946; reprint, New York: Simon and Schuster, 1996.

_____. *The Weight of Glory, and Other Addresses.* 1949; reprint, San Francisco: HarperSanFrancisco, 2001.

Louth, Andrew. *Discerning the Mystery: An Essay on the Nature of Theology.* 1983. Reprint, Oxford: Clarendon/Oxford University Press, 2003.

———. *The Origins of the Christian Mystical Tradition: From Plato to Denys.* Oxford: Oxford University Press, 1981.

Marshall, Paul, with Lela Gilbert. *Heaven Is Not My Home: Living in the Now of God's Creation.* Nashville: Word, 1998.

Martin, Francis. "Reading Scripture in the Catholic Tradition." In *Your Word Is Truth: A Project of Evangelicals and Catholics Together,* edited by Charles Colson and Richard John Neuhaus. Grand Rapids: Eerdmans, 2002.

McDowell, Josh. *Evidence That Demands a Verdict: Historical Evidences for the Christian Faith.* San Bernardino, CA: Campus Crusade for Christ, 1972.

McGrath, Alister E. *Evangelicalism and the Future of Christianity.* Downers Grove, IL: InterVarsity, 1995.

———. "Forerunners of the Reformation? Critical Examination of the Evidence for the Precursors of the Reformation Doctrines of Justification." *Harvard Theological Review* 75 (1982): 219-42.

———. "John Calvin and Late Mediaeval Thought." *Archiv für Reformationsgeschichte* 77 (1986): 58-78.

———. *Luther's Theology of the Cross: Martin Luther's Theological Breakthrough.* Oxford: Blackwell, 1985.

———. *A Passion for Truth: The Intellectual Coherence of Evangelicalism.* Downers Grove, IL: InterVarsity, 1996.

Meijering, E. P. *Orthodoxy and Platonism in Athanasius: Synthesis or Antithesis?* 1968. Reprint, Leiden: Brill, 1974.

Milbank, John. "Only Theology Overcomes Metaphysics." *New Blackfriars* 76 (1995): 325-42.

———. *The Suspended Middle: Henri de Lubac and the Debate Concerning the Supernatural.* Grand Rapids: Eerdmans, 2005.

Bibliography

————. *Theology and Social Theory: Beyond Secular Reason.* Oxford: Blackwell, 1990.

Milbank, John, Catherine Pickstock, and Graham Ward, eds. *Radical Orthodoxy: A New Theology.* London: Routledge, 1999.

Mosser, Carl. "The Greatest Possible Blessing: Calvin and Deification." *Scottish Journal of Theology* 55 (2002): 36-57.

Nichols, Aidan. *Discovering Aquinas: An Introduction to His Life, Work, and Influence.* Grand Rapids: Eerdmans, 2002.

————. *From Newman to Congar: The Idea of Doctrinal Development from the Victorians to the Second Vatican Council.* Edinburgh: T. & T. Clark, 1990.

Noll, Mark A. *The Scandal of the Evangelical Mind.* Grand Rapids: Eerdmans, 1994.

Noll, Mark A., and Carolyn Nystrom. *Is the Reformation Over? An Evangelical Assessment of Contemporary Roman Catholicism.* Grand Rapids: Baker Academic, 2005.

Oberman, Heiko A. *Forerunners of the Reformation: The Shape of Late Medieval Thought Illustrated by Key Documents.* 2nd ed. Philadelphia: Fortress, 1981.

————. *The Harvest of Medieval Theology: Gabriel Biel and Late Medieval Nominalism.* 1983. Reprint, Grand Rapids: Baker Academic, 2000.

————. *Luther: Man between God and the Devil.* Translated by Eileen Walliser-Schwartzbart. 1990. Reprint, New York: Image/Doubleday, 1992.

O'Connor, Flannery. *Mystery and Manners: Occasional Prose.* Edited by Sally and Robert Fitzgerald. 1957. Reprint, New York: Farrar, Straus and Giroux, 1970.

Ogg, George. "The Age of Jesus When He Taught." *New Testament Studies* 5 (1958-59): 291-98.

O'Keefe, John J., and R. R. Reno. *Sanctified Vision: An Introduction to Early Christian Interpretation of the Bible.* Baltimore: Johns Hopkins University Press, 2005.

Osborne, Thomas M. "Faith, Philosophy, and the Nominalist Background to Luther's Defense of the Real Presence." *Journal of the History of Ideas* 63 (2002): 63-82.

Parsons, Mikeal C. "Isaiah 53 in Acts 8: A Reply to Professor Morna Hooker." In *Jesus and the Suffering Servant: Isaiah 53 and Christian Origins,* edited by William H. Bellinger and William R. Farmer. Harrisburg, PA: Trinity Press International, 1998.

Peddicord, Richard. *The Sacred Monster of Thomism: An Introduction to the Life and Legacy of Réginald Garrigou-Lagrange.* South Bend, IN: St. Augustine's, 2005.

Pelikan, Jaroslav. *Whose Bible Is It? A History of the Scriptures through the Ages.* New York: Viking, 2005.

Penner, Myron B., ed. *Christianity and the Postmodern Turn: Six Views.* Grand Rapids: Brazos, 2005.

Pinckaers, Servaes. *The Sources of Christian Ethics.* Translated by Mary Thomas Noble. Edinburgh: T. & T. Clark, 1995.

Portier, Bill. "Here Come the Evangelical Catholics." *Communio* 31 (2004): 35-66.

Potworowski, Christophe F. *Contemplation and Incarnation: The Theology of Marie-Dominique Chenu.* Montreal: McGill-Queen's University Press, 2001.

Raschke, Carl A. *The Next Reformation: Why Evangelicals Must Embrace Postmodernity.* Grand Rapids: Baker Academic, 2004.

Rogers, Eugene F. "How the Virtues of an Interpreter Presuppose and Perfect Hermeneutics: The Case of Thomas Aquinas." *Journal of Religion* 76 (1996): 64-81.

Rowland, Tracey. *Culture and the Thomist Tradition after Vatican II.* London: Routledge, 2003.

Rubenstein, Richard E. *Aristotle's Children: How Christians, Muslims, and Jews Rediscovered Ancient Wisdom and Illuminated the Dark Ages.* Orlando, FL: Harcourt, 2003.

Russell, Norman. *The Doctrine of Deification in the Greek Patristic Tradition.* Oxford: Oxford University Press, 2004.

Schmemann, Alexander. *For the Life of the World: Sacraments and Orthodoxy.* 1982. Reprint, Crestwood, NY: St. Vladimir's Seminary Press, 2004.

―――. *Of Water and the Spirit: A Liturgical Study of Baptism.* Crestwood, NY: St. Vladimir's Seminary Press, 1974.

Smith, James K. A. *Introducing Radical Orthodoxy: Mapping a Post-Secular Theology.* Grand Rapids: Baker Academic, 2005.

―――. *Who's Afraid of Postmodernism? Taking Derrida, Lyotard, and Foucault to Church.* Grand Rapids: Baker Academic, 2006.

Stackhouse, John G. "Defining 'Evangelical.'" *Church and Faith Trends* 1, no. 1 (October 2007): 1-5.

Sweetman, Robert. "Univocity, Analogy, and the Mystery of Being according to John Duns Scotus." In *Radical Orthodoxy and the Reformed Tradition: Creation, Covenant, and Participation,* edited by James K. A. Smith and James H. Olthuis. Grand Rapids: Baker Academic, 2005.

Tamburello, Dennis E. "Calvin and Sacramentality: A Catholic Perspective." In *John Calvin and Roman Catholicism: Critique and Engagement, Then and Now,* edited by Randall C. Zachman. Grand Rapids: Baker Academic, 2008.

Tavard, George H. *Holy Writ or Holy Church: The Crisis of the Protestant Reformation.* London: Burns and Oates, 1959.

Taylor, Charles. *A Secular Age.* Cambridge, MA: Belknap/Harvard University Press, 2007.

Te Velde, Rudi A. *Participation and Substantiality in Thomas Aquinas.* Leiden: Brill, 1995.

Tillard, J.-M.-R. *Flesh of the Church, Flesh of Christ: At the Source of the Ecclesiology of Communion.* Translated by Madeleine Beaumont. Collegeville, MN: Liturgical, 2000.

Turner, Denys. "How to Read the Pseudo-Denys Today." *International Journal of Systematic Theology* 7 (2005): 428-40.

Vanhoozer, Kevin J. "Into the Great 'Beyond': A Theologian's Response to the Marshall Plan." In *Beyond the Bible: Moving from Scripture to Theology,* edited by I. Howard Marshall with Kevin J. Vanhoozer and Stanley E. Porter (Grand Rapids: Baker Academic, 2004).

―――. *The Drama of Doctrine: A Canonical-Linguistic Approach to Christian Theology.* Louisville: Westminster John Knox, 2005.

Bibliography

———, ed. *Dictionary for Theological Interpretation of the Bible*. Grand Rapids: Eerdmans, 2005.

Voderholzer, Rudolf. *Meet Henri de Lubac*. San Francisco: Ignatius, 2008.

Von Balthasar, Hans Urs. *Origen: Spirit and Fire: A Thematic Anthology of His Writings*. Translated by Robert J. Daly. Washington, DC: Catholic University of America Press, 1984.

———. *Presence and Thought: An Essay on the Religious Philosophy of Gregory of Nyssa*. Translated by Mark Sebanc. San Francisco: Communio/Ignatius, 1995.

———. *The Scandal of the Incarnation: Irenaeus against the Heresies*. Translated by John Saward. San Francisco: Ignatius, 1990.

Waltke, Bruce K. *The Book of Proverbs: Chapters 15-31*. The New International Commentary on the Old Testament. Grand Rapids: Eerdmans, 2005.

Webber, Robert E. *The Younger Evangelicals: Facing the Challenges of the New World*. Grand Rapids: Baker, 2002.

Wells, David F. *Above All Earthly Pow'rs: Christ in a Postmodern World*. Grand Rapids: Eerdmans, 2005.

———. *No Place for Truth: Or Whatever Happened to Evangelical Theology?* Grand Rapid: Eerdmans, 1993.

Wengert, Timothy J. *Law and Gospel: Philip Melanchthon's Debate with John Agricola of Eisleben over Poenitentia*. Grand Rapids: Baker, 1997.

Wilken, Robert Louis. *The Spirit of Early Christian Thought: Seeking the Face of God*. New Haven: Yale University Press, 2003.

Wilken, Robert Louis, with Angela Russell Christman and Michael J. Hollerich. *Isaiah: Interpreted by Early Christian and Medieval Commentators*. The Church's Bible. Grand Rapids: Eerdmans, 2007.

Williams, A. N. *The Ground of Union: Deification in Aquinas and Palamas*. Oxford: Oxford University Press, 1999.

Wood, Susan K. *Spiritual Exegesis and the Church in the Theology of Henri de Lubac*. Grand Rapids: Eerdmans, 1998.

Wright, N. T. *Christian Origins and the Question of God*. Vol. 1, *The New Testament and the People of God*. Minneapolis: Fortress, 1992.

———. *The Climax of the Covenant: Christ and the Law in Pauline Theology*. Minneapolis: Fortress, 1991.

———. *Justification: God's Plan and Paul's Vision*. Downers Grove, IL: InterVarsity Academic, 2009.

———. *Surprised by Hope: Rethinking Heaven, the Resurrection, and the Mission of the Church*. New York: HarperOne, 2008.

Young, Frances M. *Biblical Exegesis and the Formation of Christian Culture*. Peabody, MA: Hendrickson, 2002.

Zimmermann, Jens. *Recovering Theological Hermeneutics: An Incarnational-Trinitarian Theory of Interpretation*. Grand Rapids: Baker Academic, 2004.

General Index

Abelard, Peter, 159
Accommodation, 28, 32, 99, 129-30, 175n.11
Agricola, Johann, 93
Albert the Great, 36
Alger of Liège, 118
Allegory. *See* Scripture and spiritual interpretation
Allen, John L., 120n.1
Anagogy, 148
Analogy, 70-74, 167, 172, 185-88
analogia entis (analogy of being), 70-74, 164, 167, 186
analogia veritatis (analogy of truth), 164, 167
Andrewes, Lancelot, 103
Anselm, 26, 30, 86, 95, 159, 181
Apophatic theology, 160-62, 180
Aquinas, Thomas, 13-16, 36, 59, 64, 72-74, 76-79, 86, 109, 152n.31, 165, 167, 171, 174, 176-79, 182; on analogy, 72-74
Aristotle, 36, 58, 59n.7, 64, 90
Arius, 142-43
Athanasius, 41, 44-47, 49, 72, 142
Augustine, Aurelius, 6-8, 28, 30, 33n.26, 34n.28, 53, 69, 71, 95, 109-11, 113-15, 118-19, 126, 139-40, 149, 152-53, 159, 182, 188; and allegory, 109-11; and Eu-

charist, 109-11, 118-19, 139-40; and (neo-)Platonism, 6-7, 33n.26; 34n.28, 53, 126, 188; and sacramental time, 126; on *uti-frui* distinction, 30, 69
Autonomy, 28, 36, 56, 60, 64-66, 76, 90, 154, 159, 190
Axel, Gabriel, 170

Babette's Feast, 170-72, 179, 184
Balthasar, Hans Urs von, 13, 152n.30
Barth, Karl, 13, 127-28
Baius, Michael, 65
Bebbington, David W., 137n.1
Bellarmine, Robert, 65, 109-10
Berengar of Tours, 57-58, 62, 117-18, 158-59
Berengarian controversy, 64, 116, 118, 158
Bernard of Clairvaux, 86
Bible. *See* Scripture
Biel, Gabriel, 78
Boland, Vivian, 188
Bordeianu, Radu, 32
Bouillard, Henri, 13, 165-68; on the analogy of truth *(analogia veritatis)*, 164, 167
Bradshaw, David, 35n.31
Byassee, Jason, 143-44

General Index

Cajetan, Thomas, 65
Calvin, John, 8n.12, 31n.20, 84, 87-94, 96, 98, 107, 111
Chenu, Marie-Dominique, 14, 58-61, 174-84; on action and contemplation, 182-84; on faith, 179-81; on Scripture, 177; on theology, 170-84; on tradition, 175-77; on wisdom, 180-82; and worker-priest movement, 183
Coleridge, S. T., 103
Congar, Yves M.-J., 14, 54-56, 61-63, 88, 105, 122-26, 128-32, 141; on development of doctrine, 133-34; on juridicism, 54-56; on sacramental time, 124-27; on Scripture, 61-63, 105, 131-32, 141; on time of the Church, 124; on tradition, 61-63, 105, 131-32
Copleston, Frederick, 80

Daniélou, Jean, 12-13, 152n.30, 157, 159-63, 168; on Gregory of Nyssa, 159-63; on participation, 160-63
De Lubac, Henri, 12-13, 57-58, 61-62, 64-67, 87, 106-19, 122-23, 127-30, 139-40, 144-50, 153, 157-59, 163, 165-66, 168, 175; on development of doctrine, 127-28; on Eucharist and Church, 107-19, 139-40, 157-59; on nature and the supernatural, 107-8, 111; on spiritual interpretation, 12, 139-40, 144-50, 153
Denys the Areopagite, 33n.26, 36-37, 178-80
Derrida, Jacques, 95, 156
Descartes, René, 155
desiderium naturale. See Natural desires for the supernatural
Development of doctrine, 127-28, 133-36
Dionysius. See Denys the Areopagite
Dooyeweerd, Herman, 33n.24
Du Perron, Jacques, 109-10
Dupré, Louis, 68, 79, 82, 91-92

Ecumenism, 10, 67, 84, 86, 97-99, 121, 123, 128, 153, 169, 189; Congar on, 14.

See also Evangelicals and Catholics Together (ECT)
Eliot, T. S., 103
epektasis, 162
Equivocity, 165-67, 169
Eucharist, 8-9, 25-26, 51-52, 57-58, 84, 89, 101, 105, 107-19, 125n.7, 139, 140, 158-59, 168, 174-75, 189
Evangelicalism, 1-3, 9-10, 24, 27-29, 33n.24, 35, 38, 67, 85-86, 95, 97, 99, 101, 104-5, 116, 120-22, 129-30, 132-37, 143, 152-53, 156, 169, 171-72, 177, 184, 186-90
Evangelicals and Catholics Together (ECT), 98. See also Ecumenism.
Exegesis. See Scripture
Extrinsicism, 55-56, 63-65, 78, 96, 108, 111, 116, 176

Fee, Gordon, 141
Foucault, Michel, 96, 156
Francis of Assisi, 86

Garrigou-Lagrange, Réginald, 163
Grace. See Nature and the supernatural
Greeley, Andrew, 10-11, 99
Gregory of Nyssa, 13, 27, 33n.26, 34n.29, 41, 47-51, 53, 95, 151, 159-63, 165-67, 169, 180, 183-84; and apophatic theology, 160-62, 165-66; and epektasis, 162; on mystical knowledge, 160-63
Gregory the Great, Pope, 54
Grumett, David, 106
Guarino, Thomas G., 134, 166n.14

Hagens, Gunther von, 29
Harnack, Adolf von, 38, 146
Hauerwas, Stanley, 173n.6
Henry IV, 54
Henry of Ghent, 62
Hollon, Bryan, C., 21n.4, 106
Hopkins, Gerard Manley, 21
Hunsinger, George, 112-13
Hus, John, 62

General Index

Radical Orthodoxy, 20n.3, 68, 75, 82
Raschke, Carl, 95-98
Realism, 80
Real presence, 23, 25, 26, 51, 57, 107-14, 140, 158, 168, 184
Recapitulation, 42-44
ressourcement, 9, 12-16, 54, 59, 64, 68, 83, 103-4, 106, 152, 159, 163, 169, 176, 190
Rufinus of Aquileia, 39

Sacrament, 8-10, 22-23, 39, 52, 56-58, 62-63, 69, 101, 105, 124-30, 134-38, 149-51, 158, 164, 171, 174-75, 178-79, 185, 187-89; and time, 124-30, 134-36
Sacramental interpretation. *See* Scripture and spiritual interpretation
Sacramental ontology, 9-12, 15-16, 19-22, 24-25, 32, 50-52, 54-56, 58, 61, 63, 68-71, 75, 82, 104, 111-12, 116, 126, 144, 169, 186-87, 189
Sacramental participation. *See* Participation
Sadolet, Cardinal James, 87
Sander, Placidus, 31n.23
Schmemann, Alexander, 8-9
Scotus, John Duns, 62, 74-75, 77-78,
Scripture, 2, 12, 15, 20-21, 34-35, 38, 61-64, 66, 78, 84-85, 88, 95, 98, 101, 105-6, 108, 113, 119-24, 128, 130-53, 174-77, 182, 187; and church, 61-64, 88, 105; and historical-critical exegesis, 138-39, 141, 147, 150, 152; and spiritual interpretation, 12, 137-53; sufficiency of, 61-63, 120-24, 130-37; and tradition, 61-63, 130-36, 174-75
Simons, Menno, 84
Smith, James K. A., 74-75, 82
Suárez, Francisco, 65
Symbol, 1, 22-24, 60, 86, 111-13, 158-59, 166, 175

Tavard, George H., 61
Taylor, Charles, 126
Taylor, Jeremy, 103
Tertullian, 38, 86
Thorndike, Herbert, 103
Tillard, J.-M.-R., 112
Time. *See* Congar: on sacramental time; Congar: on time of the Church; Sacrament and time
Tradition, 61-63, 130-36, 174-75
Trent, Council of, 122, 132, 135

Univocity, 68-69, 74-79, 81-82, 104, 112, 125-26, 129, 151, 166-67, 169; and John Duns Scotus, 74-76

Vanhoozer, Kevin, 130-36, 141; on development of doctrine 133-34; on Scripture and tradition, 131-34
Vatican Council II, 14, 103, 119, 121, 134-35, 169
Voderholzer, Rudolf, 106
Voluntarism, 77-79, 81

Waltke, Bruce K., 142, 143
Ward, Graham, 69
Wells, David F., 121
Wilken, Robert Louis, 38
Wright, N. T., 3-4, 33n.24, 86n.1, 142n.12
Wycliffe, John, 62

Younger evangelicals. *See* Evangelicalism

Zwingli, Ulrich, 84

Scripture Index

Scripture Index